⌐ *P*

English place names

Kenneth Cameron

English place names

New edition

B T Batsford Ltd, London

To the memory of my Mother and Father and of Kath

First published in Great Britain 1996

© Kenneth Cameron 1996
Reprinted 2001

A CIP catalogue record for this book is available from the British Library
ISBN 0 7134 7378 9

Printed in Great Britain by The Bath Press, Bath

For the Publishers
B.T.Batsford Ltd
9 Blenheim Court
Brewery Road
London N7 9NY

A member of the Chrysalis Group plc

Contents

Preface

When *English Place-Names* first appeared in 1961, the Fourth edition of Eilert Ekwall's *Concise Oxford Dictionary of English Place-Names* had just been published and the English Place-Name Society's Survey had issued 29 volumes. Today, A.D. Mills' *A Dictionary of English Place-Names* has to a large extent replaced Ekwall's monumental work, the Place-Name Survey has published 69 volumes, and several very important books on aspects of English place-name studies have appeared. At the same time the new Cambridge Dictionary of English Place-Names is eagerly awaited. The two most important works are from the pen of my friend Dr Margaret Gelling, noted along with other valuable contributions in the Select Bibliography at the end of this book. The importance of field-names has at last received due recognition, both in the volumes of the English Place-Name Survey and in the works of John Field and others.

Since 1961, the English Place-Name Society has published full surveys of the place-names of the West Riding of Yorkshire, Westmorland, Gloucestershire, Berkshire and Rutland, together with one, almost complete, for Cheshire, and volumes on Dorset, Staffordshire, Norfolk, Lincolnshire, and *Cornish Place-Name Elements*, the first authoritative book on the local nomenclature of that county. The resulting collection and analysis of a vast amount of material is of vital importance both to the interpretation of individual names and to the significance of groups of place-names.

Clearly, the time had come when addendums to individual chapters of *English Place-Names* were insufficient and revision was called for. The book has not been rewritten, rather it has been revised. Particular attention should be paid to Chapters Three, Five, Six and Ten, where so much new evidence has been discovered that a deal of re-writing had of necessity to be done. While Chapters on topographical place-names – Fifteen, Sixteen, and Seventeen – remain substantially the same so far as examples are concerned, the meanings of the topographical elements have been extensively revised in the light of field-work by Margaret Gelling and Ann Cole. Details of this work are to be found in *Place-Names in the Landscape* and in a series of articles in *The Journal of the English Place-Name Society*. A new and illustrated edition of the former, which will be a collaborative effort by Dr Gelling and Mrs Cole, will be a must for all interested in our place-names.

Chapter Thirteen is similarly unchanged so far as the examples quoted are concerned, but it includes more detailed comments on the meanings of the second elements from which these names are derived. It is a pity that these chapters read, for the most part, like lists of place-names, but unfortunately I could not find a better way of including the large numbers of examples readers would be looking for. From letters received, it was clear that to have cut these lists would have caused more disappointment – hence the decision to follow the pattern of the original edition.

I decided that the chapter on 'Place-names and Archaeology' had to go. This was, principally, because so much new archaeological evidence has been accumulated in the meantime, that only a specialist archaeologist could keep abreast of new developments and could have handled the exciting new material. This I am not competent to do. That chapter has been replaced by one on 'Modern Place-names', made possible by Adrian Room's *A Concise Dictionary of Modern Place-Names in Great Britain and Ireland* from which examples have been taken. Here, too, I offer my thanks to Mr Ambrose Clifton who kindly supplied details of the naming of Brookenby, the most recently formed place-name in this book.

The final chapter, that on 'Field-names' has been changed in one essential. I decided to select certain types of name from a single county, Shropshire, using H.D.G. Foxall's splendid *Shropshire Field-Names* for the purpose. As a result, I hope that this might encourage readers to attempt similar studies, even ones dealing with a single parish or a group of parishes. This is well within the compass of enthusiastic amateur collectors.

In 1961, I paid tribute to many scholars whose works I had used freely or who had been especially influential. That debt remains the same and I must reiterate how much I owe in particular to two of these, the late Sir Frank Stenton and the late Professor Kenneth Jackson. I owe more to them than I can express in words. My personal debt is even greater to two others, both my teachers in the 1940's, Professor R.M. Wilson and the late Professor Bruce Dickins. I can pay no greater tribute to them than to paraphrase the words of the *Beowulf* poet – "each stood in the place of a father to me". Without them this book would never have been written in the first place.

From 1967 until 1993, I was fortunate enough to be Honorary Director of the English Place-Name Survey. Here, I acknowledge the debt I owe to my colleagues in that Survey – Miss Aileen Armstrong, Professor Barrie Cox, Mr John Field, Dr Margaret Gelling, Mr A.D. Mills, Mr O.J. Padel, Dr Karl Inge Sandred, and my successor Mr V.E. Watts, as well as Mrs M.D. Pattison our former Publications Officer and Administrative Secretary. This is particularly the case with my friend and former student, Dr John Insley, who with Mr John Field, has collaborated with me in my work on Lincolnshire place-names.

I am particularly grateful to Mrs Janet Rudkin, currently Publications Officer and Administrative Secretary of the Society, who has typed the text of this book onto disc. This is a most arduous and time-consuming task and I extend to her my best thanks. Whatever errors still remain are entirely my own.

Kenneth Cameron

County abbreviations

(after The English Place-Name Society)

Bd	Bedfordshire	**Nt**	Nottinghamshire
Bk	Buckinghamshire	**Nth**	Northamptonshire
Brk	Berkshire	**O**	Oxfordshire
C	Cambridgeshire	**R**	Rutland
Ch	Cheshire	**Sa**	Shropshire
Co	Cornwall	**Sf**	Suffolk
Cu	Cumberland	**So**	Somerset
D	Devon	**Sr**	Surrey
Db	Derbyshire	**St**	Staffordshire
Do	Dorset	**Sx**	Sussex
Du	Durham	**W**	Wiltshire
ERY	East Riding of Yorkshire	**Wa**	Warwickshire
Ess	Essex	**We**	Westmorland
Gl	Gloucestershire	**Wo**	Worcestershire
Ha	Hampshire	**WRY**	West Riding of Yorkshire
He	Herefordshire	**Wt**	Isle of Wight
Hrt	Hertfordshire		
Hu	Huntingdonshire		
K	Kent		
L	Lincolnshire		
La	Lancashire		
Lei	Leicestershire		
Ln	City of London		
Mx	Middlesex		
Nb	Northumberland		
Nf	Norfolk		
NRY	North Riding of Yorkshire		

Abbreviations and pronunciation of old english and old norse spelling

The following abbreviations have been used in the text:

ODan Old Danish
OE Old English
OFr Old French
ON Old Norse
ME Middle English
PrW Primitive Welsh

The equivalents, given below, are from Standard English except where stated and are purely approximate. In some case they are of necessity simplified. They are intended as a *guide* to the pronunciation of the Old English and Old Norse (Scandinavian) words quoted in the text.

Vowels:

Old English. (It should be noted that the Old Norse letters probably had nearly the same value as those of Old English, but one or two letters used only in Old Norse are added below. The sign ¯ indicates a long vowel in Old English and ´ a long vowel in Old Norse.

a	German M*a*nn	ī	s*ee*
ā	h*a*t	o	h*o*t
æ (Æ)	h*a*t	ō	French b*eau*
ǣ	f*a*re	u	f*u*ll
e	s*e*t	ū	f*oo*l
ē	German S*ee*	y	French t*u*

i	s*i*t	ȳ	French p*u*r
	Old Norse.		
ę	s*e*t	ǫ	h*o*t

Diphthongs:

The Old English diphthong was pronounced as a single glide, but each of the vowels from which it was formed was heard. It will be sufficient for the purpose to assume that the pronunciation of each part was the same as that of the vowel itself. The Old Norse diphthongs, found in words quoted in the text, can be represented as follows:

au ǫ+u   ei e+i   ey e+y

Consonants:

All the Old English consonants were pronounced, so that ng = n+g, hl = h+l (compare Welsh 11), wr =w+r. They were pronounced like their modern equivalents in Standard English with these (simplified) exceptions:

c	before *e* and *i*, and after *i*, as in *ch*ild; elsewhere as in *c*old
cg	as in *j*u*dg*e
g	before *e* and *i*, and after *æ*, *e* and *i*, as in *y*et; elsewhere as in *g*o
h	initially as in *h*at; elsewhere as in Scots lo*ch*
sc	as in *sh*all
f	usually as in *f*ill; between vowels as in o*v*en
s	usually as in *s*it; between vowels as in *z*est
þ, ð	between vowels as in fa*th*er; elsewhere as in *th*in

These last two letters (called *thorn* and *eth* respectively) are written indiscriminately in Old English manuscripts to represent the two sounds noted above. In this book, and following recent English Place-Name Society practice, þ is used initially, ð medially and finally, though such a distinction is purely graphic. Two additional Old Norse symbols may be noted:

j	as in *y*oung
v	as in *w*ill.

one

The technique of place-name study

The basic aim of the student of English place-names is to determine the etymology of a name and to propose from this, if possible, a meaning for that name. The principles involved in this study are well established and involve two interrelated premises. First, the vast majority of English place- and river- names are very old. We know this of the names of places because of the survival of Domesday Book (DB), written down in 1086, where there are references to a very large number of what are today the names of hamlets, villages, towns and cities. But, documents also survive from the Anglo-Saxon period and in addition a few texts which record the names of Romano-British towns and stations, as well as rivers both Celtic and pre-Celtic. So, it can be claimed that the vast majority of the names of our rivers and of our cities, towns, villages and hamlets were already in existence before the battle of Hastings in 1066. What is more we can be reasonably certain that many of these were already old when we first come across them in written form. Indeed, it is now believed that some of our river-names, like the Soar (Lei), Don (Du, WRY) and Tamar (Co-D), go back to the time of the first Stonehenge and the men of the long barrows. Welland (Nth-L) and Witham (R-L) are equally likely to be pre-Celtic names, since Celtic scholars regard a Celtic origin for these as at best highly doubtful.

Second, languages are constantly changing: phonetically, i.e. in their sounds; grammatically; semantically, in the meanings of words; and in their vocabulary. English is no exception. Old English (OE), the term used for the language spoken by the Anglo-Saxons extending from the first settlements here to about 1150, was an inflected language, whereas now English only retains inflexions like those of the possessive cases, the plural of nouns, and the present and past tenses of verbs. So, taking these two premises together, it is clear that the modern spelling of a place-name will not necessarily give us a clue to the original spelling and meaning of the name. Of course, sometimes it can be shown that it does, as with Fleet (Do, Ha, L, Mx), provided the dialect use of *fleet* 'a stream' is known, or Cowbridge (Ess) which is self-explanatory. More often than not the modern form is misleading or downright unintelligible, as with Tottenham (Mx), 'Totta's homestead' or Kimbolton (He, Hu) 'Cynebald's farm, estate'.

Moreover, even when the modern form does represent accurately enough the original form, we may have to take into consideration changes in the meaning of words from which the name is formed. *Field* normally has the sense of 'enclosed piece of land' today, but OE *feld* the word from which it is derived, means 'open land', so that names like Ashfield (Nt, Sa, Sf) and Broadfield (He, Hrt) had a different meaning from that suggested by the modern form of the word. Ashfield (Nt) is in fact a district name today and occurs in Kirkby in Ashfield and Sutton in Ashfield. There, clearly its earlier sense of open land is preserved.

We must always bear in mind that the giving of a river- or place-name is the result of human activity; the need is felt to distinguish, for example, a settlement in a valley, like Denton, (at least 11 counties), Dalton (Du, ERY, La, La, Nb, NRY, We, WRY) and the Danish Dalby (L, Lei, NRY), or one on a hill or hillside like Clifton (at least 17 counties), Hilton (Db, Hu, NRY, St) and Dunham (Ch, Nf), or one in a wood or a tract of woodland like Witton (Nb, Nf, NRY), the common Wootton, or Wotton (Bk, Gl, Sr). A need was felt to give a name to a physical feature, and one only has to consider the importance of a river-crossing for early settlers and find them reflected in so many names in -ford in our English place-nomenclature to realise the fact.

When names were given in this way, those who gave them were people like ourselves, and they used their everyday vocabulary and current grammatical forms – they used in fact the dialect of their own district. So, when Anglo-Saxons referred to a place, they sometimes used the preposition *æt* (modern *at*), which took the dative case. This is probably similar to our own frequent use of place-names with a locative function as in 'London', short for at 'London'. A number of place-name survive as a testimony to it, for such names show traces of the old dative singular or plural form. Bede, in the Latin of his *Ecclesiastical History of the English People*, 731, refers to Barrow upon Humber (L) as *in loco qui dicitur Ad baruae*, as if *ad* were part of the name. He goes on to say *id est Ad Nemus* 'that is at the grove'. Though he wrote in Latin, Bede spoke Old English and knew what *bearu*, dative singular *bearwe*, meant. Now, when the Anglo-Saxon translator towards the end of the 9th century turned his work into Old English he called the place *Æt Bearwe*, and it is that form which has given us *Barrow* today, just as it has in Barrow (Ch, Db, Gl, Sa, St, So). Clearly these locative forms must have been in current use when the names were given.

And so, in order to deduce the etymology and meaning of a place-name, we have to make, from our earliest records down to the present day, a collection of the forms or spellings of the place-name, tracing the history of the spelling of the name from its current form back to its earliest recorded one, in many cases that found in DB. Such a collection will show just how the name has developed during its recorded history, with many names stretching back over 900 years, sometimes more. From this collection we can trace the linguistic history of the name over the centuries and we can see exactly how it has changed. But we can also be pretty certain that the vast majority of these names must have had a longer or shorter history before we find them first in written records, some going back to Romano-British times and even earlier, others to the Anglo-Saxon period and still others to the period after the Viking settlements of the late 9th century. In comparison with the vast number of English place-names, comparatively few are recorded in pre-conquest documents and it is only in the latter that we have Old English spellings to help us deduce an etymology. For the rest, our earliest form will be that in DB or in a later source. As a result, in order to establish the likely original form of such a name, from which we can deduce its likely meaning, we must work backwards from our earliest recorded spellings into the unknown. Our collection of spellings will have enabled us to trace the linguistic development of our name and using that and our knowledge of the ways in which the English language developed in the Anglo-Saxon period we can suggest what the likely form would have been in Old English, though this will of course be purely hypothetical. What our hypothetical form must be is the one which would explain, as it were, the development of our written collection; it must be the one we would have expected from all the evidence we have collected. We do not know as much as we would like about the vocabulary of the Old English language, for there are many broad areas, like occupational terms, animal and bird names, which are not well-represented in the surviving corpus of Old English texts. However, in spite of this, when we have deduced the hypothetical Old English form of our name, it is possible in a very large number of cases to suggest an etymology and from this indicate the likely meaning of the name. The gaps in our knowledge, nonetheless, are such that there is a hard core of place-names, which, with our present state of knowledge, defy explanation, like Palterton (Db), recorded as early as 1002 as *Paltertune*. We have not the slightest idea what *Palter* means, for it cannot be explained in terms of either known or suspected Old English *or* Celtic roots.

Sometimes, too, we only know linguistically the general meaning of a word. Old English *wæsse* can be presumed to mean 'a wet place, a swamp, a marsh'. It is found as the second element of a group of names in the West Midlands, Alrewas (St), Bolas, earlier *Bolwas* (Sa), Broadwas (Wo), Buildwas (Sa), Hopwas (St), Rotherwas (Sa), and Sugwas (He). One day a colleague was passing through Buildwas and there in a loop of the Severn, the flat area, was a broad lake. Clearly this was the marsh or swamp from which -*was* was derived. On the return journey the following day the water had disappeared, just as if a plug had been pulled out, as she herself said. This turned out to be the general topographical feature of the other names in -*was* and now we can be fairly certain that *wæsse* is a word with a *specialized* meaning, not just a marsh or swamp but 'riverside land which floods and drains quickly'. What is becoming clear, as the study of place-names progresses, is that the Anglo-Saxons had a very large topographical vocabulary in which there were few synonyms. Detailed study has shown that their words for hills, valleys, woods, streams, marshes and the like referred to different shapes and types of these features, as we have seen with the example of names derived from *wæsse*. The etymological meaning sometimes tells only a part of the story and by examining the topography of groups of places it may be possible to give a more precise meaning to a word forming part of the names.

It may be as well at this point to give some indication of the more important sources from which the forms or spellings of place-names are obtained. The earliest for our knowledge of Romano-British names are the *Geography* of Ptolemy, a Greek text dated about A.D. 150, the *Antonine Itinerary* of about A.D. 300, and the *Cosmography* of the anonymous geographer of Ravenna about A.D. 670, both Latin texts. These naturally for the most part record the names of Roman towns and forts, but also rivers, and since these are of pre-English, mainly of Celtic (i.e. Primitive Welsh) origin, they give us early forms of such names, though in the *Antonine Itinerary* and the *Cosmography* in latinized spellings.

For the Anglo-Saxon period one important source is *The Anglo-Saxon Chronicle*, a history in annalistic form from the birth of Christ to 1154. The first sections appear to have been drawn up towards the end of the 9th century, but some of the earlier entries may well include data derived from a much older written or oral tradition. Even more important is a long series of nearly 1900 charters, which, though often written in Latin, contain early forms of place-names and details of the boundaries of estates in Old English. Some of our southern and western counties are well represented but comparatively few deal with places in the North of England or the North Midlands. Many of our extant charters are preserved only in later copies, especially in collections of them, known as cartularies, made during the 12th to the 14th centuries and even later. The spellings found in such manuscripts are not always accurate copies of the spellings of the originals and some can certainly be shown to have been 'modernized' by later scribes. Of course, such forms are less reliable than those from originals or early copies, unless they can be shown to have been made by careful copyists. The vast majority of village and parish names, however old they may be, are not recorded till Domesday Book. It is as well to remember, however, that the scribes were Norman and that they would tend to represent English sounds by the nearest equivalent in their own language. As a result the spellings of Domesday Book have sometimes to be treated with considerable caution, though most of them can be satisfactorily explained. In general, however, it is fair to say that when the DB form is not supported by later spellings it is best to disregard it.

The most important sources for the Middle English (ME) period (c.1150 to c.1500) are collections of official documents preserved in the Public Record Office, beginning with Pipe Rolls in the mid 12th century which deal with payments due to the King from the sheriffs of the various shires as collectors of his Revenues, and also from various individuals, towns and cities. Others include Charter Rolls, dealing with royal grants and confirmation of grants of various kinds which had been executed in the presence of witnesses; Close Rolls, concerning royal business addressed to individuals and so-named because they were folded or closed up; and Patent Rolls, containing royal documents of a public nature written down and delivered on open sheets of parchment. In addition there are Assize Rolls, which record causes heard by the travelling justices; Coroner's Rolls, dealing with judicial cases of interest to the Crown pending action by the King's Justices; and Inquisitions *post mortem*, which deal with inquests held on the death of any of the king's tenants. Many of these have been published, but many more still remain unpublished. From such sources a representative collection of spellings for a particular place-name can be obtained. Most of this material was produced for a centralized bureaucracy for purposes of government and was therefore written down by scribes of the Chancery or of some other administrative department at Westminster. As a result their spelling may indicate a pronunciation for some particular name which was not that current in the district of the name itself.

There are also literally thousands of medieval charters, for the most part written down by local scribes, representing more accurately the local pronunciation of place-names. Often such documents include the names of fields and minor features of the landscape so their importance for the student of place nomenclature is obvious. There are also manorial court-rolls, rentals and surveys of lands, which contain similar material and are often helpful in building up a picture of the topography and development of a village. Most of these documents are unpublished and besides the Public Record Office and the British Library are to be found in County Archive Offices as well as important local, university, and college libraries, and in those of some of the great English Houses.

Some of the types of material already mentioned, such as rentals and surveys, are found in increasing numbers during the period post-1500. Indeed, these, together with Terriers which describe the site, boundaries and acreage of land, particularly in ecclesiastical possession, provide the best source of minor and field-names, which are often recorded for the first time here. Though medieval maps and plans are extant, they do not appear in any numbers before Christopher Saxon's maps of 1574, but from then on they are common enough. Plans of estates too become plentiful in the first half of the 17th century and these again are a fruitful source of minor names. In the 18th century, Enclosure Awards begin to appear in numbers and continue into the 19th, while in the 1830s and 1840s there are Tithe Awards for many English parishes. The appearance of the first edition of the Ordnance Survey maps in the 1820s marks a new and continuing source of immense value to anyone interested in a study of place-names, especially for districts which have since been urbanized.

When from such sources we have made a collection of the spellings of our place-name from its earliest recorded one down to the present day, we can trace its linguistic history and from our analysis of this suggest its likely hypothetical form in Old English, (if one does not survive) and, then suggest a likely meaning for the name. We can best demonstrate the procedure with an actual example. Preston is found in a least twenty-three counties and only that near Faversham (K) is recorded in an Anglo-Saxon charter, which happens to be unauthentic in its extant copies, so that it is clearly sensible to disregard the form found there. The earliest spellings for Preston most commonly found are *Prestetun(e)* and *Presteton(e)* and subsequent forms vary little from *Preston(e)*. The development is natural and straightforward; the vowel in the second element has simply been weakened to *-ton*, so we can be sure that its source is OE *tūn* 'a farmstead, a village, an estate'. The first element of our name shows a loss of medial *-e-* with the resultant *-tt-* being simplified to *-t-*. Such a loss of a medial vowel, even of a medial syllable, is a common feature in the development of place-names. The problem to be solved is what the medial *-e-* in early spellings represents in Old English. Using our knowledge of Old English grammar, we can say at once, probably an *-a-*, since we recognize this as a common possessive plural ending in nouns, and this weakens to *-e-* in a weakly stressed syllable. Similarly, we can hypothesize that the noun in question is *prēost*. So we can be pretty certain that our Old English form of the name would have been **Prēostatūn*, the asterisk showing that it is a deduced spelling. The meaning would then be 'the village or the estate of the priests'.

We have seen already how a comparison of the topography of a group of place-names containing the same element can throw light on the meaning of the whole group. In a similar way the spellings of one name recorded at an early date may well help suggest or confirm the etymology of another first found much later. Harwich (Ess) has been first noted as *Herwyz* in 1238, the *z* being simply a scribal form of the sound represented by our modern *ch*, then as *Herewic* in 1248. Subsequent spellings are in *Here-*, later weakened to *Her-* with the loss of medial *-e-*, the second element being spelt *-wich(e)*. The later development of *Her-* to *Har-* is paralleled by the pronunciation of Derby (Db) as if it were spelt *Darby*. From our collection of spellings it is possible to suggest that the likely OE form would have been **Herewīc*, the form actually found in 1248, the subsequent development being precisely what we would expect. There is, however, another Harwich, in Whitstable (K), which has from the 13th century a development of forms exactly parallel to that of the Essex name, but it is recorded in an

Anglo-Saxon charter dated 863 where the name is spelt *herewic*, precisely the form suggested for Harwich (Ess). The meaning of this compound is literally 'the army place', hence probably 'the camp'. By comparing the names in this way we can be pretty certain that our interpretation of the name of the Essex port is right.

To sum up, the study of place-names involves the collection of the spellings of a name which traces it back to the earliest one we can find. We can then see the way it has developed through its recorded history and using our knowledge of the ways in which the English language has changed in its various dialects, we can explain the linguistic development of the name. Working back from the known into the unknown, as it were, if the name is unrecorded before 1086, we can suggest the likely form the name would have had in Old English and from that suggest a meaning for it. And, we use this method because our place- and river-names have had such a long history and because our language in its various dialects has changed so much.

So far we have only discussed place-names in terms of their forms or spellings, for after all the names themselves have come down to us only through the *written* word, even though what changes they have undergone must have been for the most part at any rate through the *spoken* language. If the modern spelling of a name in the majority of cases is of little help in determining its meaning, in some instances the modern local pronunciation is. If, for example, that pronunciation is the one we would have expected as the direct phonetic development of the hypothetical original Old English form we can be pretty certain that our Old English form is correct. So, the local pronunciation of Loughborough (Lei) is [lufbrə] and this is precisely what we would expect given its hypothetical Old English form **Luhhedaburh* 'the fortified place, stronghold of Luhhede' (an Old English masculine personal name). The pronunciation [luf] is exactly paralleled by that of some of the Broughs, e.g. Brough (Db, Nt, We), 'fortified place' pronounced [bruf], since the *-hh-* and *-h* represent the same sound in Old English. The development shows the weakening and loss of the medial syllable and the normal tendency to reduce the final syllable, with the final vowel being that in the modern pronunciation of fath*er*, moth*er*.

Sometimes, in the known history of a place-name, developments occur which are not in line with those which we know took place in the dialectal area with which we are concerned. Other influences have played their part and an important one is that of the Danes who settled in eastern England in numbers in the last quarter of the 9th century. Old Danish contained sounds which did not occur in equivalent positions in Old English and vice versa. Because of this sometimes names already in existence before they arrived were modified by Danish influence. On occasion, it seems to be a case of a Danish sound replacing an English one, as in Skipton (ERY, WRY) for Shipton (Do, Gl, Ha, O, Sa) 'sheep farm', for Danish has no *Sh-* sound in this position, so *Sk-* was substituted for it. In others it would appear that the cognate Danish word has replaced the English one, though sometimes we cannot be sure as in Fiskerton (L, Nt) for Fisherton (W) 'the fishermen's estate', for the two words, Danish and English, differ really only in their pronunciations. We can be sure, however, in the case of Melton (L, Lei, Nf, ERY, WRY), which without Danish influence would have been Middleton (at least 17 counties) 'middle estate'. Here, OE *middel* has clearly been replaced by the cognate Old Danish *meðal*, both having the same meaning. Similarly, we can be sure that we are dealing with a word replacement in Carlton and Carleton (at least 14 counties), which without Danish influence would have given us Charlton (at least 18 counties) 'estate of the husbandmen', where Danish *karl* has replaced English *ceorl* (modern churl).

The Norman Conquest had comparatively little effect on name-giving for there are few names of French origin compared with the vast number of place-names in this country. However, the influence of Anglo-Norman scribes, and of the Anglo-Norman language spoken here was for long thought to have had a considerable effect on the early spellings of some existing names. This is currently the source of considerable debate and it will be some time before a definite conclusion can be reached. It was for long claimed that when Anglo-Norman scribes, who were used to or trained in copying Latin and Anglo-Norman itself, came across sounds or combinations of sounds which were unfamiliar to them, they sometimes tended to substitute the nearest sound or sounds they knew. It still appears, in spite of the current debate that the medieval spellings of some English place-names were changed in this way. Though in individual names many such changes did not persist, in others the spellings have been permanently affected. It still seems likely that the loss of S- in Nottingham is to be explained in terms of Anglo-Norman influence. The name is first recorded as *Snotengaham* in 868 and initial Sn- persists till 1086 and appears on Anglo-Saxon coins struck at the mints there. The subsequent loss of S- in later forms seems likely to be due to Anglo-Norman influence by which S- followed by -

n- is sometimes lost, so that *Snotengaham* 'homestead of Snot's people or followers' has become Nottingham, instead of Snottingham.

Both Scandinavian and Anglo-Norman influences are ones we are reasonably well aware of, but there are others which are sometimes difficult to *explain* even though they can usually be recognised with reasonable certainty. Principally, these are due to popular etymology or euphony. Forest Hill (O) literally means 'ridge-like hill', and presumably should have come down to us as Forsthill. The first element, *forst* seems to have been a rare word and by the early 13th century at latest its meaning had apparently been lost, and so in order to make it intelligible it became Foresthill. A clear instance of euphony is Belgrave (Lei), which is recorded in Domesday Book as *Merdegrave* and in 1135 as *Merthegrava*, probably 'martens' grove'. The first element appears to have been associated by the Normans with *merde* 'filth, shit' and so was duly replaced by *bel* 'beautiful'.

It will have been noticed that several mentions have been made of dialectal developments in discussing the known history of English place-names. I have emphasized that a study of the meaning of such names is based on the analysis of a collection of spellings in the light of the historical development of English sounds in the dialectal area in which they occur. But, of course not all English place-names are of English origin; some are Pre-Celtic, Celtic, Scandinavian or French. This does not, however, affect the validity of the technique used and for a simple reason. Once a river- or place-name, whatever its origin, has been adopted in English, it becomes 'naturalized', as it were, and from then onwards it develops just like a name of Old English origin, subject to the changes that would affect the English sound in the position in which it occurs and in the dialectal region of the name itself.

When pre-English names were passed on by Primitive Welsh speakers into Old English, sometimes a linguistic development known as 'sound-substitution' took place, a feature which has in fact already been noted. The same sounds are not always found in the same position in different languages; for example English has no equivalent to the sound represented by modern Welsh *ll*, as in Llandudno, 'church (of) St. Tudno'. Sound-substitutions are found in names of pre-English origin when they were adapted into Old English. The name Eccles (La, Nf) is derived from Primitive Welsh (the term used of the form of the Celtic language which the Anglo-Saxon settlers met here) *eglēs*, itself borrowed from Latin *ecclēsia* 'a church'. The Primitive Welsh form had the main stress on the second syllable, as is normal today in Welsh place-names. When the name was passed on into Old English sound-substitution took place for the latter had no single *g* in this position, with the result that [k] was substituted for it. A change in the stress pattern of the name also *naturally* took place, since in English the main stress occurs on the first syllable of the name; so, we have the modern form Éccles and not Eglés.

As has been stressed earlier, it is essential to remember a very important fact, that so many documents in which names appear from the 12th century onwards were produced by and for a centralized beaurocracy for purposes of government, and were written down by scribes of the Chancery or of some other administrative department at Westminster. Even though it is certain that in some cases the original drafts from which these documents were prepared were written down locally, some of the spellings in Westminster documents indicate a pronunciation for a particular name which was not that current in the district in which the place-name occurs. We can call these 'official' documents, and clearly on occasion the evidence from such sources will be less valuable for etymological purposes, because they would tend to be spelt in what might be called the 'conventional Westminster manner'. Such spellings are certainly much less valuable than the spellings found in local documents, those which we can be pretty certain were actually written down locally and therefore are much more likely to reflect the forms of a name *used* locally. If, therefore, and it does occasionally happen, that a particular spelling occurs only in 'official' sources it is clear that we should not attempt to construct an etymology on the basis of such a spelling or spellings, and that is certainly the case with Litton (Db) 'farm, estate on the slope'. The early spellings are all in *Lit-*, *Lyt-*, except for three forms in *Lut-* each found in an 'official' source *completely* unsupported by those from 'local' documents, suggesting at best that the official spellings are suspect and can hardly be of importance for deducing the meaning of the name.

It will be clear that the modern spelling of a name is more often than not of little value in indicating the original meaning of a name, even though some occasionally do. It may be guessed that Otterbourne (Ha) and Otterburn (Nb, WRY) have to do with otters and a stream, that Coates (C, Gl, L, Nt, Sx) and Cotes (Lei) have to do with cottages or sheds, or that Woodhouse (Lei, WRY) has to do with a wood and a house, but one could not deduce from the present-day form that Bedwyn

(W) means 'place where bindweed grows', that Easter (Ess) means 'sheepfold' or that Tring (Hrt) means 'slope on which trees grow'.

Place-name study, then, is essentially a linguistic discipline but, as we shall see in some of the following chapters it is interdisciplinary, for frequently one has to take into consideration local topography, soil-types, archaeology, ecology and local history. It is clearly no good suggesting a topographical explanation for a particular name if local geography does not bear out that interpretation. The lime-trees may have disappeared from the ridge at Lindridge (K, Wo), but the stony ground can not have done so from many of the numerous Stantons, Stauntons or Staintons. There is little point in suggesting, as has been done that the first element of Worldham (Ha) is an Old English word meaning wood-grouse or capercaillie, when the locality has been shown to have been thickly forested and cannot ever have been capercaillie country. Its meaning is more probably 'homestead of Wærhild' (an Old English feminine personal name). In a similar way, the evidence of archaeology can often confirm or otherwise a suggested etymology or it can define more precisely the significance of an element like *ceaster* 'a Roman camp, station'. Most names derived from the latter can certainly be shown to be former Roman camps or stations; Woodchester (Gl), however, is the site of a Romano-British villa and Chesterblade (So) is near to a prehistoric camp. The second element in the latter is OE *blæd* 'blade or leaf' presumably used in some transferred topographical sense.

Similarly, the place-name student can find the answer to certain problems by using the evidence provided by sources commonly used by local historians. There are many places in England which have a second name prefixed or added to the village name. Often these are used to distinguish nearby places with the same name but this is not invariably the case. In a group of this type the affixed name is that of the family which held the manor at some time or other. This is the explanation of Mandeville and Poges in Stoke Mandeville and Stoke Poges (Bk). Local historical sources show that the former was held by the Mandeville family in the 13th century and the latter by the Poges (or Pugeis) family in the same century. The family names have been added to the existing place-name Stoke (a common name) 'place, meeting-place' to distinguish them from other places of the same name. There are literally hundreds of place-names of this and similar types, for which a knowledge of local history is needed in order to explain the origin of the distinguishing addition.

The process of name-giving has continued certainly from pre-English times and still goes on today. All the names in -ville, apart from an odd one or two which are the result of popular etymology or the like, such as Wyeville (L), earlier *Wyewelle* 'spring near a heathen temple', are 18th or 19th century formations, like Ironville (Db) first recorded in 1837. Ironbridge (Sa) is of course named from the first cold cast iron bridge in the world built in 1778, Nelson (La) and Waterlooville (Ha) from public houses, Peterlee (Du) from Peter Lee a mining trade union leader and given to the new town designated in 1948, while Telford has only been in existence since 1968 when the name of the Shropshire new town was given commemorating the Scottish civil engineer Thomas Telford. Occasionally the place-name student is lucky to come across the explanation of an odd-looking name, as did a colleague with Nanpantan (Lei). Its -tan ending makes it look as though it must be an old name, but in fact on a map of 1754, there in the right spot a house is marked and beside it the name *Nan Pantain's*. So, it turns out that the modern Nanpantan is simply derived from the name of a lady, whose name, as it were, is perpetuated for posterity in the name of a place.

two

Types of place-name formations

Place-names, whether of English, Scandinavian or Celtic origin, can be divided into two main types, habitative and topographical. There is, however, among names of English origin, a third – group or tribal names, discussed in a little detail later. Habitative names from the beginning denoted inhabited places, homesteads, farms, enclosures, villages, or estates. They include Higham (at least 12 counties) 'high homestead', Norton (at least 24 counties) 'north farmstead, villages' and Wandsworth (Sr) 'Wændel's enclosure'. Here the second element describes the type of habitation, the first being a descriptive word, a personal name or that of a group of people. These examples, like those which follow, are of English origin, but most of the place-name formations themselves occur also in Celtic or Scandinavian names. Those found only in the latter are discussed in the relevant chapters.

The second type of name consisted originally of a description of some topographical feature, natural or artificial. Greenhill (in most counties) 'green hill' and Blackburn (La, Nb) 'dark stream' are obvious examples. Here too belong Allestree (Db) 'Æðelhard's tree' and Taplow (Bk) 'Tæppa's burial-mound' and these are essentially topographical rather than habitative, even though the first element is a personal name. Of course, many such names at an early date became the names of inhabited places and the stages in the consequent extension of their meaning can readily be understood. When people made their homes near some distinctive feature of the landscape, they often adopted the existing name for the new settlement. Sherborne (Do, Gl, Ha, Wa) was originally a river-name 'clear stream', but when men and women came to live near that stream they took over the river-name without changing it. So, Sherborne would come to mean 'village on the *Sherborne*'and later 'Sherborne village'. Indeed, in course of time Sherborne as a river-name may have gone out of use and the name simply denote that of a village. Nonetheless, such river- and place-names were in origin *simply* names given to physical features of various kinds. They were *not* originally settlements and this clearly distinguishes them from habitative place-names proper. Not all topographical names have developed in this way. Many still retain their original character as with Selwood Forest (So-W) 'wood where sallows grow' and Liddesdale (Cu) 'valley of Liddel Water'.

In addition to these two large classes, there is a small but important type of name of English origin indicating the settlement of a group of people or a tribe. The most numerous of these are distinguished by having an ending in -*ingas*, like Hastings (Sx), without the addition of a word denoting 'farm, village' or the like. Hastings was in origin the name of an Anglo-Saxon group, the *Hæstingas* meaning 'Hæsta's dependents, people'. Clearly, such names are not place-names proper but the names of groups of people. They subsequently became place-names when the group so-called became associated with a particular site. Because of their historical interest they will be discussed in a later chapter. Some names in -*ingas* have as their first part an appellative or older place-name and the suffix -*ingas* has apparently developed a meaning 'dwellers at or in'. Meering (Nt), in spite of its loss of final -*s*, seems to denote 'dwellers by the pool' or 'at *Mere*'. If the latter is correct, *Mere* 'pool' would then be a lost place-name, but in either case the meaning is topographically appropriate.

Other examples of group- or tribal names, like Norfolk and Suffolk, will be found in the chapter on English shires. But, in addition, there are few names which appear to have been originally the names of Anglo-Saxon tribes like the *Gyrwe*, a name apparently derived from a word meaning 'mud, fen', perhaps therefore 'people who lived in or near a fen'. It is this tribal name which has given us Jarrow (Du) today. Ripon (WRY) is derived from the dative plural of the name of a tribe known as the *Hrype*, who also gave their name to Repton (Db) 'hill of the *Hrype*'. Hitchin (Hrt) is a similar dative plural formation of *Hicce*, a tribe known to us from a 7th century document *The Tribal Hidage*, as are the *Undalas*, who gave their name to Oundle (Nth). Wales (WRY) belongs here too since it simply means 'Welshmen' and so is identical with the name of the Principality itself. All these names are those of groups of people, no doubt of different sizes, whose names have been transferred to become those of the places in which they lived.

Most place-names fall naturally into different parts, usually called 'elements'. Those which cannot be divided in this way are *simplex*, as with Stoke (found in most counties) meaning 'place, settlement'. In the same way Week (Co, Ha, So, Wt), Wick (Brk, Gl, So, Wo) and Wyke (Do, Sr) are from OE *wīc* 'trading centre, salt-production centre, dairy-farm' and Worth (Ch, So, K, Sx) from OE *worð* 'enclosure, homestead'.

The vast majority of names, however, are *compound* and consist of two or more elements joined together. These are sometimes two nouns as in Marston (at least 20 counties) from OE *Mersctūn* 'marsh farm, estate' or Oakley (at least 12 counties) 'oak-tree wood or glade'. At other times it is an adjective and a noun as in Weston, a very common name, from OE *Westtūn* 'west farm, estate' or Widnes (La) 'wide headland'.

In some compound names the first element was originally in the genitive case. This usually, though by no means always, signifies personal or group association. Old English was an inflected language and the ending of the genitive varied according to the declension of the particular word or personal name. The genitive singular endings in -*es* and -*an* have left traces in the modern forms of place-names as in Edgbaston (Wa) 'Ecgbald's farm, estate', Kingston (at least 20 counties) 'king's estate' and Bickerston (Nf) 'beekeeper's farm'. The genitive singular in -*an* remains as -*n* or -*en* when followed by a vowel or *h* as in Bardney (L) from OE *Bardanēg* 'Barda's island of land', Itchenor (Sx) OE *Yccanōra* 'Ycca's shore' and Tottenham (Mx) OE *Tottanhām* 'Tota's homestead, village'. But when the -*an* was followed by a consonant it usually leaves no trace at all, as the case with Laxfield (Sf), earlier *Laxanfeld* 'Laxa's open land'.

There are also a number of examples of names in which the first element is a personal name and which never seem to have had a genitive ending, like Alkmonton (Db) 'Alhmund's farm, estate' instead of Alkmonston, Kinwarton (Wa) 'Cyneward's farm, estate' instead of Kinwarston. We do not know why such formations occur or what their significance is. All we can do is to note that names of this type seem to occur most frequently in the North and North Midlands.

On the other hand, we occasionally find the genitive used when we would not normally expect it. It occurs sometimes when the first element is a river-name as in Wyresdale (La) 'valley of the River Wyre' and this is perhaps readily understandable. But why we should find it in a name like Alresford (Ha) literally 'ford of the alder', Farnsfield (Nt) 'open land of the fern or bracken', and Beaconsfield (Bk) 'open country of the beacon' is difficult to say. It is just possible that *Alre*, *Farn* and *Beacon* were older simplex names meaning '(place at) the alder', 'fern-, bracken-covered place' and 'the beacon' respectively. If this is so the modern names would mean something like 'ford at *Alre*', 'open land around *Farn* ' and 'open country around *Beacon*' respectively.

There is a small group of names consisting of two elements in which the order of these elements is reversed. These are known as *inversion* compounds. This is the case with some names of Celtic origin, but the formation is also found particularly in Cumbria, where men of Norwegian descent settled. Many of them had come to England from Gaelic speaking areas, and following Celtic custom they formed some place-names by reversing the order of the elements. So, for example, we have Kirkoswald (Cu), literally 'church Oswald', as compared with the 'normal' word order in Oswaldkirk (ERY).

A few place-names contain three elements and most of them follow a similar pattern. In several the medial element was originally OE *ford*, as in Wotherton (Sa) literally 'wood ford farmstead, village'. The most likely explanation of this name is that it was originally a topographical one, *Woodford* 'ford by a wood', as in Woodford (Ch, Co, Ess, Nth, W). When a settlement was made near the ford, OE *tūn* 'farm, village, estate' was added to the existing name, itself a compound place-name, so that in fact Wotherton really means 'farm, village, estate near *Woodford*' and the name Woodford has subsequently been lost. In such names the third element is a later addition to an already existing name, and there seems to be no proven examples of original triple-compound place-names. However, the third element must have been added early and therefore this type is to be distinguished from the large group of names, which we have already briefly noted, in which the addition called an *affix* was made later. Whether prefixed or added it often still remains as a separate word. The affix in East and West Drayton (Nt), Great and Little Wilbraham (C) and Lower and Upper Shuckburgh (Wa) has been added to distinguish adjacent places of the same name. Many such additions are the names of the holders of the manor in medieval times as with Manningford Abbots and Manningford Bohun (W). The former was held by the abbey (hence Abbots) of Hyde, Winchester, while a family called Bohun held the manor of Manningford Bohun in the 13th century. These descriptive words and names are not only used to distinguish neighbouring villages, as we shall see in a later chapter. Sometimes they differentiate places of the same name which, though in the same county, are many miles apart. This is so with King's Norton and Bredons Norton (Wo). The former, which was held by the King in 1086, is near Birmingham, the latter near Bredon. In may other cases, however, their use seems to be quite irregular and occasionally a place-name may have had two different affixes in the course of its history.

A further aspect of the formation of place-names has already been noted in the opening chapter. As we saw there, place-names are normally used in locative or adverbial contexts, chiefly indicated by a preposition such as *at*. As a result, in the early Anglo-Saxon period OE *æt* seems to have been regarded almost as an integral part of the name. So, in *The Anglo-Saxon Chronicle* there is a reference to "a place which is called *æt Searobyrg* (Salisbury, W)", where it is clear that *æt* is considered as part of the name. It is impossible to know when this form became obsolete, but in the later part of the period we believe that is was used in documents as a written formula. The colloquial use of *æt* with the place-name in the dative is clearly shown, however, by the number of dative forms in modern place-names, as we saw earlier in the case of Barrow (L). The Old English dative singular ending most frequently found in place-names is *-e*, which has often been lost today. Nonetheless, it sometimes survives in simplex names like Sal*e* (Ch) 'at the sallow, willow' and Clev*e* (D, He) and Cleev*e* (Gl, He, So, Wo) 'at the river-bank, escarpment'. In the South-west, especially in Devon, when it is preserved it is often spelt *-a* as in Fludd*a* 'at the water-channel' and Wood*a* 'at the wood' but occasionally *-er* as in Braund*er* 'at the burnt place', and Ford*er* 'at the ford'. In compound place-names traces of this dative singular ending have normally been lost.

The dative plural ending in Old English was *-um*. It seems that its use in place-names was far commoner in the North and Midlands than in the South. Further, it appears to occur more frequently in simplex than in compound names. The dative plural ending is reflected in names like Coat*ham* (Du, NRY), Cot*ham* (La, Nt), Cott*am* (ERY, Nt), Cot*on* (at least 8 counties) and Cott*on* (Ch, Nth, Sa), all derived from *æt Cotum* 'at the cottages, sheds'. Here, the endings *-ham, -am, -on* are modern reflexes of OE *-um*. Similarly there is Down*ham* (La, Nb) 'at the hills', Lane*ham* (Nt) 'at the lanes', and Lyt*ham* (La) 'at the slopes'. Other modern spellings include *-holme* in Hipperholme (WRY) 'at the hippers, osiers' and *-om* in Millom (Cu) 'at the mills'. The variety of modern spellings from the OE dative plural *-um* shows us very clearly how important early spellings are in place-name study. The modern spellings of the names above would have been completely misleading in the absence of early forms. Indeed, this is the most important fact to be appreciated by all interested in the meanings of place-names. The original forms have so very often changed greatly during their history that without a collection of early spellings it is difficult, if not impossible, to determine the original meaning.

Finally, there is a group of place-names formed with a preposition as first element and these are often referred to as *elliptical* names. They will be discussed in more detail in a later chapter, so that only a couple of examples need be given here. OE *bī*, modern *by*, which took a dative, occurs in Byfield (Nth) literally 'by, near the open land'. It is quite clear that here it is used elliptically and some word like 'place' or 'village' is to be understood. So a fuller translation would be '(place, village) by or near the open land'. Similarly OE *binnan* (from *be innan*) 'inside, within' occurs in Bembridge (Wt) literally 'within, inside the bridge', that is, '(place) within or inside the bridge', apparently a reference to the situation of Bembridge at the end of a peninsular, which in early times could only be reached by sea or by the bridge at Brading. Although only a comparatively small group, these elliptical place-names are naturally of considerable interest because of their distinctive linguistic formation.

three

Celtic place-names and river-names

The earliest place- and river-names in England for which etymologies can be suggested are those of Celtic or British origin. There are, however, some names which, with our present state of knowledge, appear to be neither Celtic, nor Anglo-Saxon nor Scandinavian, and so may well be earlier. Just as the Britons passed on some of their names to the Anglo-Saxons so some of those given by even earlier inhabitants of this country may still persist. This is without doubt a real possibility, but even when we can suggest likely examples we certainly cannot suggest etymologies, for we know little of the language or languages of such people. The R. Wey (Ha-Sr, So) and R. Wye (Db, Wales-He) appear to be of identical origin but they cannot be derived from any known or suspected word in Celtic or English, though related words appear in languages akin to these. Other names seem to derive from roots found in various parts of Europe. Bovey (Do) apparently contains the same root as Bobbio in Italy, Tamar (D/Co) as Tambre in Spain and Don (WRY) as Don and Danube in eastern Europe. It is not surprising, therefore, that such names have sometimes been referred to as 'Old European' and here we have at least four English names which were probably given by pre-Celtic settlers in this country.

Just as these names names would be passed on or taken over by the Britons, so Celtic names were passed on to the Anglo-Saxons. This did not happen all at the same time, since different parts of England were occupied at different times, from the middle of the 5th century in Kent and coastal areas of the East and South-east to the 9th in Cornwall. The very fact that names were passed on presupposes the survival of Celtic speaking people in the districts where the names occur. Exactly how the names passed from one language to the other is not known for certain, but there are strong indications that they passed into English through people who spoke both languages and it is more likely that these were bilingual Britons. It seems certain that there was intermarriage between the two people at the highest social level, as is indicated by the fact that *walh* 'a Briton, Welshman' appears in English both as a simplex personal name *Walh* and as the second element of compound personal names. Similarly, some Old English personal names are wholly of Celtic origin, like *Cæbæd*, whose name appears in the royal genealogy of the kings of Lindsey, *Cædmon*, the earliest name of an Anglo-Saxon poet we know, and *Cædwalla*, the name of a West Saxon king; and it may not be pure coincidence that the latter's brother was called *Mūl* 'the half-breed'. Further, the occurrence of a small group of names in which a Celtic plural is represented by a plural in Old English is certainly an indication of bilingualism. Otherwise it it is difficult to explain linguistically how a plural in one language could be represented by a plural in a very different language. For example, Dover (K) was originally a plural form in Celtic meaning 'the waters', and the OE *Dofras* is similarly a plural form. In the same way, Wendover (Bk) 'white waters', the name of a chalky stream, is also represented by a plural form in Celtic and in Old English. Though some Anglo-Saxons may well have known Celtic, it is much more probable that the bilingual speakers were Britons, since after all they eventually gave up their own language and spoke English. The likelihood is, therefore, that names of Celtic origin were *passed on* to the Anglo-Saxons rather than being *borrowed*.

A further point to be noted is that the sound-systems of Celtic and Old English differed in some respects; certain sounds or groups of sounds which occurred in Celtic were not found in English. If a Celtic name containing a sound that did not occur in an equivalent position in a name in Old English was passed on, then sound-substitution took place and the unfamiliar sound was replaced by the nearest equivalent in Old English. So, Eccles (Db, La, Nf) is derived from Celtic *egles* 'a church', but at that time English had no medial -*g*- and -*c*- was substituted for it. The stress in Celtic was on the final syllable, whereas in English it was on the first so that a change of stress eventually took place giving us our modern *Eccles*. Eccles is also found in a number of compound names, the second element of which is an Old English word, and four such names are repeated more than once. Eccleston 'village, estate' is found four times, three examples being in Lancashire and one in Cheshire. There are similarly four instances of Eccleshall, two in

Warwickshire, and one each in Staffordshire and the West Riding of Yorkshire. The second element here is OE *halh*, the basic meaning of which is 'nook'. Two instances of Eccleshill 'hill' are found in Lancashire and the West Riding of Yorkshire and two with a second element *feld*, 'open land', in Ecclesfield (WRY) and Eaglesfield (Cu). Three other names occur only once, Eccleswall (He) 'spring', Egglescliffe (Du) 'bank', and Exley (WRY) 'glade, clearing'. Recently it has been suggested that *ecles* should be interpreted as 'a Celtic Christian community' and that Eccles indicates the former presence of a British population with an organized Christian worship and further, that the *Eccles* names constitute an important body of evidence for co-existence between the two peoples.

There is a further group of names usually referred to as tautological compounds which consist of a Celtic word and an Old English word with the same meaning. The first element of Penhill (NRY) means 'hill', while the second is the English word *hill*. In fact, in Pendle Hill (La) *hill* has been added twice, for Pendle itself is from an earlier *Penhill*. By the time it had developed to Pendle the original meaning of the second element had been forgotten and a further explanatory *Hill* was added. Further examples of tautological compounds include Chetwode (Bk), where both elements mean 'wood', Bredon (Wo) and Breedon (Lei), where both words mean 'hill', and Brill (Bk) again 'hill'. Such names suggest that the meaning of the Celtic name was unknown to the Anglo-Saxons, who added, by way of explanation, their own word for the particular topographical feature. Unlike the Eccles names, the tautological compounds do not provide us with evidence for the co-existance of the two races.

The names of some of the important Roman towns and stations, as recorded in Latin sources such as the *Antonine Itinerary*, appear in forms in which the original Celtic name has been Latinized. This is the case with *Lindum Colonia*, modern Lincoln, *Pennocrucium*, now Penkridge (St), and *Londinium*, London. The modern forms of such names are derived from the Celtic and *not* from the Latinized forms found in documents, since these names would have been passed on to the Anglo-Saxons by Celtic-speaking people.

Before considering the various groups of Celtic names, we may note Albion, an old name for Britain, which perhaps means 'the world', a very early example of British insularity, as the late Professor Kenneth Jackson pointed out.

The modern names of Roman towns and forts form an interesting and important group. The Celtic names from which they were derived may be either simplex or compound, and either type might have an English or Scandinavian word added to it. In the following examples the Romano-British forms will be given where they are known.

Names wholly Celtic in origin include Lympne (K), *Lemanis*, 'river in the elmwood', Reculver (K), *Regulbium*, 'great headland', London, *Londinium*, the meaning of which is still uncertain, while the Romano-British name of Carlisle (Cu), *Luguvalium* probably means 'Luguvalos's town'. The Celtic form was passed on into English and in early forms is spelt *Luel*. By the 9th century Celtic *cair* 'fortified town' had been prefixed to the Old English form and this has given the modern Carlisle. Catterick (NRY), *Cataractonium*, seems to be ultimately derived from Latin *cataracta* 'waterfall, rapids'. It has been suggested that from the Latin word a Celtic river-name was formed with the addition of a British suffix *-ono-* and that this was the name of the R. Swale. The name refers in all probability to the rapids near Richmond. Catterick would then have been named from the river.

However, in most of the names of Roman towns an Old English word has been added to the original Celtic name. The one most frequently found is *ceaster*, *cæster* 'city, (Roman) town', itself borrowed from Latin *castra*. This has happened in the following examples, for which the meaning of only the Celtic part has been given. Several are named from the river on which they stand: *Corinium*, Cirencester (Gl), 'town on the Churn' *Danum*, Doncaster (WRY), and *Isca Dumnoniorum*, Exeter (D), both of which are river-names, Don and Exe, used unchanged as place-names in Roman times. Churn and Exe are of uncertain meaning, but Don is 'the rapidly flowing river'. On the other hand, *Mamucium*, Manchester (La), perhaps means 'town on the round, breast-like hill', while the meanings of *Uiriconium*, Wroxeter (Sa) and *Venta*, in *Venta Belgarum*, now Winchester (Ha) are quite unknown. *Durobrivae* 'walled town at the bridges' was the Romano-British form of the modern Rochester (K), but when it was passed on into Old English the first syllable of the Celtic name was lost, so that the *first* element of Rochester represents the *second* syllable of the earlier name, that is *-rob-*. Colchester (Ess) means 'the Roman fort on the R. Colne' and Colne itself is a pre-English name of unknown meaning. The earlier name of the place was *Camulodunum* 'fortress of Camulos', the war-god of the Britons, and it is only by chance that, although the old British name of Colchester has been lost, the modern one is still partly pre-English in origin.

Other Old English words, such as *burh* 'fortified place', were occasionally added to Celtic names in the same way. Probably the most interesting of these is Salisbury (W), the Romano-British form of which was *Sorviodunum*. The meaning of *Sorvio-* has never been explained, though the second element means 'fort'. The name originally denoted Old Sarum, but when the move to the present town took place the name was retained. When the name was taken over into Old English *-dunum* was replaced by *burh*, a word having a similar sense, and it has early spellings such as *Searobyrg* and *Searesbyrig*. The latter is, however, the one which has survived, but a change of the first *r* to *l* took place, apparently due to Anglo-Norman influence, hence the modern Salisbury. The present form of Old Sarum is due to a mistake. In medieval documents it normally appears in the Latinized form *Saresburiensis*, often abbreviated. The abbreviation for *-resburiensis* was the same as that used in Latin documents for *-rum* and it was consequently taken to represent that form. As a result it was expanded to *Sarum* instead of the correct *Saresburiensis*, as was pointed out long ago by Dr. L.C. Hector, and the form *Sarum* has survived to the present day.

Only a few other Old English words have been added to the names of Roman towns, but Lichfield (St) is worthy of note. This was formerly *Letocetum* 'grey wood', and to the Celtic name was added OE *feld*, 'open land'.

A Celtic etymology has been suggested for some of the present or former names of districts. Arden (Wa) is probably from a word which means 'high, steep', topographically appropriate for the Forest of Arden; Leeds (WRY) may orignally have been a folk-name, 'dwellers on the violent river'; Maund (He) may have had the original sense 'the plain'; The Weald (K-Sx-Ha) was in Old English *Andredesweald*, literally 'large tract of land of *Andred*', *Andred* representing Romano-British *Anderita* 'great fords', renamed Pevensey (Sx); but the meaning the district-name Chiltern is quite uncertain.

Celtic names can be divided into three main groups. The largest comprises the names of rivers, usually the larger ones; a smaller group is that of hills, and the smallest that of woods. There are comparatively few of the older Celtic names denoting a habitation and those that do occur refer to some important form of settlement like names containing *dūno-* 'fort' and *duro-* 'walled town'. It was, therefore, thought that place-names did not provide us with a single example of a British habitation name. It was assumed that Celtic names were simply those of rivers and natural features some of which were transferred to later settlements nearby. Only comparatively recently has it been realised that this misinterpreted the evidence. It seems clear now that the Britons defined their settlements in terms of adjacent topographical features without using a term denoting a settlement in contrast to later Anglo-Saxon usage, when a word like *tūn* 'farm, village', 'estate', was in vogue. This, of course, suggests a continuity of settlement and place-names like Crich (Db), 'hill', and Mellor (Ch, La), 'bare hill', must have had a continuous history, as the names of habitations, from Romano-British times. It has been rightly said that this is a considerable gain for historians in search of evidence for continuity of settlement from Romano-British to Anglo-Saxon times.

Many names of Celtic origin especially those of rivers have survived without any change of form. With others an Old English (or Scandinavian) word has been added, as in the notable series Exeter, Exminster, Exmouth, Exmoor, and Exwick in Devon, all named from the R. Exe. The connection between the river-name and the place-name is usually obvious, but in some cases it has been obscured by later linguistic changes, as in Frome and *Framp*ton (Do, Gl), Avon and *Ave*ton Giffard (D).

In the past a Celtic origin has been suggested for several river-names, as for example, Amber (Db), Clun (Sa), Hodder (WRY-La), Humber (ERY-L), Itchen (Ha, Wa), Kennet (Sf-C, W), Neen (Sa) and Nene (Nth-L), Ouse (Nth-Nf, NRY-ERY), Parret (Do-So), Soar (Wa-Nt), Tees (Du-ERY), Test (Ha), Till (Cu-Nb), Tweed (Scotland-Nb), Tyne (Cu-Nb), Ure (NRY), Wear (Du), Welland (Nth-L), and Witham (R-L). Research by the late Professor Kenneth Jackson has, however, shown that such a derivation is at least doubtful, and in some cases linguistically certainly wrong. They are, without doubt, all of pre-English origin and may well in fact belong to the group of *pre-Celtic* names mentioned at the beginning of this chapter.

Sometimes, even when a name is certainly Celtic, no meaning can be suggested for it, because of gaps in our knowledge of the early British languages. This is the case with Aln (Nb) and Ellen (Cu), along with the place-name Alne (NRY), named from a lost river-name, and Severn (Wales-Cl), mentioned already as *Sabrina* by Tacitus in the second century A.D.

Tame (NRY, Wa-St, WRY-Ch), Team (Du) and Thame (Bk-O) are apparently of identical etymology, and, from the same root but with the addition of various endings, are Teme (Wales-He) and Thames (Gl-Ess/K), Romano-British *Tamesis*, *Tamesa*. The meaning of the root is uncertain, but may be something like 'dark river'. It may be noted that the *h* in Thames had never been pronounced and was inserted by 17th-century antiquarians in an attempt to make the name more classical in appearance. Tarrant (Do) and Trent (St-L) are also identical and diffi-cult names. Perhaps they mean 'strongly flooding' and this would certainly be appropriate enough for the Trent.

Often when a meaning can be suggested it is only a very general one, such as 'river', as in Avon (D, W-Gl, W-Ha, Nth-Gl). 'Water, stream' is the only one we can give to the root occurring in Dore (He), Dover (Beck) (Nt), and the place-names *Dover*court (Ess) and *Dover*dale (Wo), each derived from lost river-names. This name appears as the second element of Calder (Cu, La, WRY) 'rapid stream' and in place-names taken unchanged from the old names of streams on which they stand, like Andover (Ha) perhaps 'ash-tree stream', Candover (Ha) 'pretty stream', and Toller (Do) perhaps 'stream in a hollow'.

'Water, river' may be the meaning of the root found in Esk (Cu, NRY) and Exe (So-D), and of the second element of Dalch (D), Dawlish (D), Divelish (Do), Douglas (La), Dulas (He), as well as the place-name Dowlish (So), all of which mean 'black stream'. The Celtic adjective meaning 'black', found as the first element in this last group, is also the source of Dove (St/Db), NRY, WRY), literally meaning 'the black one'.

Celtic adjectives form the base of several other river-names such as Cam (Gl) 'crooked', Carant (Gl) perhaps 'pleasant', Cray (K) 'fresh, clean', Frome (Do, Gl, He, So-W) perhaps 'fair or brisk', Laver (WRY) 'babbling', Taw (D) 'silent, calm'. That in Peover (Ch) and Perry (Sa) means 'bright, beautiful', but in both cases OE *ēa* 'river' was added later, though it has since been lost in Peover. Here too may be noted Ivel (Bd-Hrt) 'forked river', identical to which is Yeo (So).

Several Celtic river-names are derived from the names of trees and plants which grew there. It is possible that these may originally have been adjectives, with some such meaning as 'abounding in', which came to be used of rivers. So Warren (Burn) (Nb) may mean 'abound-ing in alders', Cole (Wa-Wo) 'abounding in hazels', Leam (Nth-Wa), Lemon (D) and Lymn (L) 'abounding in elms', Darwen (La), Dart (D) and Derwent (Cu, Db, NRY-ERY, Nb-Du) 'abounding in oaks'.

A few are derived from nouns which occur also in Celtic place-names. Cerne (Do), Char (Do) and Charn (Brk) came from a word meaning 'rock, stone', hence perhaps 'stony, rocky stream' and a similar sense is likely for Crake (La), though this is derived from a different word.

A particularly interesting name is Hamps (St), which apparently means 'summer-dry', appropriate enough for a stream which flows partly underground. Where it disappears it has also a bed on the surface, which is often dry in summer, but fills in winter when the underground stream cannot take the flow of water.

Besides river-names, there are a good many hill-names of Celtic origin, most of which are derived from words which mean simply 'hill', as in the simplex Bar, now Great Barr (St). A derivative of this meaning 'hilly' is found in Barrock (Fell) (Cu). Another British word meaning 'hill' is that which appears in modern Welsh as *bre*. It occurs in the simplex form in Bray (D), while an English word meaning 'hill' has been added to form tautological compounds, as we saw earlier in this chapter. An OE word *wudu* 'wood' has similarly been added to give Brewood (St). *Bre* is also found as the second element in Clumber (Nt) 'hill above the R. Clun' (from which Clowne in Derbyshire is named and which is now called the R. Poulter), but in Kinver (St), however, the first element is uncertain. Similarly, the word now appearing in Welsh as *bryn* has given Bryn (Sa) and is the second element of the compound name Malvern (Wo) 'bare hill'.

A particularly common Celtic hill-name was that represented by modern Welsh *crug* 'hill, ridge, barrow'. It is found as a simplex name in various forms like Creech (Do, So), Crook (D, Do) and Crutch (Wo); as the second element of compound Celtic names in Evercreech (So) perhaps 'yew-tree hill' and Penkridge (St) 'chief ridge'; and as the first part of tautological compounds such as Churchdown (Gl), Church Hill (So), Crichel (Do), Crook Hill (Db), as well as Crookbarrow (Wo) and Crooksbury (Sr), where both elements apparently have the sense 'barrow, burial-mound'. An English word *tūn* 'farm, village, estate' has been added in Christon (So) and Cruckton (Sa); another Old English word *ærn* 'house' has similarly been added in Crewkerne (So), while *heath* and *field*, the latter in the sense 'open land', are found in Crickheath (Sa) and Cruchfield (Brk) respectively.

The Celtic word *penno-* now represented by Welsh *pen*, seems to have had a variety of meanings – 'head', 'end', 'hill'. It is used in the sense 'hill' in Penn (St) and the Somerset Pendomer and Penselwood, the endings of which are derived from a family name and Selwood Forest respectively. *Pen* is found occasionally in Celtic compounds such as Pentrich (Db) and Pentridge (Do) 'boar's hill'; but the meaning is probably 'end' in Pencoyd (He), Penge (Sr) and Penketh (La) 'end of the wood', and in Penrith (Cu) 'end of the ford'.

It may be noted, however, that the name of the Pennines is not an authentic Celtic name at all. It appears first in the chronicle attributed to Richard of Cirencester by Charles Bertram (1723-65), but this is certainly a forgery by Bertram. Where he got the name from is unknown, nor do we know any name for the whole range before the 18th century.

Wood-names comprise the smallest of the three main groups of Celtic names in England. As has been seen earlier in this chapter, some of the names used later of forests, such as Arden, were not originally forest-names at all. Most of those which do occur are derived from the word which has given *coed* 'wood' in modern Welsh, as in Chute (Forest) (W). This is the second element of a Celtic compound in Culcheth (La) and Culgaith (Cu) 'narrow wood', of Lytchett (Do) 'grey wood' and of Melchet (Forest) (W) 'bare wood'. Tautological compounds include Cheetwood (La) and Chetwode (Bk) in which the words from both Celtic and English mean 'wood'. In Chatham (K) and Cheetham (La) OE *hām* 'homestead, village' has been added.

Other Celtic words for topographical features are found in (King's) Lynn (Nf) 'pool', derived from the same word which occurs in *Lin*coln. Ince (Ch, La) means 'island'; Cark (La) 'stone, rock', as does the related word which has given Carrock (Fell) (Cu). Crayke (NRY), Creake (Nf) and Crick (Nth) each means 'rock, cliff' and the same word appears in the Celtic-English hybrid names Creaton (Nth) and Creighton (St), the second element of which is OE *tūn* 'farmstead, village, estate'. Another hybrid is Charnwood (Forest) (Lei) derived from Celtic *carn* 'cairn, heap of stones' and OE *wudu* 'wood'. Roose (ERY), Roose (La) and Ross (He, Nb) have the same etymology, though the meaning may be either 'moor, heath' or 'hill, promontory'. The same word is the second element of the Celtic compound Moccas (He) 'swine moor', with the loss of the medial *r* in the modern form.

The compound names discussed so far are of the usual Germanic formation, in which the defining element comes first. There is, however, also a distinctively Celtic type of compound, usually called an inversion compound, in which the defining element follows. Professor Jackson has shown that place-names of this type were not given at all during the

British period and that they probably first appear no later than the 6th century. The reasons for suggesting this date are that they occur in the more westerly areas of England and in districts settled late by the Anglo-Saxons and that they must have been prominent here by the time of the Breton migrations from south-west England, which took place in the late 5th and again in the late 6th century. They are of course common in Wales and Cornwall as also in Brittany. One feature of the inversion compounds is important. Their modern form often has the stress on the second element in contrast to the stress pattern of names of English and Scandinavian origin. So, we have Glendúe (Nb) literally 'valley dark' and Tretíre (He) 'ford long'; this stress pattern is a characteristic of later Celtic names and is almost a sure sign of Celtic origin.

Examples of inversion compounds include Cardew (Cu) literally 'fort black', i.e. 'black fort' and Maisemore (Gl) 'field big', i.e. 'big field'. Castle Carrock (Cu) is 'castle fortified', Landican (Ch) 'church (of St.) Tecan', Lancaut (Gl) 'church (of St.) Cewydd', with which can be compared the well-known Llandudno 'church' (of St.) Tudno', Caradoc (He) 'fort (of) Caradoc', Pensax (W) 'hill (of the) Saxons' and Dunchideock (D) 'fort wooded'. It has already been noted that such names occur in the more westerly parts of England and in districts settled late by the Anglo-Saxons. Research has shown that they occur particularly in Cumberland and the neighbouring part of Northumberland, in Lancashire, Cheshire, Shropshire, Herefordshire west of the Wye, in the border parts of Worcestershire and Gloucestershire, and in Cornwall, all areas of late English settlement. In Herefordshire and Shropshire there are also some purely Welsh place-names like Nant Mawr (Sa) 'valley big' and these are probably due to late Welsh migrations. Similarly, some names in north Cumberland are probably due to British reoccupation from the north in the 10th and 11th century.

This type of compound is very common in Cornwall where local names are overwhelmingly Celtic and where English settlement did not occur till the 9th century. The native language remained in use till the end of the Middle Ages in most of the area and in part of it till at least the 18th century. Only a small selection of Cornish place-names can be given and in the main they are those of well-known places.

Many of the inversion compounds contain Cornish *lann* 'enclosed cemetery'. Oliver Padel has shown that about fifty parish churches are known to have had names derived from this word and that some twenty are formed with the name of the patron saint. However, another twenty apparently have a person name, other than a saint's name, as part of the place-name. Likely examples of *lann* compounded with a saint's name appear to be Lemellan 'Maelwin', Lamorran 'Moren', Lanhydrog 'Hydroc' and Lanivet 'Nivet'. Launceston may belong here if it is derived from St. Stephen as has been suggested; in any case OE *tūn* 'farmstead, village, estate' has been later added. The names of many Cornish saints are apparently obscure and this seems to be the case with the saint-names found in Landulph, Laneast, Lanlivery, Lansallos and Lewannick.

Cornish *eglos* 'church' occurs in Laneglos which may mean 'church in the valley' and Egloshayle 'church on the estuary'. The name of the county-town, Bodmin, may also have religious associations if it means 'dwelling of the sanctuary', though Padel notes that Cornish *meneghy*, the source of the second element, came to mean 'glebe land'. He points out that if this is so the name is not significant for early church history.

There are numerous inversion compounds containing Cornish *tre*, *tref* 'estate, farmstead' and these include Tregair and Tregear the second element of which means 'fort', Tremaine 'stone', Trenowth 'new' and Trerose 'moor or promontory'. Other habitative names are Gweek 'village', Tywardreath 'house on the sands' and Helston formed from a Cornish name meaning 'ancient court' and OE *tūn*. A particularly interesting name is Marazion, with its modern alternative Market Jew, though the two were originally separate names. It is situated opposite St. Michael's Mount, and among early grants made to the monastery there was the right to hold a Thursday market. This was held on the mainland and gave its name to Marazion 'small market' and also to Market Jew which actually means 'Thursday market'.

Cornish *pen* occurs in Penare, Penryn and Pentire, each meaning 'headland, promontory', as well as Penzance 'holy headland'. Other coastal names include Towan 'sand-dune', Treath 'ferry', Porth 'harbour' and Porthallow, probably 'harbour on the R. *Alaw*', this last a lost river-name. In addition we may note Ennis 'island', Landrake 'clearing', Menna 'hill' and Restormel perhaps 'ford by the bald hill'.

Over the past fifteen years a number of studies have been published throwing light on the relations between the Anglo-Saxon settlers and the British population in the early period of large-scale Germanic settlement. Dr. Margaret Gelling has shown that in the southern parts of England the Anglo-Saxons came into direct contact with Latin speakers and that they borrowed Latin words into Old English, using those words to form place-names. One of these words is OE *wīc*, a loan-word from Latin *vicus*, the term used for the smallest unit of government in the Roman provinces. By the 4th century, however, it had come to mean as much or as little as our term *village*. OE *wīc* itself subsequently developed a variety of meanings 'dwelling, building, farm, dairy-farm' even 'salt-works'. In the compound *wīchām*, as in Wickham (Brk 2x, C, Ess 3x, Ha, K 5x, Sf 3x, Sx 2x, W), Wykeham (L 2x, Sx), Wykham (O, Sf) and Wycomb (Gl, Lei), however, it seems to have had a more specialized meaning. It has been shown that a significant number of the Wickhams and Wykehams are situated near to Romano-British habitation-sites and that there are too many examples of this for it to be purely coincidental. So, it is highly probable that here we have a group of names which has a direct connection with small Romano-British settlements. The exact significance and meaning of these names is uncertain, but they certainly seem to denote small settlements in the neighbourhood of or associated with a *vicus*. The least we can say about them is that they indicate some direct communication between Romano-British and Anglo-Saxon settlers in England. There is, moreover, an additional bonus to be gained from this group of names, in that it confirms in a striking way the early use of the word *hām* in our place-names.

There are other names which seem to demonstrate the likelihood that Anglo-Saxons settlers came into contact with Romano-British institutions and probably borrowed certain other words found in place-names. One of these is *camp*, a loan-word from Latin *campus* 'a field', and which incidentally is not found in all Germanic languages, though it does occur in Old Frisian and Old Saxon. It is the source of Camps (C), in the plural, and is the second element of Addiscombe (Sr) from the personal name *Æddi* and Barcombe (Sx) 'barley', and as the first element of Campsey (Sf) and Campsfield (O). Again, we have places closely associated with known Romano-British settlements. Further it is noteworthy that two of these names are in genitival composition, Campsey 'island of the *camp*' and Campsfield 'open land of the *camp*', and this would be perfectly consistent with the concept that *camp* could well have been originally a simplex place-name *Camp*. There seems to be a sufficient correlation between these names and known Romano-British settlements for the place-names themselves to belong to a very early period of Anglo-Saxon settlement in the areas in which they occur.

The same can be said of OE *port* 'harbour', a borrowing from Latin *portus*, and found in such coastal names as Porlock (So) 'enclosure', Portishead (So) 'headland', Portland (Do) 'tract of land, estate', Portslade (Sx) 'stream' and Portsmouth (Ha) 'mouth'. Again it seems that most of the names derived from *port* are associated with Romano-British sites and can be assumed to have a similar significance to the *camp* names.

A third word which probably belongs here, too, is OE *funta* 'spring' found only in place-names and not in other Old English sources. This would appear to be a direct borrowing from Latin *fontāna*, a view supported by the distribution of names containing the word – they are found in close association with other types of names we have already noted. It is certainly worthy of note that at least five names derived from *funta* are in a rough circle around London, Bedfont (Mx) and Bedmond (Hrt) both 'spring with a tub, butt' (the meaning also of Bedford, which survives as a street-name in Eastbourne in Sussex), Chalfont (Bk) 'calf spring'. Cheshunt (Hrt) 'spring by the Roman fort' and Wansunt (K) apparently 'Wont's spring'. All are closely associated with Romano-British sites or Roman roads. There are also small clusters in Hampshire, Boarhunt 'spring by a stronghold', Havant 'Hāma's spring' and Mottisfont perhaps 'speaker's spring', presumably referring to the holding of assemblies there, and in Wiltshire, Fovant 'Fobba's spring', Telfont 'boundary spring' and Urchfont 'Eohric's spring', as well as a single example, Tollshunt in Essex 'Toll's spring'. Again these all show similar correlations which can hardly be coincidental.

Together with other names we have already noted it seems that a very good case can be made out for contact between Anglo-Saxons and Latin speakers in an early period of English settlement. The question naturally arises, why should the Anglo-Saxons borrow the word *fontāna* when they already had perfectly good words of their own for a spring, especially OE *wella*? The answer is we do not really know, though it is reasonable to assume that there must have been something special about these springs for them to have been singled out in this way. Perhaps a clue is provided by the fact that three of them have as first element a word meaning 'tub, butt', which could well refer to a trough for collecting essential drinking water for the settlements. It may be further noted that many of the *funta* place-names are the sites of springs with a strong flow.

Three further names should be considered here. The first element of Croydon (Sr), 'valley where saffron grows', is likely to be OE *croh*, a loan-word fróm Latin *crocus* 'saffron', a plant thought to have been a Roman introduction into Britain. It is probable that this word, too, was borrowed from Latin speakers and would be a further piece of evidence for continuity from Romano-British to Anglo-Saxon times. A similar argument can be made for Dovercourt (Ess), the first element of which is a Celtic river-name, as has already been noted. It has been suggested that the second element is OE *corte*, borrowed from Latin *cohors*, *cohortem* in the sense 'enclosed yard'. Again we appear to have a word borrowed directly from Latin speakers. Thirdly, the first element of Faversham (K) is OE *fæfer*, a loan-word from Latin *faber* 'smith', a word found only in this one place-name and not in independent sources in Old English. Since the word appears here in the possessive singular it is certainly possible that it is a nickname or personal name Fæfer, derived from the noun. So, the meaning of Faversham is either 'village of the smith' or 'village of Fæfer (i.e. 'smith')' and it may well be relevant that Faversham was almost certainly a centre for metal-working in the early Anglo-Saxon period. Again we must face the possibility that here we have a third word borrowed by the Anglo-Saxons from Latin speakers in an early stage of Anglo-Saxon settlement in Britain, as Dr Margaret Gelling has suggested.

There has been considerable argument over the survival of Britons in Anglo-Saxon England. From the earlier view that they were exterminated or driven westwards, it is now believed that many more Britons survived than had been suspected. My own study of OE *walh* has demonstrated that place-names containing this word are widely distributed in England. OE *walh* means 'foreigner, Briton or Welshman' and later 'serf, slave'. The earlier meaning 'foreigner' has surived in *walnut* 'foreign nut'. It was thought that it was difficult to distinguish the meanings 'Briton, Welshman' and 'serf, slave' when the word occurred in place-names. However, it seems to be universally accepted that I have been able to 'prove' that the sense is in fact 'Briton, Welshman' in a corpus of some one hundred names, including many now lost. There are, however, numerous names with a present-day spelling Wal- which are derived from either OE *wall* 'wall' or OE *wald* 'woodland, high forest-land'. The problem of distinguishing names in *walh* from those in *wall* or *wald* is made easier because the former frequently appear in the genitive plural in contrast to *wall* and *wald*. The genitive plural of *walh* is *wala* and this gives medieval forms in *wale*. So, to make a collection of names certainly derived from *walh*, only those with Old English spellings in *Wala-*, Middle English *Wale-* can be included. Before we consider such compounds, it should be noted that Wales, the name of the Principality is derived from the plural form, *Walas*, and this is repeated in Wales (WRY), while a derivative is also found in Walredden close to the boundary of Devon and Cornwall 'the community of Britons, Welshmen'. One name Walford near Ross in Herefordshire is derived from *walh* in an uninflected form and literally means 'Welshman ford', presumably, that is, 'Welsh ford'. Otherwise all the other place-names containing this word are derived from the genitive plural OE *Wala-*, ME *Wale-* with a second element. As will be seen these names are distributed widely throughout the country, though there are some gaps, most notably in the extreme north-west and north-east. *Walh* is found with a word meaning 'brook, stream' in Walbrook (Mx) and Walburn (NRY), 'cottage, shed' in the common Walcot, as well as Walcote (Lei) and Walcott (Nf), 'valley' in Walden (Ess, Hrt, NRY), 'ford' in Walford (near Quantock, So), 'enclosure' in Walham (Gl) and 'island' in Wallasey (Ch). The second element means 'pool, lake' in Walpole (Sf), 'copse' in Walshaw (WRY) and 'farm, village, estate' in Wallington (Brk, Ha, St), Walton (Ch, Db 2x, Ess, K, La 4x, Lei 2x, Sa, Sf, St 3x, Sx, WRY 4x), as well as Walton on the Wolds (Lei) and Walton on Thames (Sr). Walmer (K) means 'pool of the Welshmen' and Walworth (Du, Sr) 'Welshmen's enclosure'. Further, it is interesting to note that a nickname or personal name *Walh* was formed from the noun and it has been suggested that this was perhaps equivalent to our present-day Taffy. The nickname is the source of about ten place-names, including Wallingford (Brk) 'ford of the people of Walh', Walshford (WRY) 'Walh's ford', Walsall (St) 'Walh's sheltered place', Walsham (Nf 2x, Sf) 'Walh's homestead, village' and Walsworth (Gl) and Wellsworth (Ha) 'Walh's enclosure'. The overall impression of the distribution and situations of all these names is that most denoted small settlements, and in many cases we can indicate a relationship between a Wal-place-name and an important Anglo-Saxon settlement in the neighbourhood. Many of the undisputed names in Wal-are situated on marginal soil or sometimes in minor valleys running from the major valleys where Anglo-Saxon settlement has taken place. The distribution clearly suggests that these Welshmen cannot have been other than a small, but nonetheless distinctive feature of the racial complex in the areas in which the names occur. Some are found in the west of England where the English language cannot have been in the ascendency much before

BRITISH RIVER NAMES
—— Certainly or probably Celtic
·········· Possibly Celtic

the end of the 7th or the early 8th century. This raises the possibility, at least, that at that time there were still small groups of Welshmen recognizable as such in areas further to the east. It cannot be doubted that there was a much greater survival of Britons in Anglo-Saxon England than was thought even twenty years ago.

Another word which points in the same direction, but which has not been subjected to such a thorough study, is OE *Cumbre*, a borrowing from the word which is represented today by Welsh *Cymro* 'Welshman'. It is the word which has given Cumberland 'land of the Welshmen'. *Cumbre* appears in such place-names as Comerbatch (Ch) 'stream, valley', Comberford (St) 'ford', Comberhalgh (La) perhaps 'sheltered place', Comber Mere (Ch) 'mere, pool', Comberton (C, He, Wo 2x) as well as Cumberton (Ess) 'farmstead, village, estate'. It also survives in the self-explanatory Cumberhill (Db), Cumberwell (W) and Cumberwood (Gl), as well as Cumberlow (Hrt) 'mound, hill' and Cumberworth (L, WRY) 'enclosure'. A personal name or nickname *Cumbra* is recorded in Old English and could well be the first element of some of the names quoted above, but this does not affect the argument, since it would parallel *Walh* derived from the noun *walh*. The evidence provided by this group of names reinforces that of Wal- names. It will be noticed, however, that here there is a marked tendency for Comber-, Cumber- place-names to occur chiefly in the West Midlands, but this is not exclusively the case, for single examples are found in Cambridgeshire, Essex, Hertfordshire and Lincolnshire, all areas well to the east of the main body of the names. Clearly, British or Welsh survival was far greater than was once believed and it is certainly possible that at least small groups of recognisable Welsh men and women survived in many parts of England and were recognizable as such as late as the end of the 7th century.

Finally, in spite of reservations, the distribution of Celtic names here provides significant evidence for the course of the Anglo-Saxon settlements. In 1953 the late Professor Kenneth Jackson made a fundamental contribution to this subject, by showing that, on the evidence of Celtic river-names alone, the country can be divided into four areas. Place-names fit so well into this distribution pattern that it is clear that, even when all English shires have been fully surveyed, the final conclusions will not be very different. County volumes published by the English Place-Name Society since Jackson wrote fully support his findings.

In Area I Celtic river-names are rare. They consist mainly of the large and medium-sized rivers, with occasional examples of other types, and the proportion of doubtful, but pre-English names, is high. This area corresponds fairly closely with the extent of primary English settlement to about the first half of the 6th century and in the south perhaps as early as about 500. Here the surviving British population was comparatively small, but, even so, was probably larger than was at one time supposed. Some districts here did not attract the new settlers, such as the Chilterns and perhaps the Fens, where enclaves of Britons lived on in some numbers.

Area II is an intermediate area, where Celtic names are markedly more common than in Area I and there are more names of small rivers. There are also names of hills and woods. This area corresponds to the next stage of Anglo-Saxon settlement, which Jackson places in the second half of the 6th century in the south and down to the first half of the 7th in the North. He points out that the hilly districts between Tyne and Tees were probably among the last parts of the area to be settled and should perhaps be placed in Area III. Indeed, he subsequently informed me personally that the map should be redrawn accordingly and the Tyne-Tees included in that area.

The third area really consists of three parts. Four particular points should be noted about Celtic names here. They are comparatively common, the number for which a certain Celtic etymology can be given is greatest, there are more names of hills and woods than to the east and there are plenty of examples of the inversion type like Blencarn, Pensax and Dunchideock. Jackson further points out that Area III comprises the final phase of Anglo-Saxon settlement, except for Cornwall; as he put it, the middle and third quarter of the 7th century in the north, the middle and second half of the same century in the Marches and the middle of the 7th century and the earlier part of the 8th in the south-west. He argued that the reason for the survival of so many names of Celtic origin here is not simply a matter of chronology, but must be rather of comparative numbers. In other words, smaller numbers of Anglo-Saxons must have been present than in areas to the east, while the 'native population' survived in considerable numbers.

The final area comprises Wales, Monmouthshire, the southwest corner of Herefordshire and Cornwall, where place-names are overwhelmingly Celtic.

The study of place-names over the past forty years has added considerably to our understanding of the nature of the relations between the Britons and the Anglo-Saxons and has demonstrated that the Britons survived in much larger numbers than had previously been allowed. It has certainly shown that, in all probability, there were groups of Welsh men and women recognizable as such, and probably in enclaves, in some parts of England certainly at the end of the 7th or early 8th century. However, it has succeeded in providing only two 'new' Celtic names. Professor Richard Coates has shown that Leatherhead (Sr) is one, such a name meaning 'grey ford', and that another is Lewes (Sx), 'slope(s)', and that this was perhaps a pre-English name for the South Downs. As Margaret Gelling notes now "it seems clear that there is no major body of such (i.e. Celtic) names awaiting discovery". Indeed, it should be stressed that, on the contrary, many more names have been deleted from the corpus of Celtic place-names than added to it. Names like Avenbury, Dinmore and Mintridge in Herefordshire seem to belong here, and certainly this is the case with Parwich (Db). I, myself, had interpreted this as 'farm on the R. *Peover*', a lost river-name identical with Peover (Ch), a name noted earlier in this chapter. Parwich should be a salutary reminder to all interested in the study of place-names of the importance of early spellings. The etymology and meaning I suggested seemed sound enough from the evidence of forms from Domesday Book onwards. However, in 1983 a hitherto unknown Anglo-Saxon charter dated 963 was discovered and the Old English spelling for Parwich found there shows conclusively that the first element *cannot* possibly be the Celtic river-name, though truth to tell its etymology is obscure. Nonetheless, there still remains a wealth of authenticated pre-English names, both Celtic and pre-Celtic, which helps to throw light on the relations between Britons and Anglo-Saxons from the first Germanic settlements here to at least the early 8th century.

four

The anglo-saxon kingdoms, the English shires, hundreds and wapentakes

The Germanic tribes who invaded and settled in Britain during the 5th century are traditionally divided into the Angles, Saxons and Jutes. We owe this classification to Bede, who in 731, describes the invaders; "They came from three very powerful nations of the Germans, namely the Saxons, the Angles and the Jutes. From the Jutes are the people of Kent and the people of Wight, that is the race which holds the Isle of Wight, and that which in the province of the West Saxons is to this day called the nation of the Jutes, situated opposite the Isle of Wight. From the Saxons, that is, from the region which is now called that of the Old Saxons, came the East Saxons, the South Saxons and the West Saxons. Further from the Angles, that is from the country which is called *Angulus*, and which from that time until today is said to have remained deserted between the provinces of the Jutes and Saxons, are sprung the East Angles, Middle Angles, the Mercians, the whole race of the Northumbrians, that is those people who dwell north of the River Humber, and the other peoples of the Angles".

It seems very likely that here Bede is drawing on genuine tradition, for the names alone would not have told him, for instance, that Kent had been occupied by the Jutes or that they had settled in part of Hampshire, or that the Mercians and Northumbrians were Angles. There is independent evidence, too, to support his classification. The kings of Mercia claimed descent from kings known to have reigned in *Angulus*, while the memory of the Jutes in Hampshire survived long enough for a late 11th-century chronicler to tell us that the New Forest was called *Ytene* 'of the Jutes', i.e belonging to the Jutes, by the English, and this is confirmed by the evidence of place-names. In the 1840 Tithe Award of the parish of East Meon there is a field-name *Eadens*, and this is the modern reflex of *Ytedene* recorded in documents dated 1263, 1301, and 1452, and of *Itedene* in a similar document of 1350. The meaning of this name is 'the valley of the Jutes'. This is the only name in Hampshire so far discovered referring to the Jutes but it clearly demonstrates their presence there. It may be noted, however, that Bede makes no mention of the Middle Saxons who gave their name Middlesex, or to any of the smaller tribal groups whose names we know from other sources. Furthermore, he does not include the Frisians, another Germanic tribe, who according to the 6th century historian Procopius also took part in the settlement of Britain. Although they have left traces of their presence in such names as Frieston (L) and Fryston (WRY) 'a farm, village of the Frisians' we have no evidence that such names definitely go back to the days of the early settlements. On the other hand, Swaffham (C, Nf) 'homestead of the Swabians' might well indicate that members of that tribe, also mentioned by Bede, were in fact among the early invaders of Britain.

By the time Bede was writing there were seven Anglo-Saxon kingdoms in existence, the so-called Heptarchy. Of these, in the southeast was Kent 'the land of the *Cantii*', apparently derived from a British tribe, the original meaning of which is unknown but might be 'the Hosts'. As we have seen it was the Jutes who settled here, but they also settled in the Isle of Wight, Romano-British *Vecta* or *Vectis*, a Latinization of a British name of uncertain origin and meaning. The Old English form of the name was *Wiht* and from this the modern form of the name is derived.

The kingdom of Sussex, corresponding more or less with the modern county, lay to the west; further west was Wessex, a name revived by 18th-century antiquarians, and across the estuary of the Thames was Essex. All three (as well as Middlesex) were originally folk-names, 'the West Saxons', 'the South Saxons' and 'the East Saxons' respectively, the group-names coming to be used of the districts in which the tribes had settled. The meaning of 'Saxon' itself is uncertain, but it may be derived from *seax* 'knife, sharp single-edged sword or dagger', the tribe taking its name from the characteristic weapon it used.

East Anglia is merely a Latinized form of OE *Ēast Engle* 'East Angles', originally a folk-name applied to the district they occupied. The Angles seem to have derived their name from *Angel*, the district Bede tells us from which they came. It probably included part of Jutland and the adjoining islands. The name itself seems to be connected with OE *angel* 'fish-hook', used in some transferred topographical sense such as 'bend of a river, land in the bend of a river'. Little is known of Bede's Middle Angles and their kingdom has left no trace in place-names. By the 7th century the district they occupied formed part of the kingdom of Mercia, itself a Latinized form of OE *Merce* 'boundary people', a word better known with reference to the later *marches* of Wales and Scotland. We do not know for certain which *boundary* is meant, but either the western one with the Welsh or the northern with Deira is most likely.

Northumbria is another Latinization, this time of OE *Norðhymbre* 'the people living north of the Humber'. At the height of its power it included the north of England, east of the Pennines, and also much of the lowlands of Scotland. The district was called *Norðhymbraland* 'land of the Northumbrians', the name still surviving in the modern county of Northumberland. Northumbria, itself was formed by the amalgamation of the kingdoms of Dere and Bernicia, named from the Celtic tribal names *Dere* and *Bernice*, which have left no trace on the modern map. It is clear that both were ultimately British or Celtic district names; *Dere* may be derived from a Primitive Welsh word meaning 'waters' and if this is so it would perhaps suggest that the centre of the original kingdom was along the rivers flowing into the Humber. *Bernice* may mean 'people of the land of mountain passes' and, if so, this would be appropriate enough for those who lived in and around the Pennines.

The Anglo-Saxon kingdoms were, however, only the final result of a gradual amalgamation of small tribes into larger units. The names of some of the smaller tribes are known, partly by the trace they have left in the place-names of the area and partly from the *Tribal Hidage*, an 11th century copy of an earlier document, which gives what appears to be the contributions due by the various districts and peoples to the 7th-century Mercian kings. Some of these names were noted in Chapter 2.

Middlesex, 'the middle Saxons', as we have seen, are not mentioned by Bede, but must have occupied a central position between the East Saxons of Essex and the West Saxons of Wessex and their territory probably included both modern Middlesex and Surrey. Little is known of the Middle Saxons historically, though 'Middlesex' was later a province of the East Saxon kingdom, but they must have been sufficiently important for a district to be named after them.

England, as we know it today, was only slowly conquered by the Anglo-Saxons and in many parts British kingdoms survived for some considerable time. For example the Anglian settlement of Cumbria was comparatively late, but Carlisle was firmly in English hands by 685. Devon was not altogether overcome before the 9th century and the occupation of Cornwall was even later and never fully carried out, while the British kingdom of Elmet in Yorkshire survived until the 7th century. Its name still survives as an affix in Barwick in Elmet and Sherburn in Elmet (WRY).

Of these names Cumbria was really a convenient geographical term before its use as that of a 'county' in 1974. The base of Cumbria occurs as the first element of Cumberland 'land of the Cymry', and *Cymry* itself is a Primitive Welsh name meaning 'men of the same country, the (joint-) countrymen'. Devon and Cornwall have both retained their Celtic names. OE *Defnas* is the Anglo-Saxon version of British *Dumnonii* 'the deep ones', *perhaps* a reference to the mines there, while Cornwall, OE *Cornwalas*, has as first element British *Cornovii* 'the promontory folk', the second being *walas*, the plural of OE *walh* 'Welshman'. On the other hand, the etymology of Elmet is quite obscure.

The division of England into administrative units called shires took place for the most part during the 9th and 10th centuries. OE *scīr* denoted 'a division of the people', but at a comparatively early date seems to have come to refer to the district inhabited by this division. From this it developed the sense 'a division of the kingdom for administrative purposes'. *Shire*, of course, appears in the name of some but not all our counties. It is also used of smaller districts which were formerly administrative units like Hallamshire (WRY), Hexhamshire (Nb) and Richmondshire (ERY) 'land within the juridiction of the manor of Hallam', 'of Hexham' and 'of Richmond'.

Some of the Anglo-Saxon and British kingdoms became shires, as for example Devon, Kent, Sussex and Essex, but for the most part the Anglo-Saxon shires did not correspond to the old tribal divisions. Some in the West Midlands were purely artifical divisions created for defence. So, Shropshire was formed probably in the 10th century by a union of two older tribal districts, that of the *Magonsǣtan* 'settlers around Maund (He)' and that of the *Wreocensǣtan* 'settlers around The Wrekin (Sa)'. The shire was named from Shrewsbury and was responsible for the defence of the fortification there. Maund is thought to be derived from a Primitive Welsh word meaning 'a plain', while The Wrekin probably takes its name from the hill-fort there before it was transferred to the Roman town, *Uriconium*, now Wroxeter. The meaning of *Uricon*, a name of Celtic origin is uncertain.

The earliest English shires, however, were formed certainly by the end of the 8th century and were in Wessex. Each district took its name from a town or royal estate which became the centre of local administration as in the case of Wilton for Wiltshire, Southampton (earlier Hampton) for Hampshire, and Somerton for Somerset. It would appear that the West Midland shires, as well as Oxfordshire, Buckinghamshire and Hertfordshire, were formed on the West Saxon pattern. These areas were under the control of Wessex, and the shires were probably created in the reign of Edward the Elder, 899-925, to assist in defence against the Danes. Each of them represents an administrative district responsible for the maintenance of a defensive centre, as we saw in the case of Shropshire and Shrewsbury, and similarly with Herefordshire and Hereford, and Staffordshire and Stafford.

The East Midland shires of the Danelaw also came into existence during the 10th century. These too took their names from the most important town in the area, but these towns had earlier been the headquarters of a Danish army. So, Derbyshire, Nottinghamshire, Leicestershire, Northamptonshire, Huntingdonshire, Bedfordshire, and Cambridgeshire represent the district occupied by divisions of the Danish army with their headquarters at Derby, Nottingham, Leicester, Northampton, Huntingdon, Bedford, and Cambridge respectively. Lincolnshire was formed in a similar way, but in this case it was a union of the areas under the control of two armies, those of Lincoln and Stamford, which formed the great shire taking its name from Lincoln.

The only county south of the Humber which had not come into existence before the Norman Conquest is Rutland. The southern region formed part of Northamptonshire, while the northern, from at least 1002, was regularly assigned as dower to the queen. Presumably it was this royal association which enabled a small district to become a county. It is first named as such in 1204 when 'the county of Rutland' was granted as dower by King John to Queen Isabella. However, it is pretty certain that Rutland 'Rōta's estate' was formed as such in a very early stage of Anglo-Saxon settlement in the East Midlands, and that it survived intact the Danish occupation of the 'Kingdom of the Five Boroughs', as we shall see in a later chapter.

The only pre-Conquest shire north of the Humber is Yorkshire. Considerable Danish settlement took place here from 875 onwards and like the East Midland shires it no doubt represents the district controlled by the Danish army with its headquarters at York. It *may* even be that this district comprised the old British kingdom of Deira.

Lancashire, south of the Ribble, formed part of Cheshire before the Norman Conquest, while the remainder of the pre-1974 county, together with South Westmorland and South-west Cumberland belonged to Yorkshire. Most of what was Lancashire was held by Roger of Poitou after 1066 and a group of manors under a single lord was known as an Honour. So the county of Lancashire developed out of the Honour of Lancaster, probably in 1194.

The history of the two pre-1974 counties, Cumberland and Westmorland, is obscure through much of the Anglo-Saxon period, but it is believed that in the reign of William the Conqueror they formed a border province held by the king of Scotland. It was recovered by William Rufus in 1092 and granted to Ranulf le Meschin who surrendered it to the crown when he became Earl of Chester in 1120. Most of those parts which had been previously assessed with Yorkshire were added and the whole area divided into the sheriffdoms of Carlisle and Westmorland. The 'county of Cumberland' is first recorded in the sheriff's accounts in 1177.

As we have seen, Northumberland is derived ultimately from the Anglo-Saxon kingdom of Northumbria, which was gradually reduced to the status of an earldom centred on Bamburgh. The name Northumberland is apparently first recorded in its modern sense in 1065 and during the 11th century it is used with increasing definiteness of this district, except for areas which formed part of the lands of the bishops of Durham.

The land between the Tyne and the Wear was given to the Church of St Cuthbert by the Danish king Guthred in 883 and was consequently known as 'the land of St Cuthbert'. The seat of the bishop was moved to Durham in 995 and the relics of the saint were similarly translated to the new cathedral there. Before the Norman conquest this had already become the centre of a great lordship and during the 11th and 12th centuries additional areas came into the hands of the bishops. The Bishop of Durham exercised regal rights over his lands and by the end of the 13th century they were known as a palatinate – a district, the lord of which held jurisdictions which elsewhere belonged only to the sovereign. The palatinate was abolished in 1646 but was revived after the Restoration and survived until 1836, when jurisdiction was finally vested in the Crown.

Although the shires came into existence in various ways their names fall into three separate groups, those originally tribal or folk-names, those originally district names, and those derived from the names of towns. Essex, Middlesex, Sussex, Kent, Devon, and Cornwall, as we have seen, were tribal names, whether British or Anglo-Saxon. Norfolk 'the north folk' and Suffolk 'the south folk' were named from the people who lived respectively in the northern or southern parts of East Anglia. In all these cases the original names came to be used of districts, without the addition of a word meaning 'land or district'.

The same is true of Dorset and Somerset, which were earlier also folk-names, though in these cases they are derived from place-names to which OE *sǣte* 'settlers, dwellers' was added. So, Dorset, OE *Dornsǣte*, means 'settlers around *Dorn*', a shortened form of Dorchester, the first element of which is derived from Romano-British *Durnovaria*, which has not yet been properly explained, but which is almost certainly Primitive Welsh in origin. To this Celtic name of the town the Anglo-Saxons added OE *ceaster* 'Roman fort', so giving *Dornwaraceaster*, our modern Dorchester. The OE form for Somerset was *Sumortūnsǣte* 'dwellers around Somerton' in which Somerton means 'summer farm'. Either *sǣte* was added to the first part of the name only or *tūn* was lost at an early date, the resulting *Sumorsǣte* giving modern Somerset.

In three shire-names, Cumberland, Northumberland and Westmorland, a final element *land* 'large tract of land' has been added to the genitive plural of tribal or folk-names. The first two have already benn discussed, and Westmorland means 'land of the *Westmōringas* (people who live west of the moor)', probably referring to those who lived around the upper valley of the Eden.

Four of the shire-names were from the beginning the names of districts. Kent, as we have already seen, is a Celtic (i.e Primitive Welsh) name, and so is the first part of Berkshire, which is derived from an adjective meaning 'hilly'. It is certainly possible that it was originally the name of the Berkshire Downs. Rutland and Surrey, on the other hand are names of Old English origin. The meaning of Rutland has already been noted as an old district name and so too is Surrey. It dates from the settlements of the Middle Saxons on both sides of the Thames, Surrey being the southern part of the area and appropriately called 'the southern district'.

The remaining counties with the exception of Durham have the word *shire* added to the name of an important town in the district. The county of Durham came into existence comparatively late and here the same form is used indifferently of county and town. The name seems to be an Anglo-Scandinavian formation, *Dūnholmr*, the first element being OE *dūn* 'hill', the second ON *holmr* 'island', topographically appropriate for a place situated on a hill in a prominent bend of the Wear. It seems likely that the replacement of *n* by *r* is due to Anglo-Norman influence, but it is worth noting that the Bishop of Durham still signs himself 'X Dunelm'.

The names of the counties which end in *shire*, can be classified according to the language from which they are derived – Celtic, hybrid Celtic and English, English, and Scandinavian. The first element of Lincoln, the Romano-British *Lindum Colonia* of the Ravenna geographer, is from a Celtic word, which has given *llyn* 'lake' in modern Welsh, with reference to the broad pool in the River Witham now called Brayford Pool. To this was added the British form of Latin *colonia* after the establishment here of a settlement of time-expired legionaries in succession to the earlier fortress.

The hybrid Celtic-Old English names include Cambridge, Gloucester, Lancaster, Leicester, Wilton, and Worcester. Cambridge in Old English was *Grantanbrycg*, 'bridge over the *Grante*', though the subsequent development of the name is still a matter of debate. It should be noted that in Bede it is called *Grantacaestir* ,'Roman fort on the *Grante*', and that this is not the origin of the nearby Grantchester which means 'settlers on the *Grante*'. The meaning of the river-name is obscure and it may indeed be a pre-Celtic name. Gloucester, Romano-British *Glevum*, is based on a Celtic name probably meaning 'the bright spot or place' to which was added OE *ceaster* 'Roman fort' and, like Lincoln, Gloucester was a Roman *colonia*. Lancashire is a shortening of an earlier Lancastershire, Lancaster itself being 'Roman fort on the Lune'. Lune is a Celtic river-name (found also in NRY) though its meaning is uncertain. The exact etymology of Leicester is much more difficult, though of course the second element is the same as in Lancaster. The first has been explained as a folk-name ultimately derived from a Celtic river-name, but the river in question cannot have been the Soar (itself in all probability a pre-Celtic name) on the banks of which Leicester stands. This is recorded early and always in forms such as *Soar*. It must refer rather to one of its tributaries which itself must have been called *Leire* and which gave its name to the nearby Leire (Lei). The first element would then mean something like 'dwellers on the *Leire*', but the meaning of this river-name is also not known. Wiltshire, earlier Wiltonshire, is named from Wilton (W) 'farm, estate on the Wiley', and all that can be said of Wiley is that it is a pre-English river-name of unknown etymology and meaning. Worcester means 'Roman fort of the *Wigoran*', the latter an Anglo-Saxon tribal name, which occurs also in Wyre Forest (Wo). It is thought that this name is perhaps ultimately the pre-English name of a stream or river near which the people lived, but it is impossible today to identify it, or to deduce its etymology.

Most of the names of the county towns are of English origin and five have a second element -*ford*, a clear indication of the importance of river-crossings for early settlers. The first element of Bedford is probably a masculine personal name OE *Bēda*; Hertford and Oxford are named from 'hart' and oxen' respectively, Stafford from a landing-place, and Hereford, like Hartford (Hu) and Harford (D), is literally 'army ford', though the significance of such a name is still being debated.

The modern spellings of Buckingham and Nottingham conceal the fact that the endings are of different origins, as the early forms for each show. That in Buckingham is OE *hamm* 'land in a river-bend' while that in Nottingham is OE *hām* 'homestead'. So, Buckingham means 'land in the river-bend of Bucca's people' and Nottingham 'homestead of Snot's people'. The earliest recorded spelling of Nottingham is *Snotengaham*, but the initial *S*- had been lost by the early 12th century, probably due to Norman influence, and the modern form is *N*ottingham instead of *Sn*ottingham.

Sout*hampton*, from which Hampshire took its name, and Nort*hampton* similarly appear to have the same etymology, but the latter represents an original *Hāmtūn* 'home farm', while Southampton is from *Hammtūn* in which h*amm* has been shown to denote a promontory, hence 'promontory settlement'. The two names would later need to be differentiated because of the similarity of their forms. By 962, Southampton had already been given its distinctive prefix, but that in Northampton does not seem to have appeared before 1085, after which the county also has the longer form. On the other hand, in Hampshire, the short form has survived with the loss of the medial -*ton*- although for a time *Hamtonshire* and *Southamtonshire* are found side by side. A still further shortened form *Hantescire* occurs in Domesday Book and Hants, the usual abbreviation of the county name, has developed from this. The abbreviation Northants for Northamptonshire is not, however, found in early spellings and presumably was formed later by analogy with Hants.

Huntingdon means 'huntsman's hill' but Warwick is a difficult name for which only a tentative suggestion can be made 'dwellings by the weir' though this is really uncertain. Early spellings show that Shropshire is named from Shrewsbury, OE *Scrobbesbyrig*, itself another name for which only a plausible, but uncertain, meaning 'fortified place of the scrubland' can be proposed. The difference between the present name of the town and that of the county is due to various changes having taken place in the forms of both, including the loss of the medial *-bury-* in the latter. The usual abbreviation for Shropshire, Salop earlier *Salopescire*, is derived from a Normanized form of the English name. Cheshire is a shortened form of Chestershire and is of course named from Chester 'Roman fort, city'. Its earlier name was Romano-British *Deva* 'place on the Dee', the river-name meaning 'the goddess', presumably therefore 'holy river'. Throughout most of the Roman period Deva was the headquarters of the Twentieth Legion and this is reflected in the earliest English forms of Chester, *Legaceaster*, etc., 'camp of the legion(s)'. The first part of this name was lost in the Old English period and the resulting simplex form *Ceaster* has given the modern Chester.

The only county town of definitely Scandinavian origin is Derby, though the present form of York owes much to Scandinavian influence. Early sources make it clear that Derby 'farm, village where deer are found' has replaced an earlier English name of the place *Northworthy,* 'north enclosure'. The *Chronicle of Ethelwerd*, written down about 1000, tells us how the body of the English alderman Athelwulf, killed in battle against the Danes at Reading in 871, was brought for burial "into the place which is called Northworthy, according to the Danish language, however, Derby". The earliest recorded spellings of York, *Eborakon*, *Eburacum* and *Eboracum*, are found in Greek and Latin sources. This is in origin a Celtic name perhaps meaning 'yew grove'. By the time of the earliest Anglo-Saxon settlement there it had probably become *Evorōg* and the newcomers seem to have taken the first part of the name as being identical with OE *eofor* 'wild boar' and so substituted their own word for the Celtic one. To it they added a common place-name element *wīc* 'trading centre, dairy farm', so giving OE *Eoforwīc*. During the Scandinavian occupation of the city further changes took place and the Old English name was adapted by them to *Eórvík*, later becoming *Jórvík*, York being the modern reflex of the latter. Latin *Eboracum*, however, continued to be the usual spelling in official documents and is still in ecclesiastical use when the Archbishop of York signs himself 'X Ebor'.

Yorkshire is divided into three parts, the East, North, and West Ridings. These division are of Danish origin as is the word itself, for Riding is from the Scandinavian *þriðjungr* 'third part', borrowed into English as *þriðing*. This would give an early form like *Norththriding* which would regularly become *Northriding* and so North Riding. The other divisions had forms such as *Eastthriding* and *Westthriding*. The combination of the consonants *t* and *th* would become *tt* and then *t*, hence *Easttriding*, *Westtriding* in turn becoming *Eastriding*, *Westriding* and finally East Riding and West Riding.

Lindsey, the most northerly of the parts of Lincolnshire, similarly has North, South, and West Ridings, but the term is not found in any other county. Lindsey was itself once an independent Anglo-Saxon kingdom, though its early history is obscure. The first element of the name itself is Primitive Welsh *Lindes* 'the people of Lincoln or of the pool', the base of this name being the same as that of Lincoln itself. To this was added OE *ēg* 'an island, raised land in a wet area', but its significance here is completely uncertain. The two other Parts of Lincolnshire are Kesteven and Holland. The former is a hybrid Celtic and Danish name. The first part is the Primitive Welsh word surviving as *coed* 'wood' in modern Welsh, the second being Danish *stefna* 'meeting', later 'district with a meeting-place', no doubt its meaning here. Holland (identical with Holland Ess, La, Hoyland WRY and Hulland Db) 'land by a (low) hill-spur' is of English origin, an example of a place-name becoming the name of a district.

Two other counties, Kent and Sussex, had similar major subdivisions in Anglo-Saxon times. The *Lathes* of Kent probably represent the provinces of the old kingdom and the *Rapes* of Sussex may well have a similar origin. Both are Old English words, the first meaning 'division of land', while the second is derived from the same word as modern *rope*. Its use in this sense is apparently due to the Germanic custom of enclosing the precincts of a court with ropes.

Most of the English shires were divided into smaller administrative districts called *hundreds*. These were probably formed in the 10th century, though an earlier date is certainly possible for those in the West Saxon shires. Furthermore it is equally possible that they represent much earlier land divisions. In theory the hundred represents a district assessed for purposes of taxation at one hundred hides, but in practice they were rated at a higher and a lower figure. The hide was originally the amount of land which would support a household, probably as much land as could be tilled with one plough in a year. Of course, this would vary according to the fertility of the soil, but it seems on average to have been about 120 acres. OE *hīd* has itself actually given rise to a number of place-names and these are discussed in a later chapter. Now, the hundred enjoyed particular financial and jurisdictional functions and had its own court and meeting-place, and the number of these divisions within a county varied, so that Huntingdonshire had only four while Sussex had sixty-seven.

In the Danelaw, the equivalent of the hundred was called the *wapentake*. This is the modern form of *wæpengetæc*, itself a borrowing of Sacandinavian *vápnatak*. The word originally seems to have denoted the symbolic brandishing of weapons by which decisions at meetings were confirmed. It then came to be used of the meeting itself and at a later date, but apparently only in England, of the district from which the members of the assembly came. In all probability wapentake was the regular word for this adminstrative area throughout most of the Danelaw, but in those parts of it which were early reconquered or less completely Scandinavianized the term was replaced by the hundred of the other counties. Today, the division into wapentakes is found only in the three Yorkshire Ridings, Nottinghamshire, Leicestershire, and the northern parts of Lincolnshire. However, in other counties some of the divisions now called hundreds are referred to as wapentakes in early sources, as for example in Northamptonshire and parts of Derbyshire.

In the four northern counties, as in some of the southern counties of Scotland, the division is into *wards*. This apparently meant 'district to which certain defensive duties were assigned', and its use in this sense seems to belong to the period after the Norman Conquest. Many of these wards are named from river-valleys, as in Glendale (Nb), Eskdale (Cu), and Lonsdale (We), from the Glen, Esk, and Lune; others from medieval castles or manors such as Bamburgh (Nb) 'fortified place of Bebbe (a late 6th century queen of Bernicia)', Morpeth (Nb) 'murder path', and Easington (Du, as also in Bk, ERY, NRY) 'farm, estate associated with Ēsa'; while two Wards in Westmorland are simply called East Ward and West Ward.

The names of the hundreds and wapentakes fall into three main groups according to their origin. A few have district names, usually no longer used as such; some take their name from the meeting-place of the hundred or wapentake; while the greatest number is named from a village or manor in the area. Only the second of these groups is discussed here, the district names having been dealt with already, the last group being more conveniently considered as place-names.

This second group consists of topographical names referring to hills, mounds, clearings, trees, stones, and the like. These presumably became the names of hundreds and wapentakes because they were the meeting places of the district assemblies. This is certainly the case with Barrow Hundred (Do), formerly *Hundredsbarrow Hundred* 'hundred burial-mound', i.e. 'burial-mound where the hundred meets'. The site of the meeting-place is still known, since Hundred Barrow survives as the name of a Bronze Age round barrow near Bere Regis.

A few names describe what happened at the meeting, since Spelhow (Nth) and Spelthorne (Mx) mean 'speech hill' and 'speech thorn-bush' respectively. Modbury (Do) is 'moot barrow', the name of a burial-mound on the hill near Cattistock, and the first element of this is found in a large number of widely-distributed minor names like Moot Hill, Moatlow, Mootlow, as well as Mutlow (C, Ess) all of which are named from burial-mounds. These were hills or mounds on which the assembly of the shire, hundred, or village was held. A comparable Scandinavian name is Thingoe (Sf) 'assembly mound'. Two similar names are the Scandinavianized Skyrack (WRY) 'oak where the shire meets' and the English Shirley (Ha) 'glade where the shire meets', which became the names of a wapentake and a hundred respectively. Wittery (Sa) is probably also a name of this type. It means 'wisemen's tree' i.e. 'tree where the wisemen meet', and the 'wisemen' here may well have been the members of the hundred court.

The site of the hundred assembly would have been chosen for various reasons, the most usual presumably being the ease of access from different parts of the district. A hill or mound was a not uncommon place for it and some of these, particularly burial-mounds, must already have possessed names. Unfortunately OE *beorg* and *hlāw*, could mean either 'hill' or '(burial-) mound' and it is not always easy to say which is the correct interpretation. In some cases, however, the burial-mound still survives or is recorded in earlier records or on maps, and can be identified, as in the case of Offlow (St), the first element of which is the Old English personal name Offa, though we do not know whether Offa himself was buried there. Other hundred names derived from similar personal names are Brightwellsbarrow (Gl) and Bountisborough (Ha) from Brihtwald and Blunt respectively and Huxlow (Nth) from Hōc. In some names the first element is not a personal name like Standborough (D) 'stony hill', the site of an ancient encampment, and Radlow (He) 'red mound, hill'.

A few hundred-names are derived from Old English words such as *stoc* and *stōw*, commonly used in place-names with a meaning 'place, site'. In the case of *stōw* it is certain that the word had developed the sense 'meeting-place', as in Broxtowe (Nt) 'Brōcwulf's meeting-place' and Northstow (C) 'north meeting-place'; it is probable that a similar extension of meaning had taken place with *stoc*, as in Stoke (Bk, Mx).

A further group of hundred-names have as second element OE *lēah* 'wood; glade in a wood'. As a rule the meaning here is probably 'glade' as in Bisley (Gl), Budleigh (D), and Godley (Sr) from the OE masculine personal names Bisa, Budda and Godda; Bradley (Gl, L) is 'broad, spacious glade' and Wetherley (C) 'glade where wethers are found'.

Many of the hundred-names are descriptive of some such feature like a tree or stone, no doubt one which marked the meeting-place of the hundred. Appletree (Db) is self-explanatory, but most of the -tree names have a personal name as first element, *Beohha* in Becontree (Ess), *Ēadwine* in Edwintree (Hrt) and *Wīhstān* in Wixamtree (Bd). The particular trees occurring most frequently are oak, ash and thorn as in Tipnoak (Sx) 'Tippa's oak-tree', Catsash (So) 'Catt's or wild cat's ash-tree' and Elthorne (M) 'Ella's thorn-bush'.

Usually, -stone is combined with a personal name as in Tibaldstone (Gl) 'þeodbald's stone' and Kinwardstone (W) 'Cyneward's stone', but the first element of Hurstingstone (Hu) is a folk-name meaning 'dwellers in the wood'. These must have been prominent stones at which the meeting was held, as presumably they were at Staine (C) and Stone (Bk, So), simplex names meaning simply 'stone'. A similar name is Staple (Sx, W) 'pillar, post' suggesting that the meeting-place was marked by a post, which was 'white' at Whitstable (K).

Most of the Scandinavian names refer to wapentakes and they can be classified in a similar way to the hundreds; but, three words occur particularly frequently here. ON *haugr* could mean either '(burial-) mound' or 'hill' and the problems of interpretation have already been highlighted in the discussion of OE *beorg* and *hlāw*. Grimshoe (Nf) and Wraggoe (L) are derived from the Old Danish personal names Grīm and

Wraggi respectively but it would be unsafe to assume that these were the names of men buried there. The same is true of Haverstoe (L) where the first element is the Old Danish personal name Hawarth. Here the mound in question is a pre-historic round barrow and it is highly unlikely that it was also the burial mound of Hawarth himself. Now, in the cases of Haverstoe and Wraggoe there are in the same wapentakes the place-names Hawerby and Wragby 'farm, village of Hawarth' and 'of Wraggi'. It is very likely that both the place and wapentake were named from the same man and that he was the head-man of the district. Greenow (Nf) and Langoe (L) are derived from the adjectives 'green' and 'long' respectively, and the meaning of *haugr* in these names could be either 'mound' or 'hill'. However, there can be no doubt that the meaning is 'tumulus' in Threo (L) 'three barrows', and Forehoe (Nf) 'four barrows'.

Similarly, ON *lundr* could mean either 'wood' or 'grove', particularly 'sacred grove' and this may explain why such a site was chosen for the meeting-place of the wapentake. In modern forms *lundr* sometimes appears as -land as in Aveland (L), Framland (Lei), from the Danish personal names Ave and Fráni respectively

The third of these words is modern English *cross*, ultimately Latin *crux, crucem*. The Latin word was borrowed into Old Irish as *cros* and this in turn entered the vocabulary of the Norwegian invaders of Ireland as *kross*. The Norwegians passed the word on to their later settlements in the north-west of England and from there it gradually spread southwards, eventually finding its way into the vocabulary of late Old English. In place-names *cros* is common in the North and East Midlands, but elsewhere it is usually found only in late forms from the 16th century onwards. In hundred-names it occurs as far south as Norfolk and Huntingdonshire, counties which once formed part of the Danelaw. It is the source of Staincross (WRY) 'stone cross', but most examples have a Scandinavian personal name as first element, like Osgot (Ásgautr) in Osgoldcross (WRY), Bróði in Brothercross (Nf), Gildi in Guiltcross (Nf), Vali or Valr in Walshcroft, earlier -cross, (L). Normancross (Hu) 'Northman's or Norwegian's cross', however, is a particularly significant name historically. It indicates the presence of a man of Norwegian origin in the southern part of the Danelaw, where the settlers were predominantly Danes. Such a name could only have arisen in a district where it was unusual to find Norwegians among the settlers.

Perhaps the most interesting of all the wapentake-names is Lawress (L) 'Lag-Ulfr's coppice'. The modern equivalent of this personal name would be Law-Wolf; Wolf was his name and Law his nickname. In Norway and Iceland a famous lawman was sometimes distinguished by having *Lag-* or *Laga-* prefixed to his name and our Law-Wolf must have been just such a man. Only rarely does a single place-name throw such light on the local social, administrative, and human situation. Lawress indicates that the wapentake met at a coppice named after its headman; it also indicates that this district was sufficiently dominated by Danes for them to have been able to impose their own customs upon it. Groups of Danes settled in the district which they themselves formed or took over under their lawman into the wapentake of Lawress, and they must have settled in sufficient numbers to have been able to impose their own social structure on it.

five

Early English settlement-names

In 1961 place-name scholars were agreed that the earliest English habitation-names were those derived from the OE suffix *-ingas*, surviving today as -ings in Hastings (Sx) or more frequently as -ing in Reading (Brk). They also believed that place-names derived from *-ingahām* as in Nottingham were only a little later. The general view was that such names belonged to the earliest phases of substantial Germanic settlement in Britain, traditionally associated with the second half of the 5th and first part of the 6th century. As we shall see this hypothesis is no longer believed tenable.

The theory of the high antiquity of *-ingas* place-names goes back to the historian J.M. Kemble in 1849. OE *-ingas* is the plural of the suffix *-ing*, which in genealogies and similar contexts was added to a personal name to form a patronymic, so that Alfred the Great occasionally appears as *Ælfred Æþelwulfing* 'Ælfred son of Æþelwulf'. In the plural it was added to a personal name and used to denote the name of a dynasty, so that the royal house of East Anglia was known as the *Wuffingas* 'descendants of Wuffa'. The plural form, however, seems at an early date to have developed further, to denote the dependents of, people of, as in Hastings 'dependents of, people of Hæst(a)'. This was in origin the name of a group of people associated together under a single leader and not only included blood relations but also dependents (along with their wives and children). These were unrelated by blood to the lord but bound to him by an oath of loyalty. Group-names, and the place-names formed from them, are also found in other Germanic areas on the continent, and such groups seem to have been typical of the migrations of the Germanic peoples. Since they represent a social organization which must have preceded the establishment of kingdoms, it was accepted that place-names like Reading 'dependents, people of

Read(a)', must belong to the earliest periods of settlement in this country. So, they help to define those areas first settled, and their geographical distribution will indicate the routes by which the settlers penetrated into the country.

Further, it was believed that, in spite of some discrepancies, archaeological evidence supported that of the *-ingas* place-names. When the sites of Anglo-Saxon pagan cemeteries were plotted on a map placed side by side with one showing the distribution of *-ingas* names the patterns were thought to show a "remarkable agreement", according to the Swedish place-name scholar Eilert Ekwall. Anomolies in the two distribution patterns were, however, clear enough. There are districts like the upper Thames valley where evidence of early settlement is indicated by archaeology but where *-ingas* names are rare. In others like Essex, there are over twenty *-ingas* names but the supporting archaeological evidence is to a considerable extent lacking. Nonetheless, the theory of the high antiquity of names like Hastings was so entrenched that it survived in spite of this.

It should be borne in mind that Old English place-names in which a personal name was followed by the suffix *-ingas* are not originally place-names at all; rather, they are group-names, the names of groups of people, which became the names of places when the group concerned became associated with a particular district and eventually with a particular place. Of course, several generations may have elapsed before this happened, though this was never taken into consideration when the theory was accepted as fact.

Now, the suffix *-ingas* was also used to denote the inhabitants of a place, in which case it was added to an appellative. Clearly a further development of meaning had taken place to 'people who live at, etc.' So, Avening (Gl) means 'people who live by the R. Avon', Epping (Ess) 'on the upland' and Nazeing (Ess) 'on the spur of land'. This formation, however, continued in use through the Old English period, as is shown by such a name as *West Centingas* 'men of West Kent' recorded in the *Anglo-Saxon Chronicle* in the annal for 999. It was therefore clear that only the place-names which consist of a *personal* name and the suffix *-ingas* provide certain evidence of a very early date.

The plural form only rarely survives into the present day, though in addition to Hastings, we have Cannings (W) 'Cana', Barlings (L, identical with Barling Ess and Birling K, Nb, Sx), 'Bǣrla' and Filkins (O) 'Filica'. Usually the final -s has been lost so that the current spelling is in -ing as in Read*ing*, or even -in as in Kilp*in* (NRY) 'Cyppel' or -en as in Kitch*en* End (Bd) 'Cycca'. But, early spellings are usually conclusive in demonstrating that the original Old English form was indeed *-ingas*.

Group-names, in the genitive plural, are also found compounded with other elements. The commonest of which is *hām* 'homestead, village'. So, we have Nottingham, Birmingham (Wa) from *Beormingahām* 'homestead of the *Beormingas* (people of Beorma)', and Gillingham (Do, K, Nf) 'of the Gyllingas (Gylla's people)'. Occasionally the medial syllable has been lost, hence Goodmanham (ERY) 'Gōdmund', Langham (Ess) 'Lahha' and Longham (Nf) 'Lāwa'. There are also a few examples of this type in which the first element is a topographical group-name, as in Hoveringham (Nt) 'homestead, village of the Hoferingas (dwellers on the hump of ground)', and Uppingham (R) 'of the Yppingas (dwellers on the higher ground)'. These are comparable with the topographical group-names in *-ingas* and like them were not thought to provide evidence of a very early date. They were, however, thought in general to be likely to be very old formations.

The relationship between names such as Birmingham and Hastings appeared to be so close that it was believed that both were being formed during a similar period. It was thought that the Birmingham type continued to be given for a generation or so after the Hastings type became obsolete, simply because the former are place-names in origin and not group-names which became the names of districts and later of places. Nonetheless, it was believed that both belonged to a similar broad period of primary Anglo-Saxon settlement in the various parts of England in which they are found, say from the later 5th to the end of the 7th century.

The genitive plural of a group-name is sometimes followed by other elements besides *hām*. In all the names which follow only the personal name from which the group-name is derived will be given. So, from OE *burh* 'fortified place' we have Wellingborough (Nth) 'Wendel'; from *burna* 'stream', Bassingbourn (C) 'Basa'; from *feld* 'open country', Haslingfield (C) 'Hæsel(a)'; from *ford* 'ford', Manningford (W), 'Manna'; from *lēah* 'wood, glade', Headingley (WRY), 'Headda'; from *tūn* 'farm, village, estate', Knedlington (ERY), 'Cneddel or Cnytel'; from *worð* 'enclosure', Bobbingworth (Ess), 'Bubba'. These names form a small but important class and it was thought that they belonged to a similar period to those in *-ingahām*.

The various parts of England were, of course, settled at various times and names in -*ingas* and -*ingahām* may well have been used in some areas long after they had become obsolete in others. Settlement in the South and South-east was presumed to have taken place in the second half of the 5th century and the early part of the 6th, while that in say Warwickshire and Worcestershire was later. In these two counties there are only occasional examples of names in -*ingahām* and none at all derived from -*ingas*. Indeed, in Derbyshire not a single example of either type is recorded. It was argued, no doubt quite rightly, that a group of pioneers moving westwards might still retain an earlier form of social organization and so give names like Birmingham at a time when such an organization and the place-names resulting from it had become obsolete in the South-east of England, as we have already noted. It was always believed that names in -*ingas* comprised the earliest identifiable English habitative place-names and that the -*ingahām* and other -*inga*- formations, like -*ingaburh*, were given only slightly later. The high antiquity of these types was never in dispute.

The anomalies in the distribution patterns of Anglo-Saxon pagan burial-sites and these place-names have been recognized for a long time. Already in 1935, J.N.L. Myers had noted that the place-names might represent a phase later than that of the burial-sites, but suggested that, if they were indeed contemporary, the disparity of their distribution must be caused by the non-survival of place-names and the non-discovery of burial-sites. It was not until the 1960s, however, that the two bodies of evidence were compared in detail and startling results followed.

The first study to demonstrate this was by the late John Dodgson, who examined in detail the coincidence of -*ingas*, -*inga*- names and pagan burial-sites in the South-eastern counties. It was found to be, as one scholar put it "about as little as is possible, given that both occur in substantial numbers in the same southern and eastern portions of England". Of course, there are occasional coincidences between these place-names and burial-sites, but they are comparatively rare. The overwhelming evidence from southern England shows that the supposed relationship between the two is illusory; the -*ingas*, -*inga*-names cannot, it would seem, go back to the earliest period of the Anglo-Saxon settlement, the so-called 'immigration phase', as represented by the pagan-burials.

Yet, it must be emphasized that the evidence indicates that the personal name plus -*ingas* formula is an archaic one. Even so, it is clear that in the South-east at any rate these place-names and the social organization they represent are not associated with pagan burial-sites. Rather they seem to be associated with a later phase of settlement, now referred to as the 'colonizing phase'. It would seem that the communities who gave these names used different and distinctive burial customs, which are difficult to discover. Once again, Myers had suggested a possible answer to this, that the burial places of the *-ingas, -inga-* groups may have become the Christian churchyards of the Conversion, an interpretation which has now found general favour. The significance of these names is still considerable. They may not be derived from the names of men who were among the first to settle in Britain, but they may well have been leaders of "the folk who made Britain England", as Dodgson put it, and he added "they are still sure of their eminence in some command, which ever way the speculation goes".

This hypothesis was tested in the East Midlands by a young Dutch scholar, Joost Kuurman. His detailed analysis of these groups of names supported the theory that they belong rather to a colonizing than an immigration phase of settlement. But, examining them from a topographical and geological point of view, he found that places with names of the *-ingahām* type were frequently on more attractive sites for settlement than those derived from *-ingas* and *inga-* plus another element, like *burh* for example. As a result, he suggested that place-names derived from *-ingahām*, in general, **preceded** those derived from *-ingas* and *-inga-*followed by another element, at least so far as the East Midlands is concerned. This clearly involves nothing less than a stratification within the whole group, completely contrary to that previously held.

A third study, by Barrie Cox, included a detailed examination of the sites, situations and archaeological associations of place-names derived from *hām* 'homestead, estate' in thirteen counties in the East Midlands and East Anglia. It is difficult sometimes to distinguish place-names derived from this word and those from OE *hamm* 'land hemmed in by water or marsh, river-meadow' unless very early spellings are available. Often the topography of the place will offer a clue. However, Cox included in his analysis only those which seemed indisputedly to be derived from *hām*. A comparison of the distribution and situations of these names with those already discussed seems to suggest a remarkable conclusion, that the *hām*s predate the *-ingas, -inga-* names. His findings also support Kuurman's conclusions. Doubts can be expressed about the validity of this in some areas, such as the Lindsey division of

Lincolnshire and parts of Suffolk, but in general it seems a good working hypothesis.

Now, all this sounds illogical, for it is clear that though names in -*ingas* **must** have preceded the formula -*ingahām*, they did **not** do so as place-names. The former were originally group-names, the names of groups of people, transferred to districts and then to places belonging to these groups, rather than names given to places from the beginning. Whatever 'batting-order' is eventually accepted within the four groups of names we have been discussing, it is quite clear that they all belong to an early stage of name-giving in Anglo-Saxon England, though not to the earliest, that represented by pagan cemeteries. The bulk of them presumably belong to the late 5th to 7th centuries. Names in -*ingas* and -*inga*- still form a unique and fascinating group and they remain the earliest identifiable habitative place-names, even if they seem now not to have the special significance of high antiquity which was once attached to them.

It should, however, be remembered that the etymology and meaning of these place-names is not in question – Hastings still means 'followers, dependents of Hǣst(a)' and it is still *in origin* a group-name, not a place-name proper. What is changed is the significance of the name, its status as belonging to the 'colonizing' rather than the 'immigration phase' of Anglo-Saxon settlement in Britain.

It is worthwhile, therefore, giving some examples of both -*ingas* and *ingahām* place-names, and in the two lists which follow only the name of the man from whom the group was named will be given. At the same time it should be noted that they are all masculine personal names; so far not a single example of a woman's name has been noted in this context.

Place-names derived from -*ingas* include: Angermering (Sx) 'Angenmǣr', Basing (Ha) 'Basa', Blickling (Nf) 'Blicla', Braughing (Hrt) 'Brahha', Detling (K) 'Dyttel', Ealing (Mx) 'Gilla', Gedding (Sf) and Gidding (Hu) both 'Gydda', Gedling (Nt) 'Gēdel or Gēdla', Gissing (Nf) 'Gyssa', Godalming (Sr) 'Godhelm', Goring (O, Sx) 'Gār(a)', Halling (Bk, K) 'H(e)all', Havering (Ess) 'Hæfer', Hayling (Ha) 'Hægel', Hickling (Nf, Nt) 'Hicel(a)', Nunkeeling (ERY) and Kelling (Nf) 'Cylla', the Nun- in the first is from the nuns of the Priory there, Knotting (Bd) perhaps 'Cnotta', Malling (K, Sx) 'Mealla', Matching (Ess) 'Mæcca', Minting (L) 'Mynta', Patching (Ess, Sr) 'Pæcca', Peatling (Lei) 'Peotla', Rising (Nf 2x) 'Risa', Sonning (Brk) 'Sunna',

Swefling (Sf) 'Swiftel', Tooting (Sr) 'Tota', Wakering (Ess) 'Wacer', Wendling (Nf) 'Wendel', Wittering (Nth) 'Wiðer', Wittering (Sx) 'Wihthere', Woking (Sr) 'Wocc(a)', Woolbedding (Sx) 'Wulfbeald', Yeading (Mx) 'Geddi'.

Place-names derived from *-ingahām* include: Addingham (Cu) 'Adda', Alvingham (L) 'Ælf(a)', Antingham (Nf) 'Anta', Badingham (Sf) 'Bēada or Bada', Badlingham (C) 'Bæddel', Barningham (Nf, NRY, Sf) 'Beorn', Bessingham (Nf) 'Basa', Collingham (Nt, WRY) 'Cola', Cottingham (ERY, Nth) 'Cotta', Dersingham (Nf) 'Dēorsige', Ellingham (Ha) 'Ēdla', Empingham (R) 'Empa', Folkingham (L) 'Folca', Framingham (Nf) 'Fram', Framlingham (Sf) 'Framela', Gillingham (Do, K) 'Gylla', Gislingham (Sf) 'Gys(e)la', Helmingham (Nf, Sf) 'Helm', Heveningham (Nf) 'Hefa', Honingham (Nf), Hunningham (Wa) 'Hūna', Immingham (L) 'Imma', Keyingham (ERY), Kingham (O) 'Cga', Leasingham (L) 'Leofsige', Massingham (Nf) 'Mæssa', Padiham (La) 'Padda', Pattingham (St) 'Patta or Peatta', Rockingham (Nth) 'Hrōc', Saxlingham (Nf 2x) 'Seaxel', Tillingham (Ess, Sx) 'Tilli or Tilla', Waddingham (L) 'Wada', Walkeringham (Nt) 'Walhhere', Walsingham (Nf) 'Wæls', Warlingham (Sr) 'Wærla', Whittingham (La, Nb) 'Hwæta', Willingham (C), North Willingham, Willingham by Stow (L) 'Wifel', Willingham (near Carlton Sf), Cherry Willingham, South Willingham (L) 'Willa', Winteringham (L), Wintringham (ERY, Hu) 'Winter or Wintra', Wingham (K) probably 'Wiga'.

It will be noted that most of the examples quoted above are found in southern and eastern England, areas of early Anglo-Saxon settlement.

Examples of place-names derived from OE *hām* are given in a later Chapter, where English settlement-names are discussed in some detail.

six

Scandinavian place-names

In 865 a great Viking army, principally of Danes, landed in East Anglia spending the next fourteen years in campaigns almost the length and breadth of England, as well as making a foray north into Strathclyde. The Viking army came with its kings and its earls and became a highly mobile and co-ordinated force. It conquered three of the four Anglo-Saxon kingdoms, Northumbria, Mercia, and East Anglia, and came within a hairsbreadth of overcoming Wessex too.

The earliest permanent settlements here took place in Northumbria in 876, when one part of this army had separated from the rest. It seems that these settlements were chiefly in Yorkshire, particularly in the Vale of York. In the following year a second division of the great army followed suit. After a campaign in the south-west a part of the army moved north from Exeter and went into Mercia which it partitioned. The area in which they settled later became known as the Kingdom of the Five Boroughs – Derby, Leicester, Nottingham, Lincoln, and Stamford. The remaining part of the Viking army split into two, one group turning to settle in East Anglia in 879, the rest leaving England and returning to the Continent from which they had originally come.

The boundary between English England and Danish England was decided in 886 by a treaty between King Alfred and Guthrum, the leader of the East Anglian Vikings and probably also of those in Essex and the southern Midlands. It ran from the Essex side of the Thames estuary as far as the R. Lea, up the Lea to its source, from there across to Bedford, then to the R. Ouse, following the Ouse to Watling Street, the line of the Roman road being the probable extension of the boundary through the Midlands. This boundary seems to have been almost an 'Iron Curtain', for there are few place-names of Scandinavian origin to the south of it.

Literary sources tell us no details concerning the extent and density of Viking settlement in eastern England, so that scholars have for long turned to place-names in an attempt to resolve these questions. After all there are literally hundreds of names of Scandinavian origin still here for us all to see as we travel round the countryside, names ending in -by, -thorpe, -toft, -thwaite, -holme, -kirk, and the like.

Now, the actual size of the Viking army of 865 has been disputed, but the general view accepted today seems to be that it numbered a few thousands. Yet it is clear that even three divisions of such an army could not have been responsible for settlements on the scale suggested by the place-name evidence. After all there are over 300 names derived from *bȳ* 'a farm, a village' and over 100 from *þorp* 'a secondary settlement' recorded in Domesday Book in the East Midlands alone.

As a conquering army, of course, the Vikings no doubt took over existing villages without altering their names in any way, especially when the names presented no phonetic difficulty. After all, we know they took over centres like Cambridge, Leicester, Lincoln, Northampton, Nottingham, and Stamford without modifying the names at all, though since these were the names of important places, their names might have been resistant to change in any case.

There are very few *recorded* examples, however, of the Vikings taking over English settlements and re-naming them, but Derby is one example and was earlier called *Northworthy*. A number of names like Appleby (L, Lei, We) and Riby (L), both hybrid English-Danish formations, suggest that they may well be partial Scandinavianizations of English names, perhaps Appleton (Brk, Cu, K, NRY, WRY) and Ryton (Du, Sa, Wa). When we compare the sites and situations of places with Danish names in -by with neighbouring English-named villages we can often demonstrate that the latter have more preferable situations for agricultural exploitation than the nearby Scandinavian-named places. On the other hand, there are some examples where it is impossible to distinguish meaningfully between their sites and situations, and this seems to be the case with the Applebys and Riby. However, it is particularly so with the so-called Grimston-hybrids, names in which the first element is a Scandinavian personal name, the second OE *tūn* 'village, estate'. The reason why these were called Grimston-hybrids was because the largest single group consisted of places called Grimston 'Grīm's village, estate'. However, as it has been shown that all the Grimstons do not fit into a single pattern, it would be preferable to call them perhaps Toton-hybrids, from Toton (Nt) 'Tovi's village, estate'. This nomenclature is adopted here and examples of these hybrids are given at the end of the chapter.

The striking features of the distribution pattern of Toton-hybrids are that, in general, they are found in areas where *bys* are absent, they occur in the valleys of the important rivers, like the Trent and, most significant of all, their sites and situations are closely similar to adjacent English-named villages. A detailed study of names in the Trent valley in Nottinghamshire demonstrated clearly that the hybrids appear to represent earlier villages taken over and partially renamed by the Vikings. It confirmed the late Sir Frank Stenton's conclusion that the Toton-hybrids denoted English villages "acquired by a Danish owner when the Great Army of the Danes divided out the land which it had chosen for settlement". Further, it is as certain as can be with material of this kind, that they belong to the earliest phase of Viking settlement here. I subsequently suggest that the men who bore the personal names occurring in these hybrids were leaders in the armies stationed in the Five Boroughs and that their association with the villages named after them was rather "manorial" than "occupational". In other words, they were overlords of the places rather than actually living permanently there, – a suggestion which seems to have received general acceptance.

The evidence of place-names, then, points clearly to Scandinavian settlers taking over land not occupied at the time, frequently on less attractive sites, as well as occupying some villages *without* changing their names. We can call this colonization in the strict sense. It would appear that, besides veterans from the victorious Viking army settling here, there must have been others, immigrant farmers from the homeland, who came into Eastern England, especially during the period following the army settlement. The patterns of place-names in Yorkshire and the East Midlands point to Danish settlers taking over vacant plots between existing villages in marginal areas; they were responsible for the fragmentation of existing estates and also for the reclamation of land once occupied, but then deserted.

The variety of Scandinavian words for different pieces of land and of terms for different types of fields is striking, and such field-names are found in places with English names too. Widely scattered among the minor names and field-names of eastern England are *Beck* 'stream', *Brigg* 'bridge', *Carr* 'marsh', *Dale*, especially in the plural, 'share of land', *Garth* 'enclosure', *Gate* 'way, road, street', *Holme* 'isle, higher ground in marsh', *Ing* 'meadow, pasture, *Intake* 'piece of land taken in or enclosed', *Kirk* 'church', *Lathe* 'barn', *Rigg* 'ridge', *Roe* and *Wroe* 'corner of land, secluded spot', *Stang* and *Stong* 'pole (measure of land)' and *Wang* and *Wong* 'garden, in-field'. These are all from words of Scandinavian origin. It is interesting, as well as significant, to note how many street-names in *Gate* there are in towns in eastern England, a clear indication of Scandinavian influence. All this is, indeed, impressive evidence of the influence Scandinavian settlers have had on the local place-nomenclature, influence which can only be the result of settlement on a very considerable scale, and by settlers, too, who must have been farmers, not only soldiers.

Of course, there are some districts where settlement was much greater than in others, like the Wreak valley in Leicestershire and the Wolds in Lincolnshire. In Rutland, however, there is a *dearth* of Scandinavian place-names and none at all derived from *bȳ*. There are fourteen derived from *þorp*, only five of which are recorded in Domesday Book, and they are all confined to the borders of the county. Glaston 'Glaðr's village' is the only Toton-hybrid and even that is not strictly of this type, for Glaðr is a Norwegian not a Danish personal name. A full-scale place-name survey of Rutland has only recently been completed and the discussion here is largely derived from it. There it is pointed out that such Scandinavian influence as exists affects the early Middle English dialect and personal name stock of the district rather than being direct settlement by Scandinavians. All this is in remarkable contrast to the surrounding areas of the East Midland Danelaw. It suggests in fact that Rutland was never part of the Danelaw proper. It is argued that when Mercia was partitioned in 877, its king, Ceolwulf, retained Rutland "intact as an Anglo-Saxon possession" and it may well be that the large estate called Rutland had been dower lands of the queen of Mercia, a royal association noted in Chapter Four. Furthermore, by the end of the 9th century Rutland had passed into the control of the Norwegian Scandinavians of York, and this would explain the Norwegian settlement at the prime site of Normanton, 'the village of the Norwegians'. The Norwegian hold on the county must have come to an end after the recovery of the Danelaw, 918-21 and "what was once the dower land of the queen of Mercia became that of the queen of a united realm". Whatever the exact sequence of events was, it is perfectly clear from place-name evidence alone that Rutland was never settled by numbers of Scandinavians, unlike its neighbours,

Leicestershire, Nottinghamshire, Lincolnshire, and to a large extent Northamptonshire.

The situation in East Anglia, too, seems to have been different from that further to the north. In Norfolk, for example, Scandinavian settlement seems to have been restricted to certain areas and there appear to have been far fewer settlers. It may well have been much more a purely military settlement than, say, in Lincolnshire. Current place-name research will soon enable us to pinpoint the areas of Danish settlement more precisely and definitively. At the moment we can certainly point to some districts, like the Hundreds of East and West Flegg, south of the R. Thurne and north and east of the Bure, where Danish place-names in *bȳ*, for example, are more numerous than in other parts of Norfolk.

The settlers in eastern England are usually referred to as Danes. Indeed, the presence of Norwegians and Frisians among the settlers here is attested by such place-names as Normanby (L, WRY) 'village of the Norwegians', as well as Normanton (Db, L, Lei, R, WRY), of similar meaning, and Firsby (L) and Frisby (Lei) 'village of the Frisians'. Norwegians and Frisians must clearly have formed an unusual, but distinctive, feature of the racial complex of the districts in which the names occur. The same must be true of Ferrensby (WRY) 'village of the Faroese', as well as Irby (Ch, L, WRY). This denotes the presence of Irishmen or of Norwegians from Ireland, as too does the hybrid Ireton, which occurs twice in Derbyshire and which is comparable in form to Normanton. In some areas, the Danes themselves must have been a distinct but notable minority, otherwise we would not find such names as Danby (NRY), Denaby, (WRY) and Denby (Db) 'village of the Danes'. On the other hand, they must have settled in numbers in south Derbyshire where the name Ingleby 'village of the English' suggests there was an enclave of Englishmen.

Scandinavian settlement, however, was not restricted to the Danelaw. In the north-west of England – Cumberland, Westmorland, Lancashire, and Cheshire – settlements were made by men of Norwegian stock, most of whom must have been descendants of men and women, who a hundred years or so earlier had settled in Gaelic-speaking areas – Ireland, the Isle of Man, Strathclyde. The earliest known settlement here was in the Wirral in Cheshire in 902 by Norwegians from Ireland, but there were others in Cumberland and parts of Lancashire during the first half of the 10th century. Norwegians from Dublin subsequently established a Norwegian kingdom at York, but such place-name evidence as there is for this is found in the North Riding, much less so in the East and West Ridings.

The place-names of north-west England show some distinctive characteristics not found in the Danelaw. One such is the inversion compound in which the order of the elements, as found in names of English and Danish origin, is reversed, and this follows Celtic practice. So, there is Aspatria, a latinized form of Aspatric, 'ash-tree Patric', i.e. 'Patric's ash-tree', Bewaldeth 'homestead Aldgȳð', an OE feminine personal name, and Seatoller 'shieling alder' in Cumberland; Brigsteer 'bridge Styr', i.e. 'Styr's bridge' and Rigmaiden, apparently 'ridge maiden' in Westmorland. A second characteristic is the occurrence of Goidelic personal names in place-names in the north-west and in parts of Yorkshire. Examples of these include Bueth in Boothby, Corc in Corby, Glassan in Glassonby, and Melmor in Melmerby (also NRY) in Cumberland; Maelchon in Melkinthorpe in Westmorland; Cairpre in Carperby, Gaithan in Gatenby, Maelsuithan in Melsonby in the North Riding; Dufgall in Duggleby in the East Riding and Eogan in Yockenthwaite in the West Riding. In addition, ON *ærghi* 'shieling, hill-pasture', a loanword from Irish, is found only in areas of Norwegian-Gaelic settlement. Arrowe (Ch) is from the dative singular, Arras (ERY) from the nominative plural, and Airyholme (NRY), Argam (ERY), and Arkholme (La) from the dative plural. The same word also occurs in compounds like Birker (Cu) 'birch-tree', Docker (La, We) 'valley', Mosser (Cu) and Mozergh (We) 'moss', Salter (Cu) 'salt', and Winder (Cu, La, We) 'wind, ie. windy'. It is found compounded with a personal name as first element in Golcar (WRY) Guðleikr, Grimsargh (La) Grímr, Mansergh (We) Man, and Sizergh (We) from the ON feminine Sigriðr.

In the north-west too, several distinctively Norwegian words are found which occur only rarely elsewhere. Topographical terms, like *brekka, fell, gil,* and *slakki,* will be discussed in later chapters, but here we may note that these refer to physical features of the landscape which in any case, do not occur to any marked extent in eastern England. Another word found in hilly regions of the north-west is *sætr* 'mountain pasture, shieling', as in Ambleside (We) 'river sandbank', Appersett (NRY) 'apple-tree', Selside (We) 'willow', and Summerseat (La) and Wintersett, (WRY), denoting shielings used only in summer and winter respectively. Occasionally the first element is a personal name, Arnkell in Arkleside (NRY) and Haukr in Hawkshead (La), both of

Scandinavian origin, while the Old English personal name Uhtrēd is the first element of Oughterside (Cu).

Similarly, Old Norwegian *skáli* 'temporary hut or shed', which has survived in dialect as *scale*, has given Scales (Cu, La) and Scholes (WRY), but has been noted as far south as Scole (Nf) and also in minor names in Lincolnshire. In Cumberland there is Bowscale 'hut on the curved hill', Portinscale, with a first element meaning 'prostitute', Seascale 'sea', and Winscales 'wind(y)'. In Lancashire there is Feniscowles 'muddy' and Loudscales 'on the R. Loud', in Westmorland Holmescales 'belonging to Holme', in the North Riding Gammersgill 'Gamall's hut', in the West Riding Summerscales (identical with Summersgill (La) and Winterscales, denoting huts used in summer and winter respectively.

A further significant feature of the Scandinavian place-names in the north-west and in parts of Yorkshire is the survival of the genitive singular -*ar*- as -*er*-. Becke*r*met, Bowde*r*dale, and Harte*r* Fell in Cumberland have been discussed elsewhere; in Westmorland, however, are Winde*r*wath 'Vinand's ford' and Withe*r*slack 'valley of the wood', in Lancashire Amounde*r*ness 'Agmundr's headland', Lithe*r*land 'land of the slope' and Harte*r*beck 'stream of the hart', and in Yorkshire Amothe*r*by and Bellerby, noted at the end of this chapter. Elsewhere, this formation is uncommon, but it has been noted in Dalde*r*by 'village of the valley' and Londonthorpe, earlier Londe*r*thorpe, 'outlying settlement of the grove' in Lincolnshire.

We noted early in this chapter that there were over 100 examples of *þorp* recorded in Domesday Book in the territory of the Five Boroughs alone. A detailed examination of the sites and situations of these, when compared with those of English-named villages or those derived from ODan *bý*, has confirmed that the meaning of *þorp* is indeed 'secondary settlement, dependent outlying farm or village'. Furthermore, it is common in those eastern parts of England where heavy Danish settlement has taken place, and it appears to be a distinctively Danish word. In some cases, the place-name itself indicates the particular place it was dependent on, as in the case of Ashwellthorpe (Nf) belonging to Ashwell, and Staveley Netherthorpe and Woodthorpe belonging to Staveley (Db). Similarly, some of the simplex examples of Thorpe, a name recorded in twelve counties, have been distinguished by an affix which is that of a nearby village, as for example Thorpe Langton (Lei), Kilton Thorpe (NRY), Mattersey Thorpe (Nt), and

Whitley Thorpe (WRY). It will be noticed that all these parent villages have English names and it would not be unreasonable to argue that place-names in -thorpe could well indicate that the word *thorpe* was taken over into the local dialect vocabulary and that the names derived from it need not necessarily be evidence of Danish settlement itself. Nonetheless, they must, at very least, be indicative of a widespread and considerable Danish influence, and that cannot have come from thin air. It must have arisen from something. That something must have been Danish settlement on a scale considerable enough for the word *thorpe* to have become *the* term used of a secondary or dependent settlement over the whole of the Danelaw.

The first element of many place-names derived from *þorp* is a personal name and a selection of these will be found at the end of the chapter. Several of the numerous other compounds are self-explanatory, as with Easthorpe (ERY), identical with Aisthorpe (L) and Owsthorpe (ERY), Kingthorpe (L), Newthorpe (Nt, WRY), Northorpe (L, WRY), Southorpe (L), Woodthorpe (Db, WRY), as well as Millthorpe (L) and Milnthorpe (Nt, We, WRY). Birthorpe (L) means 'outlying farmstead by the birch-trees', while Biscathorpe (L) was named from the bishop (of Durham), Copmanthorpe (WRY) from chapmen and Danthorpe (ERY) from Danes.

At this point it should be noted that there was also an OE *þrop* 'hamlet, outlying farm', the forms of which could be confused with those of ODan *þorp*. However, the Old English word very frequently appears as *Throp* in both medieval and modern spellings, whilst such spellings from the Danish word very rarely occur before the 16th century. In any case, the regional distribution will often indicate clearly enough which is the source in any particular name. Thorpe (Du, Ess, Sr), Throope (W), Thrup (O, W), Thrupp (Brk, Gl, Nth) and Drupe (D) are all derived from OE *þrop*. The same is true of the self-explanatory Castle Thorpe (Bk), as well as Eathorpe (Wa) and Eythrope (Bk) 'by a river', Souldrop (Bd) 'in a gulley', Upthorpe (Hu, Wo) 'upper', and Tythrop (O) which means 'double hamlet or outlying farm'. Abthorpe (Nth), Bigstrup (Bk) and Princethorpe (Wa) each has an Old English personal name as first element – Abba, Bicel and Præn respectively.

Another element which seems in English place-names to be a specifically Danish word is *toft* 'site of a house, messuage, curtilage'. It is common, especially in minor names in the East Midlands and Yorkshire, but is extremely rare in the north-west, if indeed it occurs there at all. It survives as Toft in at least six counties and as Tofts in Norfolk, while Fishtoft (L) was originally a simplex name to which was prefixed the as yet unexplained Fish-. The first element in a number of names is a personal name, some of which are noted at the end of the chapter, but there are others in which it is an adjective or a noun. So, in Altofts (WRY) it means 'old', in Bratoft (L) 'broad, spacious', and in Nortoft (Nth) 'north'. The Lincolnshire Huttoft, Sandtoft, and Wigtoft are situated on a hill-spur, on sandy soil and perhaps near a creek or inlet respectively, and Eastoft (WRY), Thrintoft (WRY), and Willitoft (ERY), near an ash-wood, thorn-bush, and willows respectively.

The commonest by far of all the Scandinavian elements in English place-names is *bȳ* 'farm, village', found in all parts of the Danelaw and the north-west, where it was certainly a living word in the early Middle English period. In Cumberland, Westmorland, and the North Riding it still often denotes an individual farm and it has been suggested that this usage is rather Norwegian than Danish: In the Danelaw, place-names in -by are today frequently those of small villages, as on the Lincolnshire Wolds. However, it is often really impossible to decide which is the exact sense, 'farm' or 'village'.

While *bȳ* is the commonest of all the Scandinavian words found in English place-names, there is no certain example of it as as the first element of a village-name, and it does not occur at all in the simplex form By. It is sometimes difficult to distinguish between a Scandinavian compound and one consisting of an English and the Scandinavian word. For example, Fenby (L) 'fen', Moorby (L), and Smisby (Db) 'smith', could be derived from either a Scandinavian or an English word, and in these cases the former is perhaps more likely. On the other hand, there are a few names the first element of which is definitely Old English – Walby (Cu) 'by the (Roman) wall', Wauldby (WRY) 'on the wold', and Welby (L) 'by the spring'. It is likely, as has been suggested earlier in this chapter, that in some of these names *bȳ* has replaced an earlier English word, such as *tūn*. Certainly it is remarkable that there are at least nine examples of the hybrid Willoughby (L, Lei, He, Nf, NRY), as well as Wilby (Nf), 'where willows grow'. This name may well have been originally identical with Willoughton (L), Willington (Bd, Db), and Wilton (C, ERY, He, Nf, NRY), with *bȳ* replacing *tūn*.

There is, however, documentary evidence showing that *bȳ* has replaced an OE *byrig*, the dative singular of *burh* 'fortified place', later 'manor(house)'. In these cases the similarity of the forms may be partly responsible, but at any rate it has taken place in Greasby (Ch) originally 'fortified place by a grove', Thornby (Nth) 'by a thorn-bush', as well as Badby (Nth), Naseby (Nth), and Rugby (Wa), from the Old English personal names Badda, Hnæf, and Hrōca respectively, and Quenby (Lei) probably originally 'queen's manor'.

In most cases, nonetheless, the place-names derived from $b\bar{y}$ are Scandinavian compounds and some can be compared with etymologically identical names in Scandinavia itself, -Åby, Dalby, Tjørneby and Østerby in Denmark, Aby, Dalby, Thurnby and Asterby in England. A very large proportion have a Scandinavian personal name as first element – according to my own interpretations no less than 192 out of the 303 recorded in DB in the territory of the Five Boroughs. A selection of these is given at the end of this chapter.

Others are named in relation to a neighbouring place, as with Asterby (L) 'eastern', Swinderby (L) 'southern', Westby (La, WRY) and Westerby (Lei) 'western', Itterby (L) 'outer', Yearby (NRY) 'upper', and the Cumberland Netherby and Overby 'lower' and 'higher'. Some are named from a natural or artificial feature of the landscape, as in Aby (L) and Burnby (ERY) 'stream', Barby (Nth), Barrowby (L, WRY) and Huby (NRY) 'hill', Dalby (L, Lei, NRY) 'valley', Keelby (L) and Ribby (La) 'ridge', as well as Raby (Ch, Cu, Du), Robey (Du) and Roby (La) which must have been farms or villages situated near a 'boundary mark'. The Lincolnshire Grebby is 'on stony ground', and the common Sowerby on 'sour ground'. The names of trees occur only occasionally as the first element of names in -by, but lime trees grew at Linby (Nt), willows at Selby (WRY), thorn-bushes at Thurnby (Lei) and ash-trees at Asby (Cu, We) and the common Ashby, though the first element of some of the Ashbys is perhaps rather the Scandinavian personal name Aski. Animal names are only rarely found – young pigs in Grisby (L) and wethers in Wetherby (WRY). Again, terms for groups of people are rare, but noteworthy are Flotmanby (ERY) 'sailors', Hunmanby (ERY) and Hunmonsby (Cu) 'dog-keepers', and Sutterby (L) 'shoe-makers'.

In addition to place-names wholly or partly of Scandinavian origin, there are numerous English names whose forms have been modified in various ways as a result of Scandinavian *influence*. When OE *c* occurred initially before *e* or *i*, as in *cēse* or *cild*, it was pronounced as in the modern forms of these words, *ch*eese and *ch*ild. In the Scandinavian languages, however, the sound in this position was *k*. So, the initial consonant in Keswick (Cu, Nf, WRY) and Kildwick (WRY) is due to the influence of the Scandinavian sound, for these names were originally identical with Chiswick (Ess, Mx) 'cheese farm' and Childwick (Hrt) 'dairy-farm' or perhaps 'trading-centre of the young men'. In a similar way, Kepwick (NRY) perhaps meaning 'market', would otherwise have had a modern form Cheapwick or Chipwick, while Kettlewell 'bubbling spring' is in place of Chettlewell. OE *sc*, in *scelf* was pronounced *sh*, as in modern *sh*elf, or *æsc*, moden a*sh*, a sound which was unknown in the Scandinavian languages where its place was taken by *sk*. Hence, Skelton (Cu, ERY, NRY, WRY) has replaced Shelton (Bd, Nf, Nt, Sa, St) 'estate on a shelf of land', Skipton (NRY, WRY) with Shipton (Do, Gl, Ha, O, Sa) 'sheep farm', and Skipwith (ERY) and Scopwick (L) with Shopwyke (Sx) each of which has a meaning similar to that of Skipton and Shipton. Medially the same sound- substitution has taken place in Minskip (WRY), derived from OE *(ge)mœnscipe* 'community', i.e. 'place communally held', and finally in Matlask (Nf), where, however, OE *æsc* 'ash-tree' may have been replaced by the cognate ON *askr*, as was probably the case in Askham (Nt, WRY) 'ash-tree homestead'. Similarly, ON *steinn* has replaced OE *stān* 'stone' in several names such as Stainburn (Cu) 'stream', Stainforth (WRY) 'ford', Stainland (WRY) 'land', Stainley (WRY) 'clearing, glade', Stainmore (NRY-We) 'moor', and the common Stainton instead of Stanburn, Stanford, Stanland, Stanley, Stanmore and Stanton respectively. ON *rauðr*, 'red' has taken the place of the equivalent English word *rēad* in Rawcliffe (La, NRY, WRY), which otherwise would have given Radcliffe (La, Nt); and it is at least possible that ON *austr* 'east' has replaced OE *ēast* in Owston (L, WRY) 'east village', and Astwick (WRY) and Oustwick (ERY) 'east dairy-farm' or perhaps 'east trading-centre', which would then have been the equivalents of the common Aston and Astwick (Bd, Nth). The most striking example of the replacement of an English by a Scandinavian word, however, is Carlton (Bd, C, Du, ERY, L, Lei, NRY, Nt, Nth, Sf, WRY) of which there are over forty surviving instances, as well as Carleton (Cu, La, Nf, WRY). These are equivalent to the common Charlton, which occurs some thirty times in England, Charleton (D) and Chorlton (Ch, La, St). The first element of Charlton is the genitive plural of OE *ceorl* 'free peasant, freeman of the lowest rank', modern *churl*, and this has been replaced in Carlton by the cognate ON *karl* 'freeman of the lower class'. A translation of all these names would be something like 'estate of the free peasants' or, as has been suggested, 'estate of the husbandmen'. It is clear that the new settlers recognized the English names for what they were and adapted them to their own language.

The following are examples of names containing a personal name compounded with the elements discussed above:

Cheshire:

hybrid *tūn* Croxton (also C, L, Lei, Nf, St) *Krókr*, Thurstaston (identical with Thurston Sf) *Þorsteinn*

Cumberland:

bȳ Arkleby *Arnkell*, Hormsby (identical with Ormesby Nf, NRY and Ormsby L) *Ormr*, Motherby *Mōthir* (ODan), Thursby (identical with Thoresby L, NRY, Nt) *Þórir*

Hybrid *tūn* Askerton *Ásgeirr*, Orton *Orri*

Derbyshire

bȳ Stainsby *Steinn*

þorp Boythorpe (also ERY) *Boie*, Hackenthorpe *Hákun*, Oakerthorpe *Ulkel* (ODan)

hybrid *tūn* Foston (also ERY, NRY) *Fótr*, Kedleston *Ketill*, Roston *Hrosskell*, Scropton *Skropi*, Swarkeston *Swerkir* (ODan), Thurvaston (also Thoroton Nt) *þurferð*

Durham:

bȳ Aislaby (also NRY and identical with Aslackby L) *Áslákr*, Killerby (also NRY and identical with Kilwardby Lei) *Kilvert*, the exact form of which is uncertain)

hybrid *tūn* Blakeston *Bleikr*, Claxton (also Nf, NRY and identical with Clawson Lei) *Klak* (ODan), Ouston (also Nb) *Ulkel* (ODan)

Lancashire:

bȳ Formby *Forni*, Hornby (also NRY) *Horni*

hybrid *tūn* Flixton (also ERY, Sf) *Flik* (ODan), Urmston *Urm* (ODan)

Leicestershire:

bȳ Barsby Barn, Blaby *Blár*, Gaddesby *Gaddr*, Ingarsby *Ingvarr*, Kettleby (also L and identical with Ketsby L) *Ketill*, Saxby (also L)

Saksi, Saxelby (identical with Saxilby L) *Saksulf* (ODan), Sysonby *Sigsteinn*

    þorp Boothorpe *Bo* (ODan), Bromkinsthorpe *Brúnskinn*, Oakthorpe and Othorpe *Āki* (ODan), Osgathorpe *Ásgautr*, Ullesthorpe *Ulfr*

    toft Knaptoft *Knapi*, Scraptoft *Skrápi*

    hybrid *tūn* Barkestone (identical with Barkston L, WRY) *Bǫrkr*, Bilstone (identical with Bildeston Sf) *Bildr*, Grimston (also ERY, Nf, NRY, Nt, Sf, WRY) *Grímr*, Odstone *Oddr*, Slawston *Slagr*, Snibston *Snípr*, Sproxton (also NRY) *Sprok*, Thringstone *þrœingr*, Thrussington (identical with Thrislington Du) *þorsteinn*, Thurcaston *þorketill*, Thurlaston (also Wa) *þorleifr*, Thurmaston *þormóðr*

Lincolnshire:

    bȳ Aunby, Aunsby and Owmby *Auðunn*, Barnetby *Beornede* (OE), Bleasby *Blesi*, Bransby (identical with Brandsby NRY) *Brandr*, Grimsby *Grír*, Gunby *Gunni*, Haconby *Hákun*, Heminby *Hemingr*, Keaby *Keti*, Manby *Manni*, Osgodby (also ERY, NRY) *Ásgautr*, Raithby (near Louth) *Hreiðarr*, Spilsby *Spilli*, Stainsby *Stafn*, Wragby (also WRY) *Wraggi*, Wrawby *Wraghi*

    þorp Addlethorpe (also WRY) *Ardwulf* (OE), Caythorpe (also Nt) *Káti*, Gainsthorpe *Gamall*, Ganthorpe *Germund* (ODan), Grimsthorpe *Grímr*, Hasthorpe *Haraldr*, Scunthorpe *Skúma*, Upperthorpe *Hūnbald* (OE), Wilsthorpe (also Db, ERY) *Vífill*, Yawthorpe apparently *Toli* (ODan)

    toft Habertoft perhaps *Hagbarðr*

    hybrid *tūn* Baston *Bakr*, Gelston perhaps *Gifull*

Norfolk:

    bȳ Alby (identical with Ailby L) *Ali*, Clippesby (identical with Clixby L) *Klippr*, Hemsby perhaps *Hēmer*, Herringby *Hæringr*, Mautby (identical with Maltby L, NRY, WRY) *Malti* (ODan), Oby (identical with Oadby Lei) *Auði*, Rollesby *Hroðulfr*, Scratby *Skrauti*, Tyby (identical with Tythby Nt) *Tidhe*

    þorp Alethorpe *Ali*, Bagthorpe *Bakki* (ODan), Calthorpe *Kali*, Freethorpe *Frethi* (ODan), Gasthorpe *Gaddr*, Ingoldisthorpe *Ingjaldr*, Saxthorpe *Saksi*, Sculthorpe *Skúli*, Swainsthorpe (identical with Swinethorpe L) *Sveinn*

    hybrid *tūn* Aslacton (identical with Aslockton Nt) *Áslakr*, Cawston *Kalfr*, Garveston *Geirulfr*, Helhoughton *Helgi*, Kettlestone *Ketill*, Scoulton *Skúli*, Skeyton *Skeggi*, Starston and Sturston (also Db) *Styrr*, Thelveton *þialfi*, Thurgarton (also Nt) *þorgeirr*

Northamptonshire:

bȳ Catesby (identical with Cadeby L, Lei, WRY) *Káti*, Corby (also L) *Kori*

þorp Apethorpe *Api* (ODan), Gunthorpe (also L, Nf, R) *Gunni*, Wigsthorpe (identical with Wiganthorpe NRY) *Víkingr*

toft Sibbertoft *Sigbiǫrn*

hybrid *tūn* Knuston *Knūt* (ODan), Strixton *Stríkr*

Nottinghamshire:

bȳ Budby *Butti*, Granby *Grani*, Ranby *Hrani*, Skegby *Skeggi*, Walesby (also L) *Valr*

þorp Gunthorpe *Gunnhildr* (feminine), Owthorpe *Úfi*, Staythorpe *Stari*, Winthorpe *Vígmundr*

hybrid *tūn* Clipstone (also Nth) and Clipstone (also Bd, Nf) *Klippr*, Colston *Kolr*, Gamston *Gamall*, Gonalston *Gunnúlf*, Osberton (identical with Osbaston Lei) *Ásbiǫrn*, Rolleston *Hroáldr*, Thrumpton *þormóðr*, Toton *Tóvi*

Rutland:

þorp Belmesthorpe *Beornhelm* (OE), Kilthorpe *Ketill*, Tolethorpe *Toli*

hybrid *tūn* Glaston *Glaðr*

Suffolk:

bȳ Barnby (also NRY, Nt, WRY and identical with Barmby ERY) *B(i)arni*

toft Lowestoft *Hloðvér*

hybrid *tūn* Flowton (identical with Flockton WRY) *Flóki*, Gunton (also Nf) *Gunni*, Kettlebaston *Ketilbjǫrn*, Somerleyton *Sumarliði*, Ubbeston *Ubbi*

Westmorland:

bȳ Colby (also Nf and identical with Coleby L) *Kolli*, Nateby (also La) *Nati*, Soulby (also Cu and identical with Sulby Nth) *Súla*

þorp Crackenthorpe *Krakandi*

East Riding:

bȳ Gunby *Gunnhildr* (feminine), Scalby (also NRY and identical with Scawby L) *Skalli*, Thirkleby *þorgils* Uncleby *Húketill*

þorp Hilderthorpe *Hildiger* (ODan) or *Hildigerðr* (feminine), Kettlethorpe (also L) *Ketill*, Raisthorpe *Hreiðarr* hybrid *tūn* Barmston (also Du) *Bjǫrn*, Rolston *Hrólfr*, Scamston *Skammr*

North Riding:

bȳ Ainderby (identical with Enderby Lei and probably Enderby L) *Einðriði*, Amotherby *Eymundr*, Bagby *Baggi*, Battersby *Bǫðvarr*, Bellerby *Belgr*, Helperby *Hjalp* (feminine), Romanby *Reðmundr*, Slingsby *Slengr*, Thornmanby and Thornaby *þormóðr*, Ugglebarnby *Uglubárði*

þorp Agglethorpe *Ācwulf* (OE), Carthorpe *Kári*, Ganthorpe *Galmr*, Towthorpe (also ERY) *Tóvi*

toft Antofts *Aldwine* (OE)

hybrid *tūn* Oulston *Ulfr*, Scruton *Skurfa*, Sigston *Siggr*

West Riding:

bȳ Balby *Balli* Flasby and Flaxby *Flatr*, Hellaby *Helgi*, Thorlby (identical with Thoralby and Thoraldby NRY) *þóraldr*

þorp Armthorpe *Arnulf* (ODan) or *Arnwulf* (OE), Gawthorpe (identical with Gowthorpe ERY) *Gaukr*, Goldthorpe *Golda* (OE), Hexthorpe *Heggr*, Oglethorpe *Oddkell*, Streetthorpe *Styrr*, Wrenthorpe *Wīfrūn* (OE feminine)

hybrid *tūn* Brotherton *Broðir*, Thurlstone (also Sf) *Thurulf* (Dan)

seven

English place-names of French origin

The number of place-names of French origin is comparatively small when compared to the vast number of names of English origin. Some of these distinctively French names – many are those of monasteries and castles – have, no doubt, been transferred directly from names with identical origins in France itself. It is, of course, impossible always to be sure that this is the case. Certainly, Blachland (Nb) 'white, bare glade', Freemantle (Ha) literally 'cold cloak', a descriptive name given to a forest, Grosmont (NRY) 'big hill', Kirmond le Mire (L) 'goat hill', originally identical with the French Chèvremont, Montacute (So) 'pointed hill', with the modern name in a Latinized form, Richmond (NRY, WRY) 'strong hill', and Beamond End (Bd), Beaumont (Cu, Ess, Hrt, La, Lei) 'beautiful hill' all have their parallels in France. In fact, we know that the priory of Grosmont (WRY) was named from its mother house near Limoges and that Marmont (C), of uncertain etymology, took its name from Marmande (Lot et Garonne). In most cases no doubt the name was equally appropriate to the English place, as with some of the Beaumonts and with Richmond (NRY), a name given to the castle, built shortly after the Norman Conquest, on a site above the River Swale. Richmond (Sr), on the other hand, was named by Henry VII from his earldom of Richmond, when he rebuilt the palace at a place formerly called *Sheen*, which had been burned down in 1501, though the meaning would accurately describe Richmond Hill. Ridgmont (Bd, ERY) 'red hill' may well have been named from Rougemont in France and the name of the Bedfordshire place at any rate was appropriate enough, for the sandstone there has a reddish colour. Mountsorrel (Lei) 'sorrel-coloured hill' is presumably identical with the French Mont-sorel, but was no doubt named from the pinkish granite there. Similarly Egremont (Cu) is identical with Aigremont in France and 'sharp-pointed hill' is certainly as topographically appropriate for the Cumberland Castle as it is for the French places. Cause (Sa), on the other hand, is said to have been named from Caux in Normandy, which was probably the home of the Norman family which held the Shropshire place after the Conquest.

Many French place-names in England have as first element the word *bel* or *beau* 'beautiful, fine', presumably with reference to the place or to the scenery around. Among the numerous names containing one or other of these words are Beachy Head (Sx), with Head added later, and Beauchief (WRY, but formerly in Db) 'fine headland'; Beadlow (Bd). Beaulieu (Ha), Bewdley (Wo) and Bewley (Du, We) 'beautiful, fine place'; Beamish (Du) 'fine mansion'; Bear Park (Du), Beaurepaire (Ha) and Belper (Db) 'beautiful, fine retreat', the latter later replacing an earlier *Bradley*, which was subsequently lost; Beaufront Castle (Nb) 'fine brow'; Beauvale (Nt) 'beautiful valley'; Belasis (Du), Bellasis (Du, Nb), Bellasize (ERY) and Belsize (Hrt, Mx, Nth) 'beautiful, fine seat'; Belvoir (Lei) 'beautiful view'; and Butterby (Du) 'beautiful find'. An especially interesting name with a first element *bel* is Belgrave (Lei), recorded as *Merdegrave* 'martens' grove or pit' in Domesday Book. *Merde-* seems to have been associated with Old French *merde* 'filth', and by about 1135 had been replaced by French *bel*, presumably for reasons of euphony, as we have seen in an earlier chapter.

Occasionally, the French name given to a monastery has a religious significance, as in Dieulacres (St) 'may God increase it' and Gracedieu (Lei) 'grace of God'. Comparable to these are Mount Grace (NRY) and St. Michael's Mount (Co), no doubt named from its mother house of Mont-St.-Michel in France. Haltemprise (ERY) 'great enterprise' is the name given to the priory there. The priory had been founded at nearby Cottingham but was moved a year or two later to a site at Newton and given the new name Haltemprise, Newton itself being subsequently lost. Similarly, there is Landieu (Du) 'glade of God', and Vaudey (L) 'valley of God'. Rewley Abbey (O) 'royal place', however, commemorates its foundation on land which had belonged to Richard, brother of Henry III.

French names occasionally refer to some natural or artificial feature. So, Boulge (Sf) denotes 'uncultivated land covered with heather', Bruera (Ch), Temple Bruer (L) and Bruern (O) 'heath', Cowdray Park (Sx) 'hazel copse', Kearsney (K) 'place where cress grows', Salcey Forest (Nth-Bk) 'place abounding in willows'. Caidge (Ess) means 'enclosed piece of land' and Malpas (Ch) 'bad, i.e difficult, passage'. The Prae (Hrt) is 'the meadow' and the same word, with French *de la* 'of the' prefixed is found in Delapre Abbey (Nth).

Devizes (W) represents the plural of Old French *devise* 'boundary' and the 12th century castle there was built on the boundary between two hundreds. Pleshey (Ess) and the identical Plessey (Nb) are derived from Old French *plessis* 'enclosure made with interlaced fencing', the source of Plessis-les-Tours in France. The Essex name dates from about 1100 and was given to the castle built by Geoffrey de Mandeville.

A particularly interesting name is Pontefract (WRY) 'broken bridge'. This arose when a Priory of Cluniac monks was founded at a place earlier called *Kirkby*. Pontefract is found in early references in both a Latin and an Anglo-Norman form. The Latin is *Ponsfractus*, in the accusative *Pontemfractum* and in the genitive *Pontisfractis*. Early French spellings include *Pontefrayth*, *Pontefrayth*, *Pontefreit* and *Pontefret*. What is very unusual about the name is that the modern written form is derived from the documentary Latin ones, while the local pronunciations, *Pomfret*, *Pumfrit*, have developed from the Anglo-Norman, with spellings in -*m*-dating from at least the mid-15th century. It is clear from this that the Anglo-Norman form of the name was the one in use in the locality.

The French diminutive suffix -*et* was occasionally added to an older name, as in Claret Hall (Ess) 'little Clare' from the nearby Clare (Sf), the meaning of which is uncertain. Cricket (So) means 'little *Cruc*', from a lost Celtic name identical with Crich (Db) 'hill', and Hampnett (Gl, Sx) 'little *Hampton*', the older name, now also lost, meaning 'at the high farm, village'.

It would appear that the forms of some earlier Old English and Scandinavian place-names have been influenced by French. In a few cases a part of the earlier name has been replaced by a French word. For example, OFr *mond* 'hill' has apparently replaced OE *mūða* 'mouth' in Jesmond (Nb), formerly *Gesemuthe* 'mouth of Ouse Burn' with spellings in -*mond* from at least 1414; ON *mót* 'confluence' in Beckermonds (WRY) 'confluence of streams', and OE *mōt* with a similar meaning, in Eamont (Cu) 'junction of streams', with forms in *mont* first noted in 1558. The commonest alternation is that of French *ville* for OE *feld* 'open land', especially in the South and West, in names like Clanville (Ha, So) 'clean (i.e. free of weeds) open land', Longville (Sa) 'long open land', and Enville (St) 'level open land'. It is thought that in these names the *f* of *feld* was voiced to *v* and then the word was associated with *ville*. A late substitution of *ville* for OE *wella* 'spring' has taken place in Wyeville (L) 'spring with a pagan shrine'. In at least one instance, however, Caldew (Cu) 'cold river', OE *ēa* 'river, stream' was replaced by OFr *ewe,* 'water', for a spelling *Caldeu* has been noted as early as 1189. In the fens of Cambridgeshire and Lincolnshire some river-names derived from *ēa* are today spelt Eau, as in Old South Eau. The local pronunciation of Eau rhymes with *bee* and the modern forms are simply pseudo-French ones. It may be noted here that there are no early English place-names derived from *ville*, such names as Coalville (Lei) and Ironville (Db) being 19th century formations as we shall see in a later chapter.

For a long time it was believed that the spelling and pronunciation of some pre-Conquest place-names had been influenced by Anglo-Norman scribes using a language and sound-system which was unfamiliar. As a result, it was believed that they tended to substitute the nearest sounds in their own language for English ones. It has always been recognized that it is not easy to distinguish sound-substitutions of this kind from those which are the result of dialectal developments in English itself. Very recently the influence attributed to Anglo-Norman has been challenged, partly because such influence is found *only* in the forms of place-names, not in those of personal names or in the ordinary vocabulary, and partly because such modifications could well have arisen spontaneously in rapid and casual speech. In other words, they may be the result of native English linguistic tendencies and have little to do with Anglo-Norman influence itself.

Examples of the various changes thought to have been due to Anglo-Norman influence follow, but it must be clearly understood that some are now much better explained as being sporadic developments due to local English conditions which varied from area to area and place to place. As a result these changes affect some but not all place-names derived from the same element.

Firstly, some names containing OE *ceaster* 'Roman station' in which the *c-* had the sound represented by modern English *ch-*, have modern forms in *c* but pronounced *s*, as in Cirencester (Gl), Gloucester, Leicester; Worcester, as well as Alcester (Wa), Frocester (Gl), Towcester (Nth) and Wroxeter (Sa), in which *x* stands for *ks*. A similar development is to be seen in Cerne (Do), instead of Cherne, and in

Cippenham (Bk), perhaps 'homestead of the dependents of Cippa', as compared with the etymologically identical Chippenham (C), as well as in Diss (Nf) 'ditch' and Chatteris (C), in which OE *ric* 'stream' was probably added to a Celtic name meaning 'wood'.

Then there are sporadic examples of an initial T- for an etymological Th- in such names as Tingrith (Bd) 'stream where meetings are held', Turville (Bk), identical with Therfield (Hrt) 'dry open land', Turnworth (Do) 'enclosure where thorn-bushes grow', as well as Tarleton (L), Turton (La) and Turweston (Bk), in which OE *tūn* 'village, estate' is compounded with the Scandinavian personal names þaraldr, þori and þurfastr respectively. Scandinavian personal names are similarly found in Torworth (Nt) ' þorðr's enclosure' and Torisholme (La) 'þóraldr's island of land'. Spellings in Th- and T- occur in the early forms of all these names, and it is interesting to speculate on the change when the first element in five of them is a Scandinavian personal name in þ-. No satisfactory explanation has as yet been offered, however.

Further, in at least three names an earlier OE *G-* before *e* or *i*, pronounced *y* as in *y*et, has been replaced by *J-*, pronounced as in *j*u*dge*. Modern J- survives in Jarrow (Du) and Jesmond (Nb), discussed elsewhere, and in Jevington (Sx) 'farm, village, estate of Ge(o)ffa's dependents', but occasional forms in J- occur in other names originally with initial *Ge-* or *Gi-*, though none of these has survived to the present-day. In two names, Nottingham, earlier *Snotengahám*, already discussed, and Trafford (La) from OE *Strǣtford* 'ford carrying a Roman road', the original initial S- has been lost before a following consonant. The substitution of J- and the loss of S- have in the past been attributed to Anglo-Norman influence. Whether this is so, or whether they are due to some as yet unidentified developments in English itself can only be a matter of conjecture. The same is so with the replacement of r by l in the forms of Salisbury (W), which has numerous early spellings in *Saresbury*, as well as that of r for n in Durham, earlier *Dunholm*, a hybrid English-Scandinavian name, both discussed in an earlier chapter.

A further change which has been traditionally explained as due to a phonetic development in Anglo-Norman is the diphthongization of a to au when followed by n. Such spellings survive in Saunton (D), identical with Santon (Cu, L, Nf), and Staunton (Gl, He, Lei, Nt, So, Wo) with the common Stanton, each discussed elsewhere. Similarly we have Raunds (Nth) 'at the slopes or borders' instead of Rands, though the local pronunciation, as in the name of the marble, Rance Rag, quarried

there, rhymes with Standard English d*a*nce; that is without the diphthong. In Nottinghamshire there is Saundby, instead of Sandby, 'Sandi's
village, estate' and in Somerset, Taunton, earlier *Tantūn* 'estate on the
R. Tone'. Braunston (Nth, R) and Braunstone (Lei) are identical in origin with Brandeston (Sf), Brandiston (Nf) and Branston (Lei, St)
'Brant's village, estate'. Whether this development, too, has some alternative explanation is at present quite uncertain. It is clear that a good
deal of research is needed before a firm conclusion can be reached.

Without a doubt some villages which exist today did not come into
existence until after the Norman Conquest. These include a fair number
which include a personal name not in use here till after the Conquest
itself. After 1066 radical changes took place in the type of personal
name used in England. Old English names continued in use for some
time, indeed a few have had a continuous history to the present day, but
for the most part they gradually fell into disuse. The Normans introduced their own personal names, chiefly French or continental German
in origin, and also biblical names which are hardly found at all in
Anglo-Saxon England. Few place-names which have as first element
such a personal name are those of places of great importance, but their
geographical distribution seems significant. The largest single group, as
we might expect, is that compounded with OE *tūn* 'farm, village,
estate', but also 'manor'. They are apparently rare in the Midlands and
North, but we may note Williamston (Nb) from William, Howton (He)
from Hue, i.e. Hugh, Rowlstone (He, identical with Rolleston (W) from
Rolf, Walterstone (He) from Walter and Botcheston (Lei) for Bochard.
They occur occasionally in the central South, as with Mariston (Brk)
from Martel and Mainstone (Ha) from Mayhew, i.e. Matthew; more so
in Wiltshire including Faulston from Fallard, Flamston from Flambard,
and Richardson from Richard, while Dorset has Bryanston from Brian,
a Norman name of Breton origin, Ranston from Randulf, and Waterston
from Walter. In Devon and Dorset there are some places with a family
name as first element, and Devon in fact contains the largest concentra-
tion of place-names with a post-Conquest personal name. These include
Drewston, in Drewsteignton, from Drew, Johnstone from John, Jurston
from Jordan, Penson and Penstone from Pain, and Stevenstone from
Stephen. Post-Conquest personal names are only rarely found with other
English elements denoting habitations, but noteworthy is Painswick
(Gl) 'Pain's farm'. Few of the place-names dealt with here are recorded
before the 13th century, and in some case it has been possible to identify

the person after whom the place was named. This is so with Bryanston, Stevenstone, and Walterstone, as well as Painswick.

Similar personal names are also found compounded with Scandinavian *bȳ* 'farmstead, village', though no examples have been noted in the Midlands. One or two have been noted in Yorkshire, where there is Jolby (NRY) from Johel, i.e. Joel. They are not found at all in Cheshire, Lancashire, or Westmorland, districts in which considerable settlement by men and women of Norwegian origin took place. However, they are fairly common in Cumberland, particularly around Carlisle, where we have Aglionby from Agyllun, Allonby and Ellonby from Alein, Etterby from Etard, Lamonby from Lambin, Ponsonby from Puncun, Rickerby from Ricard (Richard), and Wigonby from Wigan. Some of these personal names, such as Alein and Wigan, are of Breton origin, others, like Lambin, are Flemish. This may well indicate the presence of Bretons and Flemings among the 12th-century settlers in Cumberland and in fact, we know that Flemings did indeed settle there as is shown by the place-name Flimby, 'the village of the Flemings'. In addition, there are a few names of this type which have as second element Scandinavian *þorp* 'outlying settlement', for example Buslingthorpe (L), Mablethorpe (L), Painsthorpe (ERY), Painthorpe (WRY) and Waterthorpe (Db) from the personal names Buselin, Malbert, Pain and Walter respectively. *þorp* is more associated with Danish settlement than with Norwegian and it will be noted that the examples quoted are all in the Danelaw, that part of England at one time subject to Danish Law. On the other hand, *þveit* 'clearing meadow' is commoner in areas settled by Norwegians, but there is only a single example Bassenthwaite (Cu), the first element of which is the Anglo-Norman personal name Bastun.

eight

Elliptical place-names

We have seen in the first Chapter that in Old English the preposition *æt* 'at', which took the dative case, seems to have been regarded as an integral part of a place-name. Its former use is clearly shown today, for the most part by traces of the old dative ending in the form of such a name as Barrow.

Middle English *atte* 'at the' is commonly used in personal names to indicate a place of residence, which sometimes later came to be adopted as a surname. Forms like John *atte Broke* 'John who lives by the brook', Robert *atte Halle* 'Robert who lives at or near the hall' and Richard *atte Tounesende* 'Richard who lives at the town's end (i.e. the end of the village)' often contain the earliest references to minor names like Brook Farm, The Hall and the Townsend. They are also, of course, the source of the surnames Brook, Hall and Townsend.

However, *atte* is a weakened form of the Old English masculine or neuter *æt þæm* or feminine *æt þære*, which gave *atten* and *atter* in Middle English before being reduced to *atte* and this actually survives in the present-day Havering-atte-Bower (Ess) 'at the (king's) residence'. Sometimes traces of the earlier forms can still be found today, when the name originally began with a vowel. It sometimes happens that the final *-n* and *-r* of *atten* and *atter* were taken as belonging to the following word, a process known as metanalysis, so that ME *atten Ashe* 'at the ash-tree' has become Nash (Bk, He, Sa), *atten Eccheles* 'at the land added to a village' has become Nechells (Wa) and *atten Eilande* 'at the island, land by the river' has given the modern form Nayland (Sf).

The final *-r* of *atter* has similarly survived in the river-names Ray (Bk, W) and Rea (C, Sa-Wo, Wa) from *atter ē* 'at the river' as well as Rye (Sx) from *atter ie* 'at the island', while Rock (Wo) must be derived from *atter oke* 'at the oak-tree'. Here it seems the name has been influenced by the common word *rock*, otherwise we would have expected the development to have been to *Roke*. One name is of particular interest here. Thurleigh (Bd) is recorded as *La Lega* and later as *La Leye* and *La Legh* from OE *lēah* 'wood, clearing in a wood, glade' preceded by the French definitive article. From the 13th century alternative forms in *Releye, Relegh* etc. occur side by side with those in *Leye* and then from the late 14th century spellings like *Thyrlye, Thurle* and even *Thurley alias Relegh*. It is clear that those in *R-* must has developed from some such formula as ME *at there leye* which became *at the releye*, while the form with *Th-* developed to *at therleye*, this giving modern Thurleigh. Here the definite article itself has become part of the place-name.

Other prepositions are used in the formation of some names, forming a group often referred to as elliptical place-names. For example, Biddick (Du) is derived from the OE preposition *bī, be* and *dīc* literally 'by the ditch', but it is clear that here *bī* is used elliptically and that some such word as 'place', 'village' or 'land' is to be understood. So, a better translation of this name would be '(place, village) by the ditch'. Biddulph (St) probably means '(place) by the delf, quarry', Bythorn (Hu) '(place) by the thorn-bush', Byfield (Nth) '(place) by the open land', and Bygrave (Hrt) '(place) by the entrenchments', so-named from ancient entrenchments there.

The same preposition is the first part of OE *begeondan* 'beyond', *beneoðan* 'beneath' and *betwēonan* 'between', each of which has been used elliptically in the formation of place-names, particularly in Devonshire, where the formation is comparatively common, as compared with other parts of the country. In many modern forms, however, the initial *be-* has been lost, so that today we have Indicombe '(place) on the other side of the valley', Indio '(place) on the other side of the river', Yendamore '(place) beyond the mire', and Yondercot and Youngcott, each of which literally means '(place) beyond the cottage'. From *beneoðan* are derived Naithwood '(place) beneath the wood', Neadon '(place) beneath the down' and Nethercleave '(place) below the steep slope'; and from *betwēonan*, Tweenaways '(place) between the ways', as well as Tinhay, Tinney and Twinyeo, each of which means '(place) between the streams', an exact description of the sites of the three places. All these are in Devon where such elliptical names form a small but characteristic feature of the local place-nomenclature. They are the names of individual farms or small settlements and some are recorded only on the old 6in Ordnance Survey map. Elsewhere similar names are infrequent, but at least two are the names of modern parishes, Twineham (Sx) '(place) between the streams' and Twyning (Gl) '(place) between the rivers', i.e. the Avon and Severn, both having an identical etymology from OE *betwēonan ēum*, *ēum* being the dative plural of OE *ēa* 'river, stream'.

The OE preposition *binnan* (earlier *be innan*) 'within, inside' is the first element of Benwell (Nb) '(place) within the wall', a reference to Hadrian's Wall. Bembridge (Wt) '(place) inside the bridge' seems to have been named from its situation at the end of a peninsula, which in early times could only be reached by sea or by the bridge at Brading. Bindon Abbey (Do) certainly means '(place) within the hill', a reference to the original site of the monastery at Little Bindon near Bindon Hill, while the affix Bendish in Barton Bendish (Nf) is a similar formation and one might translate the name as 'Barton inside the ditch', the village being situated west of Devil's Ditch. Sometimes it is difficult to distinguish names derived from *binnan* and those which have as first element the OE personal name Bynna. There are two names Binbrook. The example in Cambridge certainly seems to mean '(place) inside, that is enclosed by, the brook', but this does not fit the topography of Binbrook (L) which probably means 'Bynna's brook'. OE *bufan* (earlier *be ufan*) 'over, above' is used elliptically in Boveney (Bk) '(place) above the island', the island being in the Thames, and in a pair of names Bovingdon Green (Bk) and Bowden Park (W) originally identical in etymology meaning '(place) above, i.e. on top of the hill'.

Other OE prepositions used occasionally in place-names in a similar way are *fore* 'in front of', *under* 'under, below' and *uppan* 'upon, above'. The first appears in Fordon (ERY) and Forhill (Wo) each meaning '(place) in front of the hill'. *Fore* was also used in the formation of compound words like OE *foreburg* 'outwork', as in Forrabury (Co), and OE *foreland* 'headland, promontory' in North Foreland (K). OE *uppan* is apparently rare, but certainly is found in the form *uppan pylle* '(place) above the creek' in Uphill in Somerset, a county in which *pill* is recorded in local dialect of a small stream. On the other hand, OE *under* is much more common and several examples have been noted in Westmoreland like Underbarrow '(place) under the hill' and Underley '(place) below the wood or clearing', as well as Undermillbeck '(place) below Mill Beck, where Mill Beck means 'mill stream'. In Cumberland with a comparable formation is Underskiddaw '(place) below Skiddaw'; the meaning of Skiddaw is uncertain, but may be 'craggy hill'. It is also the source of Underwood (Db) and Underwood in Selston (Nt) '(place) under or within the wood' and of the affix Underwood in Weston Underwood (Db) 'Weston under or within the wood', a form comparable with Barton Bendish above.

When used in place-names the OE preposition *in* 'in' seems always to be preceded by an adverb of direction, hence north in, south in, east in, and west in the village, for it is frequently compounded with OE *tūn*, which in these cases must mean 'village'. So Norrington (in Alvediston) (W) is literally 'north in the village'. As with the use of other OE propositions this must be an elliptical usage, hence '(place, land) north in the village'. Occasionally a pair of such names is found in the same parish. Grimley (Wo), for example has a Northingtown and a Sinton, the latter meaning '(place, land) south in the village', while a parallel to Sinton is also found in Sodington also in Worcestershire. This is actually recorded as early as c. 957 as *Suðintun*. Sidington (Gl) has the same origin, but it has been argued that here the meaning is rather '(land) south in the district' and this may be the sense in other examples of this type of name. In the cases of Eastington (D, Do, Gl, Wo) the places are in fact in the east of the parish, so a translation '(place, land) east in the village' seems very suitable. The same is not true of Wessington (W), in the parish of Calne, so it must have been named 'west' in relation to some other settlement. Only a single example has been noted so far of the OE preposition *upp* 'up, higher up' used in a similar way, Upton in West Ham (Ess), originally *uppintūne*, '(place, land) higher up in the village'.

The only Scandinavian preposition found in place-names is *í* 'in'. This is used medially between two nouns in Loskay (NRY) and Loscoe (Db, WRY) 'house with a loft in the wood'. During the Middle Ages it was, however, used frequently in Lincolnshire in the same way as OE *in*, but always in a form such as Ketel *Northiby*, – *Suthiby*, – *Estiby* and – *Austiby* and – *Westiby* 'Ketil who lived north, south, east and west in the village' respectively. It is notable that both the OE and ODan forms *ēast* and *austr* 'east' have been noted in this construction. None has survived as a place-name and indeed this formation has to date only been noted once outside Lincolnshire with reference to the churches of *Northeby* and *Sutheby* in 1269 in North and South Collingham (Nt).

Some of the prepositions discussed above are also used in the distinguishing additions, usually called affixes, to older names, as in Barton in the Clay (Bd), Barton under Needwood (St), and Barton upon

Humber (L). Since, however, most medieval documents are in Latin, prepositions used in this way will often appear in such sources in their Latin equivalents and sometimes the Latin preposition has survived in the modern form of the name. Latin *juxta* 'near' occurs in Bradwell juxta Coggeshall (Ess) and Langton juxta Partney (L), where the second name is that of a neighbouring village, though that is not invariably the case, as in Bradwell juxta Mare (Ess) 'by the sea'. Similarly *sub* 'below, underneath' survives in Stratford sub Castle (W) 'below the castle (i.e. Old Sarum)' and Thorpe sub Montem (WRY) 'at the foot of the hill', where the full Latin form has survived. *Super* 'on' remains in Weston super Mare (So) 'on sea' as compared with St Annes on the Sea (La), and Sutton on Sea (L). Latin *in* 'in' is very common in the early forms of place-names and is followed by the ablative case. It certainly survives in the affixes Easton in Gordano and Weston in Gordano (So), where Gordano is the ablative singular of the Latinized form of English *Gorden*, probably meaning 'muddy valley'. Since the Latin and OE forms are the same, i.e. *in*, it is usually impossible to be sure which of them is represented in the modern spellings of such names as Shotton in Glendale (Nb), or Henley in Arden (Wa), but it is in all probability the English. Latin *cum* 'with' occurs in the names of joint parishes like Chorlton cum Hardy (La), Sutton cum Duckmanton (Db), Langar cum Barnstone (Nt). Compare its use in Woodford cum Membris (Nth) 'Woodford with its dependencies' where the full Latin form has survived. Occasionally the English form *with* survives, as in Tiddington with Albury (O), but this seems comparatively rare.

The French preposition *en* 'in', followed by the definite article *le* is used in the same way as the corresponding English word in Alsop en le Dale (Db) 'in the valley', Chapel en le Frith (Db) 'in the hunting forest', and Stretton en le Field (Lei) 'in the open country'. Often the form is simply today Barnetby le Wold (L) or Hamble le Rice (Ha) where the *le* only appears at a comparatively late date. In Barnetby le Wold, for example, it has not been found before 1824 and not a single example of *en le* has been noted at all. There has been insufficient study on this particular feature of place-names and all that can be said is that its occurrence appears to be purely sporadic.

We have already seen the adverbial use in place-names of north, south, east, and west. In Old English these could be either adjectives, as in the common Norton, Sutton, Aston, and Weston, *or* adverbs, but their derivatives *norðan*, *sūðan*, *ēastan*, and *westan* were adverbs only. In the early forms of names they were sometimes preceded by *bī*, used elliptically, in a name like Norney (Sr) '(place lying) north of the marshy ground' or Nornay (Nt) '(place lying) north of the river'. Siddington (Ch) is '(place lying) south of the hill', Southover (Sx) '(place lying) south of the bank', Eastney (Ha) '(place lying) east of the island', Eastnor (He) '(place lying) east of the ridge', Westbourne Park (Mx) '(place lying) west of the stream', and Westwood (K) '(place lying) west of the wood'. Occasionally, a trace of the preceeding preposition *bī* survives, as in Bestwall (Do) '(place lying) east of the wall', the old east town-wall of Wareham.

A special use of OE *wiðinnan* and *wiðūtan*, 'within' and 'without' respectively, is found in particular in London when there were two wards of the same name, one inside the city walls, the other outside. So, there is Cripplegate Within and Without, and Farringdon Within and Without, while in Carlisle there is St Cuthbert Without, the part of the parish lying outside the city. In Latin sources the English words will normally be translated as *intra* and *extra* and these are occasionally still used as in Romsey Intra and Extra (Ha). It seems highly likely that the Latin forms mentioned here, as also *juxta*, *sub* and *super*, were used in official documents and probably never had any real currency among ordinary people. It may not be insignificant that most of these are 'official' forms today.

OE *sundor* 'asunder, apart' has two elliptical senses in place-names. Its basic sense is 'something detached or separated from somewhere else' and so could mean 'remote' in Sundorne (Sa) 'remote house', and Sundridge (K) 'remote pasture'. It seems also to have been used in the sense 'privileged or private', one of the meanings of OE *sundorland*, the source of Sunderland (Cu, Du, La). However, it is just as likely that *sunderland* denoted 'land separated from the main estate'. This sense seems to be supported by the fact that in the reference to Bede's birthplace in the lands of the monastery of Wearmouth and Jarrow the Anglo-Saxon translator of the original Latin renders *in territorio* by OE *on sundurlonde*.

Similarly, OE *upp* 'up, higher up' was used in two senses in place-names. It means 'higher' in contrast to some other place lower down in habitation, names like Upham (Ha) 'higher homestead' and the common Upton 'higher farmstead, village, estate'. A similar sense is found in topographical names like Offord (Hu) 'higher or upper ford', though which ford this refers to is unknown, and Upwood in the same county, the contrast here being to lower woodland west of the village. However, *upp* is clearly used elliptically when the second part of the name is that of a river, as in Upwey (Do) '(place) higher up the R. Wey'. In this particular case *upp*, which has not been noted before the mid 13th century, was used to distinguish Upwey from other places, like Broadway, each originally simply called *Wai(a)*, from the river-name itself.

As was the case with prepositions, adverbs are sometimes prefixed to a village-name as in Down Ampney (Gl), the lower of the four Ampneys, which take their name form a stream called Ampney Brook 'Amma's stream'. In the same county is a pair of such names, Down and Up Hatherley, 'hawthorn clearing', clearly named in relation to each other, Up Hatherley being about three miles further up Hatherley Brook than Down Hatherley.

nine

Affixes in place-names

Many of the older village names, especially common ones such as Norton and Sutton, have a word either prefixed or added to them. This may be a descriptive word, or a personal name or a family name, and is often used to distinguish two places with the same name as in Bishop Norton and Norton Disney (L), and Sutton by Macclesfield and Sutton by Middlewich (Ch). In some cases, however, the use seems to be entirely arbitrary. Some affixes are very old and others, which have not survived occur in medieval documents. Indeed, some villages have had different affixes at various times, and those which, if any, have come down to the present-day are largely, it would seem, a matter of chance. Those no longer current, however, are of the same type as those still used and will not therefore be considered here.

The most important contribution to this aspect of place-names was made back in 1924 by James Tait in the first volume published by the English Place-Name Society, and his general conclusions still in the main hold good today.

These distinguishing affixes usually appear as separate words and are of two main types: those descriptive of the village, whether of its situation, shape, size, or its proximity to some hill, valley or the like, or to some more important place; and those containing the name of the holder or owner of the manor, whether lay or ecclesiastic.

Affixes of the first type are often adjectives, particularly common being those describing the cardinal points of the compass. In these cases the names often occur in pairs, as in North and South Weston (O) and East and West Anstey (D), but occasionally all four are used as in North, South, East, and West Brunton (Nb). Common too are Middle in Middle Claydon (Bk), and Nether 'lower' and Over 'upper' in Nether and Over Haddon (Db), but in modern names Nether has sometimes been replaced by Lower, and Over by Upper, as in Lower Caldecote (Bd) and Upper Heyford (Nth). In medieval documents, however, the Latin equivalents are often used and these survive unchanged in Walton Inferior and Superior (Ch). High is also common and so we have High Barnet (Hrt) and High Wycombe (Bk), while it is sometimes contrasted with Low in High and Low Worsall (NRY). *Haut*, the corresponding form in medieval French records, has apparently only survived in Ault Hucknall (Db). Another common adjective of situation is Hanging 'situated on sloping ground', found in Hanging Grimston (ERY) and Hanging Langford (W), the latter so-named from its situation below a steep hillside. Hutton Hang (NRY), however, with a suffix ultimately from the same root, has adopted its suffix from the nearby Hang Bank 'wooded slope', and this gave rise to the name of Hang Wapentake.

Other affixes refer to the size or shape of the village, as with Great and Little Rissington (Gl). Again, these sometimes appear as Magna and Parva in medieval documents, the Latin words surviving in Appleby Magna and Parva, Glen Magna and Parva and Wigston Magna and Parva in Leicestershire. OE *micel*, *mycel* 'big' has been prefixed in Mitcheldean (Gl) and the shortened form Much in Much Wenlock (Sa), Much Woolton (La) and Much Hadham (Hrt). The mickle in Mickleover and Mickle Trafford (Ch) has been either influenced by or is derived from the corresponding ON *mikill*. Long is commonly used of a straggling village as in Long Buckby (Nth); Broad, perhaps in the sense of spacious, appears in Broad Chalke (W) and Broadwindsor (Do); while Round is apparently found in Acton Round (Sa), though this is pure speculation for there is nothing particularly circular in the topography of the place.

Old appears occasionally as in Old Sodbury (Gl) and has survived as *All* in All Cannings (W). New, however, is rare and where it occurs, as in New Waltham (L), it refers to a comparatively modern building estate.

Sometimes the affix refers to colour, as in Black and White Notley (Ess), where a contrast between different types of soil is probably intended. The reference is also likely to be to the colour of the soil in Black Callerton and Black Heddon (both Nb), but at Black Torrington (D) it is said to refer to the river, for the editors of *The Place-Names of Devon* were informed that the river here has a blackish colour which it loses three miles further down stream. In some instances, such as White Roding (Ess) and White Staunton (So), it is thought that white describes the church or some other prominent building. The Blank in Aston Blank (Gl) is from French *blanc* 'white, bare' and here the references may well be to poor vegetation. OE *gylden* 'golden' is also found occasionally as in Guilden Morden (C) and Guilden Sutton (Ch), but the exact sense of this affix is uncertain, though it is said to mean 'splendid, wealthy'.

The soil at Clayhidon (D) is clayey, as it is around Holton le Clay (L). It is fen at Mareham le Fen and Thornton le Fen (both L), while the adjective fenny is found in Fenny Bentley (Db) and Sutton Veny (W), which has dialectal *v* for *f.* The neighbourhood is stony at Middleton Stoney (O), Stony Middleton (Db) and Stoney Stoke (So), and sandy at Sand Hutton (NRY). The affix in Chislehampton (O) means 'gravel, shingle' and that in Barton Turf (Nf) presumably indicates a district where good turf was obtained.

Dry probably refers to dry higher ground often in marshland, as in Dry Doddington (L) and Dry Drayton (C), the latter contrasting with Fen Drayton, while Latin *sicca* 'dry' has survived in Marston Sicca (Gl) as an alternative to Long Marston. The suffixes in Thornton Watless (NRY) and Willoughby Waterless (Lei) both have the same meaning 'waterless'. The Watless in Thornton Watless, however, was originally the name of a separate place and is derived from ON *vatnlauss*, a word corresponding to OE *wæterlēas* in Willoughby Waterless. Westley Waterless, on the other hand, is misleading since there is no lack of water here and Waterless is for *Waterlees* 'water, wet meadows'.

Cold, usually referring to a village in an exposed situation, occurs in Cold Brayfield (Bk) and Coldmeece (St), as well as Coal Aston (Db), where Coal represents a dialectal development of cold. Another name with perhaps a similar meaning is Blo Norton (Sf), in which Blo is from ON *blá* 'cheerless, cold, exposed'.

Stocking Pelham (Hrt) has Stocking from OE *stoccen* 'made of logs' while Leaden Roding (Ess) is said to owe its affix to its lead-roofed church. In the same way a group of names has a distinguishing Steeple, like Steeple Barton (O) and Sturton le Steeple (Nt), presumably referring to the village church spire. The affix in the Nottinghamshire name has, incidentally, not been noted before 1723. The presence of a castle is of course indicated by such names as Castle Ashby (Nth) and Castle Rising (Nf).

Brant in Brant Broughton (L) and Brent in Brent Pelham (Hrt) both come from the same word meaning 'burnt' and this may commemorate the destruction of the places by fire. The form in Brant

Broughton has been influenced by the name of the river on which the village stands, the R. Brant, the meaning of which is uncertain.

A few miscellaneous affixes may be noted here. English Bicknor (Gl) and Welsh Bicknor (He) are on opposite sides of the R. Wye. Port in Milborne Port (So) means 'market town', and a small group of names like Eaton Socon (Bd) and Walton le Soken (Ess) has OE *socn* as affix. This is modern English *soke* 'district under a particular jurisdiction'. The Bierlow in Brightside Bierlow and Ecclesall Bierlow in the West Riding of Yorkshire is from a Scandinavian word used in England of a small adminstrative district. Latin *ambo* 'both' has been added in Fulfords Ambo (ERY) and Wendens Ambo (Ess), usually at a later date, to indicate two villages with the same name forming a single parish. With these can be compared the West Riding Bradleys Both and Marstons Both. Two other Latin affixes are *forinseca* 'lying outside the bounds' and *intrinseca* 'lying inside the bounds, the latter surviving in Ryme Intrinseca (Do) as contrasted with the lost *Ryme Extrinseca*. An earlier Forinseca appears as Foreign in Rye Foreign (Sx), the name of a larger area which included the corporate liberty of Rye.

One or two affixes are perhaps contemptuous, for example Full Sutton (ERY) 'dirty Sutton', Stratton Strawless (Nf) 'without straw' and Thorpe Thewles (Du) 'immoral'. Other affixes indicate some former pursuit for which the village was famous and often there is only a single example. Iron Acton (Gl) was noted for old iron-workings in the vicinity, Cole Aston (Lei) for coal, Glass Houghton (WRY) for glass-making and Kirkby Overblow (also WRY) for smelting for Overblow means 'of the smelters'. The existence of former potteries is attested by Potter Hanworth (L), Potters Marston (Lei) and Potter Somersal (Db). Husbands Bosworth is apparently 'husbandmen's Bosworth' and is in a farming area, distinguishing it from Market Bosworth 'Bosworth with a market'. This last is commonly found for example in Market Lavington (W) and Market Rasen (L), while OE *cēping* also 'market' is not only the source of the simplex name Chipping (La) but has been prefixed in Chipping Warden (Nth) and Chipping Wycombe (Bk). The Latin word is *forum* and this has survived in Blandford Forum, which is also called *Chipping Blandford* in early forms. Here too may be noted Wickham Skeith (Sf) 'Wickham with a racecourse', Skeith being from a Scandinavian word.

A few places are distinguished by a term for the produce for which they were famous – beans in Barton in the Beans (Lei) and Barton in Fabis (Nt), where Leland in his *Itinerary* in the 16th century noticed the growing of beans, cress in Carshalton (Sr), flax in Flax Bourton (So), saffron (re-introduced into England in the 14th century) in Saffron Walden (Ess), and pigs in Toller Porcorum (Do) from the Latin genitive plural 'of the pigs'.

The affix in a good many village names refers to some nearby natural or artificial feature. In Borrowash (Db) and Stoke Ash (Sf) it must have been a prominent ash-tree, while Cherry Willingham (L), Hatfield Broad Oak (Ess), Barnby in the Willows (Nt) and Newton le Willows (NRY) are self-explanatory. On the other hand it is a 'building' in Botolph Claydon, a 'dwelling' in Bower Hinton (So), a 'mill' in Millmeece (St), and Corfe Mullen (Do), where Mullen is from French *molin*, and a 'bridge' in Bridge Trafford (Ch), Bridgewalton (Sa), as well as Longbridge Deverill (W) 'Deverill near the long bridge'.

In other names the affix denotes a 'stream', as in Fleet Marston (Bk) and 'water', i.e. a river, in Water Newton (Hu) and Waterperry (O), as well as Allerton Bywater (WRY) from their situation beside the Nene, Thame, and Aire respectively. One place, St. Nicholas at Wade (K), has OE *wǣd* 'ford' and Ferry Fryston (WRY) is so-named from a nearby ferry over the Aire.

Watton at Stone (Hrt) must be named from some prominent stone, which according to the editors of *The Place-Names of Hertfordshire* is reported to have been a stone under the horse trough of an Inn. Sutton at Hone (K) is also named from a stone, but here the affix is from OE *hān*, modern *hone*. The wall of Plumpton Wall (Cu) is probably that of the Roman camp *Voreda* and Heddon on the Wall is on the line of Hadrian's Wall.

Some places situated on or near a hill not surprisingly are distinguished by a word for 'hill' hence Hill Somersal (Db), Hetton le Hill (Du), and Walton on the Hill (Sr); Houghton le Side (Du) from OE *sīde* 'hill-side'; Toot Baldon (O) from OE *tōt* 'look-out hill'; and Copt Hewick (WRY) from OE *copped* 'having a peak', a reference to the hill on which the place stands. Other names indicate the situation of the village in a valley, as in Dalton le Dale (Du), Stainton le Vale (L), and Stanford in the Vale (Brk), as well as Hoe Benham (Brk) and Hetton le Hole (Du), both with OE *hol* 'hollow, valley'. Those situated in wooded country are often self-explanatory, like Wood Dalling (Nf) and Woodperry (O), but Sco in Sco Ruston (Nf) is from ON *skógr* 'wood'. Forest is sometimes used of a woodland district belonging to the king and preserved for hunting and this is reflected in Marston in the Forest and Stockton on the Forest (NRY) from the Forest of Galtres and Hesket in the Forest, and Hutton in the Forest (Cu) from Inglewood Forest.

Moor is used of a high tract of uncultivated ground, the usual sense in the North, or of marshland, hence Barnby Moor (Nt), More Crichel (Do), Thornton le Moors (Ch) and Bradley in the Moors (St). Weald or Wold 'open upland, moorland, wasteland' is found in Old Hurst (Hu), Normanby le Wold and several other similar names in Lincolnshire as well as Stow on the Wold (Gl). However, the Weald in Eyton upon the Weald Moors and Preston upon the Weald Moors (Sa) is misleading for it represents *wild*, so it is really 'on the Wild Moors'. Heath 'uncultivated land, heather-covered land' appears in Normanton le Heath (Lei) and St Giles on the Heath (D); marsh in Marsh Benham (Brk) and Welton le Marsh (L), which may be compared with Welton le Wold in the same county; and mire in Ainderby Mires (ERY) and Kirmond le Mire (L). Thorpe in the Fallows (L) is perhaps 'Thorpe in the ploughed or arable land', while Ashley Green (Bk) and Brafield on the Green (Nth) were presumably villages noted for their village-greens or commons.

Many places have added the name of the river on or nearwhich they stand. The usual form appears in Ashton on Mersey (Ch), Adwick on Dearne (WRY), and Weston by Welland (Nth), but there is also Witton le Wear, and with the river-name used alone, Danby Wiske, Eye Kettleby (Lei), and Severn Stoke (Wo) from the Wiske, Eye, and Severn respectively. Others have the name of a river valley as in the cases of Eaton Dovedale (Db) and Burley in Wharfedale (WRY).

Another group of names has that of a district as an affix. Here, the particular relationship of the place to the district is indicated by a preposition. Both Ashton under Lyne (La) and Newcastle under Lyme (St) include the name of a forest, itself apparently derived from a Celtic river-name meaning 'river where elm-trees grow'. There is a series of Warwickshire names, Bourton on Dunsmore, Clifton upon Dunsmore, Ryton on Dunsmore and Stretton on Dunsmore, which derive their distinctive form from Dunsmore Heath 'Dunn's moor'. Brampton en le Morthen (WRY) must derive its name from a district called Morthen, earlier *Morthing*, 'moorland district with an assembly', the name surviving as a place-name, Morthen in the parish of Whiston. Occasionally the district name appears without a preposition as in Higham Upshire (K) 'higher district' and Sutton Coldfield (Wa) 'open land where charcoal is burnt'. In one or two names the affix is the name of a hundred or wapentake as in Boothby Graffoe (L) 'spur of land with a grove' and

Charlton Horethorne (So) 'grey thorn-bush', though *horethorne* may well denote some specific species of thorn-bush. Carleton Forehow (Nf), however, is near Forehoe Hills 'four barrows, burial mounds' and this also gave its name to Forehoe Hundred.

Some names are distinguished by an affix which is itself a place-name, often one which is still in use today, as is the case with Kirby Knowle (NRY) near Knowle Hill 'knoll' and Kirby Underdale (ERY) close to Hundle Dale, a Scandinavian name meaning 'Hundolf's valley'. Kirkby Ireleth (La) is near Ireleth 'Irishmen's hill-slope', Perry Barr (St) near to Great Barr, a Celtic name meaning 'hill', and Stretton Sugwas (He) near to Sugwas, which perhaps means 'riverside land which floods and drains quickly where sparrows are found', a name discussed in the first chapter.

More often, however, the added name is no longer used independently, as with Burnham Deepdale (Nf) from a now lost but self-explanatory *Deepdale*, Burton Pidsea (ERY) 'pool (now drained) in the marsh', Martin Hussingtree (Wo) 'Hūsa's tree' and Silk Willoughby (L), where Silk is a shortened form of Silkby 'Silki's farmstead, village'.

Just as Preston 'priests' manor' is a common place-name, so Priest occurs as an affix to older names like Priest Weston (Sa), Preston Crowmarsh (O), and Preston Candover (Ha), named from the priests of Chirbury Priory, Battle Abbey, and Southwick Priory respectively. The Preston in the last two names is derived from the OE genitive plural 'of the priests'. In the same way monasteries and other ecclesiastical bodies owned manors during the Middle Ages and a number of affixes bear testimony to the fact. Astley Abbots (Sa), Thorpe Abbots (Nf), Abbot's Barton (Ha), and Abbot's Bromley (St) commemorate the holdings by the Abbots of Shrewsbury, Bury St Edmunds, Hyde and Burton, while the Latin *abbas* survives in Cerne Abbas and Milton Abbas (Do), both Cerne and Milton being the sites of abbeys themselves. Abbess from the Abbess of Barking has given Abbess Roding (Ess). Compton Abbas and Melbury Abbas (both Do), however, reflecting the manorial ownership of Shaftesbury Abbey, have Abbas, a reduced form of Latine *abbatissa* 'abbess'. The monks of Monks Kirby (Wa) were those of St Nicholas of Angers; those of Monks Risborough (Bk) were of Christ Church Canterbury, who had holdings here before the Norman Conquest; Monk Fryston (WRY) was held by Selby Abbey, while Monk Bretton in the same riding was the site of a Priory. Prior itself survives in Cleve Prior (Wo) from Worcester Priory, and in Priors Dean (Ha) it is Plympton

Priory which is commemorated. The nuns of Nun Appleton and Nun Monkton in the West Riding of Yorkshire had their houses at Appleton and Monkton respectively, while the prefix in Nuneaton is due to the Benedictine Nunnery found their in the reign of Stephen, 1135-54. The Knights Templar had extensive holdings in England before their suppression in 1312, hence Temple Balsall (Wa), Temple Guiting (Gl), Temple Newsam (WRY), and Temple Normanton (Db), as well as a comparatively large number of field-names in *Temple*. Finally, in this group Bishop and Bishop's are well-represented by Bishop's Cleeve (Gl) and Bishop's Norton (L) from the Bishop of Worcester and of Lincoln and Bishop's Sutton and Bishopstoke, both in Hampshire, which were so-named after the Bishop of Winchester. Cropwell Bishop (Nt), on the other hand, is somewhat misleading, for the manor of Cropwell was held by the *Arch*bishop of York.

The largest of all the groups of affixes consists of those derived from the forename or surname of some early tenant or holder of the manor. Perhaps surprisingly an Anglo-Saxon forename has survived to the present day – Abba in *Ab*kettleby (Lei), Æffa in *Aff*puddle (Do), Heca in *Egg* Buckland (D), the feminine Gōdgȳð in *Good* Easter (Ess), Mæðelgār in Tolleshunt Major (Ess), as well as Ēadgȳ in Stoke *Edith* (He) and *Edith* Weston (R). It is believed that the Edith in these names is the wife of Edward the Confessor. Some of the personal names are of Scandinavian origin – Hrafnsvartr in Crosby *Ravensworth* (We), Ketill in Stickland *Ketel* (We), Sveinn in Hoyland *Swaine* (WRY), the feminine Tola in *Tol*puddle (Do) and Vagn in Wootton *Wawen* (Wa). Welsh David occurs in Culm *Davy* (D) and Owen in Hales*owen* (Wo). Most of the personal names appearing as affixes were, however, introduced into England through the Normans, though many such names were in fact of Old German origin. Of the more common ones are Bernard in Holcombe *Burnell* (D), Richard in Askham *Richard* (WRY), Ralph in Brompton *Ralph* ((So), Roger in Strickland *Roger* (We), and Walter in Waters Upton (Sa). Here *Water* represents the regular medieval pronunciation of *Walter*. Among feminine names of Norman origin are Agnes in Burton *Agnes* (ERY) and Mauld, a common medieval form of Matilda, in *Mauld's* Meaburn (We). Less common christian names are Everard in Papworth *Everard* (C), Warin in Grendon *Warren* (He), and Otton, the usual French form of Otto, in Belchamp *Otton* (Ess). In almost every case it has been possible to trace in early records the individual from whom the affix is derived.

More frequently, however, the affix is the surname of the family which at one time or another held the manor. Few of these are of English origin, but examples include Roebuck, originally a nickname, in Appleton *Roebuck* (WRY), Walsh 'Welshman' in Shelsley *Walsh,* and Fleming 'man from Flanders' in Stoke *Fleming* (D). The Salomes of Berrick *Salome* and Britwell *Salome,* both in Oxfordshire, took their name from Sulham (Brk); the Wallops of Farleigh *Wallop* (Ha) came originally from Wallop in the same county; but the Audleys of Stratton *Audley* (O) seem to have come from Audley in Staffordshire. Sometimes the surname is itself derived from some minor place-name, as with those of the families which held *Bank* Newton (WRY), apparently from the nearby Newton Bank, and Weston *Bampfylde* (So) from some place, as yet unidentified, meaning 'bean field'.

A very high proportion of the family names which occur as affixes to older place-names are of French origin, and those interested in the meanings of such names should refer to the third edition of P.H. Reaney's *A Dictionary of British Surnames*, with corrections and additions by R.M. Wilson.

Examples, county by county are given in a list at the end of this chapter. The list also serves to indicate something of the relative frequency of affixed names in various parts of the country, for the distribution of those derived from French family names seems to agree broadly with that of affixes as whole except apparently in East Anglia. Little work on the distribution pattern of affixed names has appeared since the study by James Tait in 1924. He pointed out that, in general terms, affixes from French family names are uncommon in the North and East, except in Yorkshire. They occur increasingly in the Midlands and are more numerous still in the South, particularly in the South-west, where the high proportion is probably in part to be explained on historical grounds. Here, there were numerous small manors and where a parish was made up of a number of hamlets the various parts would need to be distinguished in some way from each other.

It is impossible at present to indicate with any degree of accuracy the dates at which various kinds of affixes become common. Full lists of early forms are not yet available for those counties still to be surveyed by the English Place-Name Society. However, both Ekwall and Mills in their Place-Name Dictionaries sometimes give the earliest dates they have noted of the affixed forms of the names included in their works. It should also be remembered that the present affix in some names is not the only one to have been attached to the particular name, while some place-names have had earlier affixes which have not survived.

Nonetheless, some general comments can be made about the dates when affixes become popular. If we leave aside those which have the name of an owner or tenant prefixed or added, an examination of the examples given above shows that in many the affix, whether it is English, French or Latin, is first found in the 13th century and a considerable number of them in the 14th. There are very few, comparatively speaking, before this date, but among them are Wooditton in 1086, and in the 12th century Chislehampton, Corfe Mullen, Fen Drayton, Over Haddon, Venn Ottery, Waterperry and White Roding. Chipping Wycombe and Potter Somersal (earlier Nether), on the other hand, have not been noted before the 15th century and others do not appear till later still, for instance *Ault* Hucknall (1535), Middleton *Stoney* (1552), Barnby *in the Willows* (1575, earlier *on Witham*) and Plumpton *Wall* (1578). The *le Wold* in Barnetby le Wold (L) has not been noted before its appearance on the first edition of the Ordnance Survey map of 1824.

A remarkably high proportion of the affixes derived from the name of the manorial holder is similarly first recorded in the 13th and 14th centuries, particularly the 13th. In some cases, however, the affix is found before 1200, as with *Aff*puddle (1086), Wootton *Wawen* (1138-47), Crosby *Ravensworth* (c. 1160), Stoke *Edith* (c. 1180) and Hooton *Pagnell* (1192). Some are not recorded until after 1400 and these include Newton *Tracey* (1402), Marks *Tey* (1439, earlier Tey *Mandeville* from the name of the holder in 1086), Barton *Blount* (1535, earlier Barton *Bagpuize),* Berrick *Salome* and Holme *Pierrepont* (1571), Ashton *Keynes* (1572), and Hampton *Lucy* (1606, earlier *Bishops* Hampton, from the Bishop of Worcester).

Some of the individuals and families whose names occur as affixes are known to have been associated with the place long before their names were affixed to the place-name. Many are first recorded as holders or tenants in the 12th or 13th century, less frequently so in the 14th. There is, however, a notable group in which an ancestor is named as tenant in Domesday Book. This includes Barrow *Gurney*, Bolton *Percy*, Drayton *Parslow*, Dunham *Massey*, Hartley *Mauditt*, Heanton *Punchardon*, Holme *Lacy*, Horsted *Keynes*, Hurst*pierpoint*, Kingston *Bagpuize*, Mansell *Lacy*, Stampford *Arundel* and Willingale *Spain*. In a very few, but nonetheless noteworthy, cases where the affix is a personal name the individual was connected with the place even before the Norman Conquest and this is the case in *Aff*puddle (987), *Tol*puddle and Wootton *Wawen* (both c. 1050), and *Egg* Buckland (in the reign of Edward the Confessor, 1042-1066).

The following is a representative collection of place-names county by county, whose affixes are composed of French family-names:

Bedfordshire: Aspley *Guise*, Higham *Gobion*, Leighton *Buzzard*, Marston *Moretaine*

Berkshire: Compton *Beauchamp*, Eaton *Hastings*, Kingston *Bagpuize*, Sulhamstead *Bannister*, Ufton *Nervet*

Buckinghamshire: Drayton *Beauchamp*, Drayton *Parslow*, Milton *Keynes*, Newton *Blossomville*, Preston *Bisset*

Cambridgeshire: Swaffham *Bulbeck*, Weston *Colville*

Cheshire: Golborne *Bellow*, Minshull *Vernon*

Cumberland: Newton *Reigney*

Derbyshire: Barton *Blount*, Marston *Montgomery*, Newton *Solney*

Devonshire: Aveton *Giffard*, Bere *Ferrers*, Bovey *Tracy*, Buckland *Tout Saints*, Cheriton *Fitzpaine*, Comb*pyne*, Heanton *Punchardon*, Newton *Tracy*, Stoke *Rivers*, Sydenham *Damerel*, Upton *Pyne*

Dorset: Bradford *Peverell*, Chaldon *Herring*, Clifton *Maybank*, Fifehead *Neville*, Haselbury *Bryan*, Hinton *Martell*, Kingston *Russel*, Langton *Matravers*, Okeford *Fitzpaine*, Tarrant *Gunville*

Durham: Coatham *Mundeville*, Dalton *Piercy*

Essex: *Marks* Tey, North Weald *Bassett*, Shellow *Bowells*, Stanford *Rivers*, Stansted *Mountfitchet*, Stapleford *Tawney*, Stondon *Massey*, Theydon *Garnon*, Wendon *Lofts*, Willingale *Spain*

Gloucestershire: Aston *Somerville*, Combe *Baskerville*, Duntisborne *Rouse*, Guiting *Power*, *Meysey* Hampton, Redmarley *D'Abitot*, Somerford *Keynes*, Stanley *Pontlarge*, Stoke *Gifford*

Hampshire: Barton *Stacey*, Hartley *Mauditt* and *Westpall*, Hinton *Admiral*, Newton *Valence*, Shipton *Bellinger*, Stratfield *Saye*, Weston *Corbet*

Herefordshire: Eaton *Tregose*, Holme *Lacy*, Mansell *Gamage* and *Lacy*, Ocle *Pychard*, Weston *Beggard*

Hertfordshire: *Furneux* Pelham

Huntingdonshire: Hemingford *Grey*, Offord *Darcy*, Orton *Longueville*

Kent: Broughton *Malherbe* and *Monchelsea*, Sutton *Vallance*

Lancashire: Heaton *Norris*, Ince *Blundell*

Leicestershire: Ashby *de la Zouch*, Aston *Flamville*, Croxton
Kerrial, Goadby *Marwood*, Kirby *Bellars*, Kirkby *Mallory*,
Melton *Mowbray*, Newbold *Verdon*

Lincolnshire: Boothby *Pagnell*, *Mavis* Enderby, Norton *Disney*

Middlesex: none surviving

Norfolk: Kirby *Cane*, Swanton *Novers*

Northanptonshire: Easton *Maudit*, Higham *Ferrers*, Marston
Trussell, Middleton *Cheney*, Stoke *Albany* and *Doyle*

Northumberland: Seaton *Delaval*

Nottinghamshire: Burton *Joyce*, Colston *Basset*, Holme
Pierrepont

Oxfordshire: Ascot *d'Oyley*, Kingston *Blount*, Newton *Purcell*,
Rotherfield *Peppard*, Sibford *Gower*, Stoke *Talmage*

Shropshire: Albright *Hussy*, Aston *Botterell* and *Eyre*, Eaton
Constantine, Hope *Bowdler*, Leegomery, Neen *Savage* and
Solers, Stanton *Lacy*

Somerset: Barrow *Gurney*, Charlton *Mackrell* and *Musgrove*,
Chilton *Cantelo*, Curry *Mallet*, *Goose* Bradon, Hill *Farrance*,
Huish *Champflower*, Kingston *Seymour*, Newton *St. Loe*,
Norton *Fitzwarren*, Sampford *Arundel*, Shepton *Mallet*,
Stocklinch *Ottersay*, Stogursey (earlier Stoke *Courcy*)

Staffordshire: Clifton *Campville*, Drayton *Basset*, Weston *Coyney*

Suffolk: Bradfield *St. Clare*, Carlton *Colville*, Stow*langtoft*,
Thorpe *Morieux*

Surrey: Stoke *d'Abernon*

Sussex: Horsted *Keynes*, Herst *monceux*, Hurst *pierpoint*

Warwickshire: Aston *Cantlow*, Hampton *Lucy*, Morton *Bagot*,
Radford *Semele*, Stretton *Baskerville*

Wiltshire: Alton *Barnes*, Ashton *Giffard* and *Keynes*, Berwick
Bassett, Easton *Grey*, Littleton *Pannell*, Marston *Maisey*

Worcesterhire: Bentley *Pauncefote*, Chaddesley *Corbett*, Croome
d'Abitot, Elmley *Lovett*, Hampton *Lovett*

Yorkshire: Thorpe *Bassett*, Wharram *Percy* (East Riding); Hutton
Bushell, Newton *Morrell* (North Riding); Acaster *Malbis*,
Allerton *Mauleverer*, Bolton *Percy*, Hooton *Pagnell*, Thorpe
Salvin (West Riding).

ten

Place-names with pagan associations

The comparatively small group of place-names connected with Anglo-Saxon paganism has for long aroused considerable interest. Five studies have already been made and it is probably true to say that we now have a pretty certain and complete corpus of these names to date, thanks to the careful analysis of Dr. Margaret Gelling. It was at one time thought that as the English Place-Name Survey proceeded more such names would be found. In fact it seems that this may not be the case. A number of names thought to belong to this category are now believed to have been wrongly interpreted; others are said to be doubtful and should therefore be omitted from the list. It is of course possible that some examples might be discovered, documented only in medieval spellings, but so far this has only occurred once or twice. It is clear today that it is most unlikely that any more *major* names will be found which contain an element denoting a pagan temple or the name of a pagan god. We can now present a corpus of certain examples and a short list of additional names in which a pagan association is possible but unproven.

There is no evidence that the Britons ever attempted to convert the Anglo-Saxons to Christianity or that Irish missionaries were at work in England before the arrival of Augustine in Kent in 597. From that time the conversion went forward gradually with occasional set-backs throughout the 7th century, but it should be remembered that the only dates we know are those which mark the acceptance of Christianity by the rulers of the various kingdoms. No doubt worship of the old pagan gods lingered long in isolated and out of the way districts, and as late as 700 there were still pagan communities in England. Place-names commemorating the older religion, however, are likely to belong to an earlier period, for as has often been argued where the name of a centre of pagan worship has survived the name must have been firmly established for it to remain unchanged despite the victory of Christianity. For the most part, therefore, they must belong to the period from the earliest Anglo-Saxon settlements in England to at the very latest the end of the 7th century. Their importance historically is clear enough.

The place-names which denote the sites of heathen worship are of two types. First, there are names which simply reflect the former existence of a pagan shrine and second, those which were cult-centres, places dedicated to a particular heathen god. In considering the evidence provided by such names, we should remember that so far no Anglo-Saxon heathen shrine has been identified and excavated and that references to paganism in Old English literary sources provide a very incomplete and very sketchy picture. The importance of place-name evidence in this field is obvious, if only because it is unique.

There are two words which are thought to mean 'heathen shrine', OE *hearg* or *hærg* and OE *wēoh* or *wīh*, *wīg*, the variant forms of the words representing dialectal differences. The first is found in Harrowden (Bd, Nth) 'hill with a pagan shrine' and in Harrow on the Hill (Mx). Harrow is first recorded in 767 as *Gumeninga hergae* 'heathen temple of the *Gumeningas* (the people of *Gumen*)' and this clearly suggests that the shrine at Harrow belonged to them or was particularly associated with them in some way. This is paralleled by the lost name *Besinga hearh*, where the charter founding the monastery at Farnham (Sr) was drawn up, which means 'heathen temple of the Besingas (people of Besa or Besi)'. The meaning of Peper Harrow (Sr) is not certain. It could mean 'Pipera's heathen temple' or 'heathen temple of the pipers'. It has been suggested that the use of musical instruments in pagan worship seems a reasonable hypothesis, but if the OE personal name Pipera is correct, then it would suggest that such shrines could be privately owned, the founder and his heirs drawing revenues form them. Such a custom is recorded in Scandinavian sources, but there is no similar independent evidence from this country. If the first element is indeed the personal name Pipera, as we shall see, there are two other place-names which would be direct parallels to Peper Harrow.

OE *wēoh*, *wīg* is a simplex form in Wye (K) and Wyham (L), an old dative plural, 'at the heathen shrines'. However, it is found more frequently as the second element of a compound name, as in Weedon (Bk), Weedon Bec and Weedon Lois (Nth) 'hill', Weeford (St) 'ford', Wheely Down near West Meon (Ha), Whiligh, in Ticehurst (Sr), Willey in Farnham (Sr), and perhaps Weoley Castle (Wo) 'sacred glade' and

Wyeville, earlier *Wyewell*, (L) 'spring'. Two further possible examples are Wyfordby (Lei) in which ODan *bȳ* 'farm, village' must have been added to a name similar in origin to Weeford, and Wysall (Nt) 'hill-spur'. In the two following instances the first element is an Old English personal name and they are therefore perhaps to be compared with Peper Harrow. Patchway, now the name of a field in Stanmer Park (Sx), is 'Pæccel's heathen temple', while in the foundation charter of Farnham mentioned above is a lost place-name *Cusanweoh* (Sr) 'Cusa's heathen temple'. However Peper Harrow is to be interpreted, here we have two names which clearly suggest that pagan shrines were privately owned on occasion.

It is pertinent to ask why the Anglo-Saxons used two different terms for heathen temples, for it has in recent years been demonstrated that they had several words for hills and valleys, for example, and that these are not synonymous. The answer to this question may well be, as has been proposed, that *hearg* and *wēoh* were used of two different types of shrine. The physical situations of the place-names derived from *hearg* and their associations with groups or tribes would suggest that this word was used for 'communal' places of worship situated on high ground, hence occupying prominent sites. Those derived from *wēoh*, on the other hand, seem to have been wayside shrines, sometimes person-ally owned, judging from their sites and from names like Patchway and *Cusanweoh*.

The second type of name reflecting aspects of Anglo-Saxon paganism denotes cult-centres, that is places dedicated to particular hea-then gods. According to the latest surveys, four such gods are com-memorated, *Tīw*, *Woden*, *þunor* and *Frīg*, whose names have given us Tuesday, Wednesday, Thursday, and Friday respectively.

The war-god *Tīw* is now thought to be the first element of Tysoe (Wa) 'hill-spur' and the lost names *Tislea* (north Ha) 'sacred grove', and Tyesmere near Cofton Hackett (Wo) 'pool'. The first of these is particu-larly interesting because of its site on either the ridge of land south of Edge Hill or one of the hill-spurs jutting out of it, and because of the adjacent valley called Red Horse Vale, where there is a turf figure cut out of the hillside. Although the name itself is not first recorded until the 17th century, such figures are thought to go back to Anglo-Saxon times. The proximity of the place-name and the turf figure led to the suggestion that the horse might well be the emblem of Tīw. Although this must be purely hypothetical of course, nonetheless it is a *reasonable* suggestion.

Woden is the god from whom most of the Anglo-Saxon dynasties traced their descent and he has given his name to a number of names in the Midlands and South. The most impressive site of a shrine dedicated to him is Wednesbury (St) 'fortification' and it is likely that here, as probably also at Harrow on the Hill, the Christian church was built where the pagan temple had been, and this is probably true of other pagan sites. Wednesfield (St) 'open land' is only five miles from Wednesbury and one cannot avoid the conclusion that this must have been a district where the cult of Woden was particularly strong. Other place-names derived from this god are Wensley (Db) 'sacred grove', Woodnesborough (K) 'tumulus', and Wenslow (Bd), the name of an administrative district, also 'tumulus'. The site of the last is unknown, but it was presumably where the district meeting-place was held.

In some ways perhaps the most tantalizing of the names commemorating Woden is Wansdyke 'Woden's ditch', the name of two linear earthworks more or less parallel to each other, one in Somerset, the other in Wiltshire, and both called *Wodnes dic* in the 10th century. It is now known that the eastern Wansdyke is of post-Roman origin and west Wansdyke presumably belongs to the same period, but the historical contexts for their construction is uncertain. Now, about five miles from the eastern end of the east Wansdyke are three further names recorded in Anglo-Saxon charter. In the bounds of Alton Priors are *wodnes beorge* and *woddes geat*, in which *-dd-* stands for *-dn-*, while in the bounds of West Overton is *wodnes dene* and all three can be identified today. The first is a neolithic long barrow, now called Adam's Grave, the second refers to a gap in the line of Wansdyke and the third to a valley crossed by it and now known as Hursley Bottom. In what particular sense Woden was associated with Wansdyke and the three neighbouring features is really uncertain and though several suggestions have been made, it seems best with our present state of knowledge to leave the question open.

Now Woden was the only one of the Anglo-Saxon gods to whom it seems likely that a nickname, *Grīm*, was applied, just as in Scandinavia Grímr was a nickname for his counterpart Othin. In Old English *grima* means 'mask' and this nickname would be appropriate for a god who had a habit of appearing in disguise. Grim is frequently associated with earthworks, somethimes linear earthworks, often with OE *dīc* 'ditch' as in Grim's Ditch (Brk, Ha, O, W), Grim's Dike (Ha), Grimes Dike (WRY) and in several names recorded only in medieval documents. The earliest reference so far noted is to a *grimes dic* in 956, which gave its name to Ditchampton in Wilton (W). Attention has been drawn to the fact that there are twice as many names derived from Grīm as from Woden, and though the connection between the two is certain, it seems likely that Grim survived the conversion to Christianity, perhaps as a pseudonym for 'the Devil'. Such a suggestion seems eminently sensible.

þunor, the god of thunder, equivalent to the Scandinavian þorr, has given his name to Thunderfield (Sr) and a lost *Thundresfeld* near Chippenham (W) 'open land', Thunderley (Ess), Thundersley (Ess) and Thursley (Sr) as well as the lost *Thunorslege* near Bexhill (Sx), *Thunreslea* near Droxford (Ha) and *Thunreslea* near Southampton (Ha) 'sacred glade' and *Thunoreshlæw* near Manston (K), *Thunreslau* near Bulmer (Ess), 'tumulus'. The last was the name of an administrative district and like Wenslow, mentioned earlier, was presumably the site of the meeting-place of the district itself. It will be noticed that all these are in the South of England and are absent from the Midlands and North, which would suggest that Thunor was essentially a Saxon or Jutish god.

It was thought that the goddess *Frīg*, the consort of Woden, had given her name to several place-names but in each case an alternative etymology has been shown to explain the early forms of the name better. In 1959, I suggested tentatively that Friden, near Ballidon (Db), might contain the goddess' name, but at that time only a single early 13th century spelling had been found for the place name. In 1983 a hitherto unknown Anglo-Saxon charter dated 963 was discovered and in the bounds of Ballidon, Friden appears as *Frigedene* 'valley of the goddess Frig', the only certain example of her name in English place-names. At the beginning of this chapter it was pointed out that occasional examples of pagan place-names might be discovered, particularly among lost names found only in occasional spellings, and Friden is the first of what may eventually prove a growing number of minor names of this type.

We have seen that there are two types of names which denote sites of pagan worship, those indicating the former existence of a shrine and those cult-centres dedicated to a particular heathen god. It is worth drawing attention to the fact that there are no place-names compounded of the name of a god *and hearg* or *wēoh*, giving such hypothetical names as Thunderharrow or Wednesway. Whatever the reason, all we can say is that none has survived.

One significant feature in the geographical distribution of pagan place-names is their complete absence from the whole area north of the Humber. This phenomenon has never been satisfactorily explained; but the late Sir Frank Stenton, in 1941, was perhaps nearest when he said that it was an open question whether their absence was due to the "lethargy of popular heathenism ... or the deliberate obliteration of heathen memorials by unusually zealous Christian kings". Evidence for the latter is perhaps to be found in the story told by Bede of the acceptance of Christianity, after debate, by king Edwin of Northumbria in 627. The chief priest then rode out on a stallion and destroyed his temple. Presumably it had a name reflecting its status as a pagan shrine, but whatever that might have been, Bede tells us that it was called Goodmanham (ERY) 'Gōdmund's homestead, estate' in his day. A further district in which no pagan place-names are recorded is East Anglia. Again, we may well never know the reasons though they could well, of course, be similar to those suggested for Northumbria.

Elsewhere, the pattern is "curiously irregular", as Dr Margaret Gelling points out. She has suggested that pagan names are not found in "areas where the earliest missionaries worked with the backing of the local ruling house", whereas such names survive in districts not accessible to early Christian missions. She draws attention to the foundation of the monastery at Farnham near which several pagan names are found and she goes on to suggest that Farnham may have been founded "with a view to mopping up an obstinate enclave of paganism". Moreover, this part of Surrey was a border area between Wessex and Kent at this date. Such a fact may well help to explain why pagan place-names have survived in some areas, like the similar borderlands between Essex and East Anglia. The names which remain in the West Midlands may reflect a later survival of popular heathenism there and it is possible that the establishment of a bishopric at Litchfield was designed for a similar purpose as that of a monastery at Farnham. We can really only speculate on what is a curious distribution pattern of a fascinating group of place-names commemorating pagan shrines; we can do little more given our present state of knowledge.

There are, in addition, some place-names which throw light on certain pagan practices, particularly the custom of burying the dead, whether cremated or not, in a mound or cemetery, accompanied by objects of various kinds. The practice of cremation had already died out during the pagan period, and with the conversion to Christianity the custom of burying objects with the dead also gradually came to an end. It would seem that several place-names illustrating this pagan custom have as second element OE *hlāw* 'tumulus, hill'. It is difficult in many cases to be certain of the exact sense, but in others the meaning 'tumulus' is confirmed by the presence of a burial-mound. This is certainly the case with the large tumulus which has given its name to Taplow (Bk) 'Tæppa's burial-mound', in which several remarkable objects were discovered and which are now on display in the British Museum. It is likely enough that Tæppa himself was buried in the mound in the churchyard there, though presumably the place had a name for the settlement before it was replaced by that of this striking physical feature. Confirmatory archaeological evidence of this kind is rare, but in Derbyshire, for example, where I noted over seventy examples of names in -low, some thirty are certainly burial-mounds. Almost one-third of those recorded early have as first element Old English personal names of the Tæppa type and some may well be the tumuli of the men after whom they are named, as with Atlow, Baslow, Hucklow, and Tideslow from Eatta, Bassa, Hucca, and Tīdi respectively. Dr Margaret Gelling has drawn attention to similar names in the West Midlands, like Offlow (St) 'Offa', Wolverlow (He) 'Wulfhere' and a wide-spread group of seven in Shropshire, for example Longslow and Purslow named from Wlanc and Pussa respectively. All these have Old English masculine personal names as first element and, though archaeological evidence is lacking, it is, as she says not too far-fetched to suggest that they were the burial-mounds of the men after whom the features were named. In other parts of England such a place-name formation is not common in major names, but Bledlow (Bk) 'Bledda', Cutslow (O) 'Cūðen', Hounslow (Mx) 'Hund', and Winterslow (W) 'Winter' seem certain examples.

For many years it was thought that 'animal-head' names in some cases reflected the pagan custom of setting the head of a sacrificed animal on a pole. Animal sacrifice, and also human, is in fact known both from the Continent and from Scandinavia, though there is no comparable evidence in English sources. These names are formed from the name of an animal in the possessive singular compounded with OE *hēafod* 'head'. In place-names *head* was often used in a transferred topographical sense of a headland, a promontory or even a hill, as well as the source of a river. Such names as Hartshead (La, WRY) and Rampside (La) are named either from hills or headlands thought to resemble a 'hart' and 'ram' respectively or from places frequented by such animals. However, it was thought that some could not be explained on topographical grounds and that a pagan interpretation was likely. However, what is striking is that well over thirty such names have been noted, whereas the list of names of pagan shrines and cult centres is numbered only in the forties. It would be surprising indeed if almost as many names survived commemorating a particular pagan custom as commemorating places of actual pagan worship. It is currently felt that judgement should be suspended on this group as a whole till a thorough examination of their sites and situations has been made. So, names like Broxted (Ess) and Broxhead (Ha) mean literally 'the head of a badger', Eversheds (Sr) 'of a wild-boar', Farcet (Hu) 'of a bull', Shepshed (Lei) 'of a sheep', Swineshead (Bd) and Swinesherd (Wo) 'of a swine' and Gateshead (Du) translated by Bede '(at) the head of a goat', but what they acutally *signify* is an open question. It may be noted that Manshead, the name of a hundred in Bedfordshire, means 'the head of a man', but this had been explained as a place where a criminal's head was exposed and so it is presumably to be compared with Thiefside (Cu) 'the head of a thief'.

Traces of Scandinavian heathenism in England are very slight. Most of the Scandinavians who settled in eastern England from the last quarter of the 9th century onwards were certainly pagan. Although they sacked monasteries in their early raids, Lindisfarne in 793, Jarrow in 794, their own religion seems to have have had little hold on them after they settled here. *The Anglo-Saxon Chronicle* describes how in 878 the Danish king Guthrum and his leading followers accepted baptism as part of the peace-terms with Alfred, but we have little evidence of how the mass of them were converted to Christianity. Hoff (We) '(heathen) temple, sanctuary' and Ellough (Sf) with a similar meaning seem pretty certain examples of Scandinavian pagan place-names, while some instances of ON *lundr* 'grove, sacred grove' may well denote sacred pagan groves, but we cannot point to any unequivocal instance. The only certain name of a Scandinavian heathen god to appear in a modern place-name is Othin in Roseberry Topping (NRY), earlier *Othenesbery*, 'hill dedicated to Othin'. The village in which Roseberry is situated was often called *Newton under Oseberry* and the initial R- of the modern name comes from the preceding prepostion by metanalysis, i.e. reinterpretation of the division between words. The affix *topping* means simply 'hill top'. Recently it has been suggested that the name of the god Thor is the first element of Thoresway (L) 'Thor's pagan shrine', a formation, as we have seen, not found in English names. If this is correct, it would be an exact parallel to the Swedish place-name Torsvi in Västergötland. Both Roseberry and Thoresway must belong to an early phase of Danish settlement in eastern England, since the re-conquest of the Danelaw here proceeded fairly rapidly in the 10th century.

Most of the English names considered so far must have been formed *during* the pagan period. On the other hand, there are some names which reflect a popular mythology, a belief in the supernatural world of dragons, elves, goblins, demons, giants, dwarfs, and monsters. Such creations of the popular imagination lived on long after the introduction of Christianity and traces of these beliefs still exist today, but we really have no idea when the place-names referring to them were given.

In Germanic mythology the dragon is represented as guarding the treasure in the burial-mound and the theme of a fight against such a dragon dominates the final section of the Old English poem *Beowulf*, while according to another Old English poem "The dragon must be in the mound, the aged one exultant over the treasures". In fact 'dragon's mound' is the meaning of Drakelow (Db, Wo) and Dragley (Beck) (La), while Drake North (in Damerham, W), first recorded as *Drakenhorde* in 940-46, means 'dragon's treasure'. The first element of these names is OE *draca*, modern *drake*, and is found also in Drakedale (NRY) 'dragon's valley' and Drakenage (Wa) 'dragon's edge'.

OE *wyrm*, modern *worm*, means 'reptile, snake' but also 'dragon' and the latter is the likely meaning in Wormwood Hill (C), formerly *Wormlow*, the name of a tumulus, and so comparable to Drakelow. Where *wyrm* occurs in other names, however, it is impossible to decide between its various senses.

Giants are particularly associated with valleys, and Indescombe (D) and Thursden (La) both mean 'giant's valley', though their etymologies are different. The first element of Thursden survives in Lancashire dialect as *thurse* and the word is found also in Thirlspot (Cu) 'giant's pot or deep hole'. *Dwarf* occurs occasionally as in Dwariden (WRY) 'valley' and Dwerryhouse (La) 'house', but *elf* is fairly frequent in minor names, in association with a hill in Eldon Hill (Db) and with valleys in Alden (La) and Elvedon (Sf).

Most supernatural beings of this kind were evil. OE *scucca* 'demon, evil-spirit' is the first element of Shobrooke (D) and Shocklach

(Ch) 'stream', with different second elements, Shugborough (St) 'fortification', Shuckburgh (Wa) and Shucknall (He) both 'hill' but again with different second elements, and Shuckton (Db) a farmstead haunted by demons. The word which survives in dialect as *scratch* 'devil' is found in Scratchbury Hill (W), a Neolithic camp presumably associated with the devil.

The OE words *grima* and *scinna* each meaning 'spectre, ghost' may occur in Grimley (Wo) 'wood, glade' and Grimshaw (La) 'copse' and Shincliffe (Du) 'steepish slope' respectively. The earlier name of Skinburness (Cu), *Skinburgh*, means 'fortified place haunted by a demon' and to this was later added *ness* 'headland'.

Various terms for 'goblin' are also used in local names. *Bug* 'bogey, boggart' is probably the first element of Bugley (W) 'wood, glade'; *hob* as in *hobgoblin* occurs in Hob Hill (Db) and Hobmoor (ERY) and is especially common in minor names in both Derbyshire and North Yorkshire; and *puck, pook*, as in *Puck of Pook's hill,* is equally common, particularly in the South, as in Puckeridge (Hrt) stream', Puckwell (Wt) 'spring', Purbrook (Ha) 'brook' and Pockford (Sr) 'ford'.

Finally, though modern *witch* does not seem to occur in old place-names, OE *hætse*, a word with the same meaning, is found in Hascombe (Sr) and Hescombe (So) 'valley', and perhaps also with reference to a valley in Hassop (Db) and to a ford in Hessenford (Co).

eleven

Place-names with Christian associations

It would appear that Godstow (O) 'place of God' is the only English place-name which without doubt refers to God, for the name was given to the 12th century abbey of Benedictine nuns there. OE *god*, however, was also used of a heathen god and so in such names as Gadshill (K) and Godshill (Wt) it is difficult to decide whether the names mean 'God's hill' or 'god's hill'.

The first element is certainly the name of Our Lord in Christchurch (Ha) 'church dedicated to Christ', where there was an Augustinian priory. Chrishall (Ess) means 'Christ's nook' on which the editor of *The Place-Names of Essex* comments that it is difficult to know how such a name could arise. The name is recorded already in DB and could perhaps have been land belonging to a church, but it might well have been a place of worship before a church was built there. The meaning of Cressage (Sa) is quite clear – 'Christ's oak-tree' – and there is a Lady Oak, first recorded in 1675, marked on maps north-west of the village. In *The Place-Names of Shropshire* attention is drawn to an account of this oak-tree. It is a young tree supporting an ancient one and it is suggested that "successive replacements could have been occurring since Saxon times". It is highly likely, it would seem, that this is the oak-tree from which the village was named.

OE *Cristen* 'Christian' appears to occur in only a single surviving name Christow (D) 'Christian place', though the exact association is not known. Perhaps a translation 'place hallowed by Christian associations' is as good as we can suggest. It is worth noting a possible parallel in the lost *Halstow* in the parish of Woodleigh in the same county, which seems to mean 'place with holy associations', the first element being OE *hālig*, modern *holy*.

It will have been noticed that three of the names above have a second element in -stow, OE *stōw* 'place, place of assembly, holy place'. In

Chapter Four, we have seen its use in hundred-names in the second of these senses, but the exact meaning in other names is not always so easily distinguished. However, the religious connection is continued in Cheristow and Churchstow 'place with a church', both again in Devon.

It has been pointed out elsewhere that there is an interesting group which refer to holy men. In Plemstall, earlier Plem*stow*, (Ch) the first element is the personal name Plegmund and there is a very early tradition that an Archbishop of Canterbury of that name (890-914) led the life of a hermit here. This tradition is reinforced by the nearby lost *Seint Pleymondes Well* recorded in 1302. Though it cannot be proved that the Plegmund of the place-name was indeed Archbishop Plegmund the association of the two seems reasonable enough. Hibaldstow (L) takes its name from St. Hygebald who was buried there, Felixstowe (Sf) from St. Felix who was responsible for the conversion of East Anglia and Wistanstow (Sa), and Wistow (Lei) from St. Wigstan, who was murdered in 849-50 and buried at Repton in Derbyshire. Edwinstow (Nt) may well have been named from St. Edwin, king of Northumbria and killed in battle in 632, but the first element may alternatively be an OE personal name *Edin*. As has been pointed out, these are named from pre-10th century saints and presumably donoted "places where they worked, died or were buried".

There are other place-names consisting of a saint's name and *stōw*, particularly in Herefordshire, Devon, and Cornwall but they are chiefly from church-dedications and so form a different group from those discussed above. In Herefordshire, for example, are Bridstow (identical with Bridestow D) St. Bridget, Marstow St. Martin, and Peterstow St. Peter; in Devon, Jacobstowe (identical with Jacobstow Co) St. James, and Petrockstow (identical with Padstow Co) St. Petroc; and in Cornwall, Michaelstow (also Ess) St. Michael, Morwenstow St. Morwenna, and Warbstow St. Werburg. Here the meaning of -stow is no doubt 'church'.

OE *stoc* is another word which means literally 'place' and it is possible that like *stōw* it also meant 'holy place'. This, however, is simply an assumption because occasionally it is the name of a place with religious associations, as in Stoke by Nayland (Sf) where there was an Anglo-Saxon monastery, and in Tavistock (D), named from the R. Tavy where there was also an abbey of early foundation.

The usual word for a monastery in Old English is *mynster*, modern *minster*, which also means 'large church'. This is the source of Minster in Sheppey, and Minster in Thanet, both in Kent, where there were Anglo-Saxon nunneries. Axminster and Exminster in Devon are named from monasteries on the rivers Axe and Exe respectively. Kidderminster (Wo) is perhaps 'Cydela's monastery', probably that for which Ethelbald of Mercia made a grant of land in 736; Newminster (Nb) is self-explanatory and is named from the monastery probably found in 1138, and Westminster (Mx) is west of London. The editors of *The Place-Names of Middlesex* point out that the site of the monastery at Westminster was traditionally known as *Torneia* 'island where thorn-trees grow', referring to an island "formed by two branches of the Tyburn at its outfall into the Thames" and first recorded in 785. Where there is no certain evidence of a monastery of early foundation in a name ending in -minster it is safest to assume a meaning 'church, large church'. There is an interesting group in which the first element is an Old English personal name, presumably that of the founder or an early owner, as, for example, Bēda in Bedminster (So), Bucca in Buckminster (Lei), Ēata in Yetminster (Do), and Pippa in Pitminster (So). 'Large church' is also the likely sense in Charminster (Do), Ilminster (So), Sturminster (Do), and Warminster (W), named from the rivers Cerne, Isle, Stour, and Were, as well as Southminster 'south' and Upminster 'higher up', both in Essex.

The usual word for 'church' in our place-names is *church* itself, OE *cirice*, the source of the simplex name Church (La) and of a large group with the second element *tūn*, here no doubt meaning 'village', hence 'village with a church'. This compound has given such varied modern forms as Cheriton (D, Ha, K, So), Cherrington (Wa), Chirton (W), Churston Ferrers (D), and Churton (Ch). As with minster a number of churches have been named from the founder or early owner – Ælfgȳð, a lady, in Alvechurch (Wo), Buna in Bonchurch (Wt), Dunn in Dunchurch (Wa), Hafoc in Hawkchurch (D), and Lilla in Lillechurch (K). Achurch (Nth) is particularly interesting in this respect, for the first element is in all probability a Scandinavian personal name, either a man's name Ási or a woman's Ása, and both are recorded as used in England in the Danelaw. If this is so this name could not have been given before say the 10th century and would therefore be at least one example of the continued practice of naming churches from the owner.

As might well be expected several names in -church have the names of the saint to whom they are dedicated as first element as in the Herefordshire Dewchurch from Dewi, i.e St. David, Kenderchurch St. Cynidr and Peterchurch St. Peter. In addition, several refer to some particular feature of the church itself. Vowchurch (He) and the affix in Frome Vauchurch (Do) denote a 'coloured church', Whitchurch, a common name, was 'white' from the colour of the stone or perhaps because it was built of stone rather than the commoner wood, which seems to be implied by the name Woodchurch (Ch, K). Berechurch (Ess) was 'made of boards', while Stockenchurch (Bk) was 'made of logs'. This must, therefore, have been the same type of Anglo-Saxon church as that which partly survives at Greensted juxta Ongar in Essex.

In the North and North Midlands *kirk*, ON *kirkja*, normally takes the place of English *church* in names like Kirkstall (WRY) and Kirkstead (L) 'site of a church', both of which are the sites of Cistercian abbeys founded in the 12th century. In Kirkham (ERY, La) and Kirton (L, Nt, Sf) both 'village, estate with a church', the second element is an Old English word and it is thought very likely that here *kirk* has replaced an original English *church*. On the other hand the Scandinavian compound *Kirkuby* has given about 40 names in Kirby and Kirkby. It must mean 'village with a church' and it is now believed that these are Scandinavianizations of earlier English names, perhaps Cheritons, Chirtons, or the like. The large number of Kirkbys, however, as compared with English Chirtons, makes one wonder whether this can be the only explanation. An examination of the sites and situations of the places now called Kirby or Kirkby certainly suggests that they were occupied before Scandinavian settlement took place, so perhaps we ought simply to say that these names have replaced or modified earlier English names.

One or two names in -kirk have as first element the name of the founder or early owner as is the case with Orm in Ormskirk (La). More frequently, however, it is the name of the saint to whom the church is dedicated – St. Chad in Chadkirk (Ch), St. Felix in Felixkirk and St. Rumwald in Romaldkirk, both in the North Riding of Yorkshire. In Cumberland, as we have seen in an earlier chapter, the order of the elements is sometimes reversed, as in Kirkandrews from St. Andrew, Kirkbride, as compared with Bridekirk in the same county, from St. Bride and Kirksanton from St. Sanctan, which is paralleled by Kirk Santon in the Isle of Man.

Both *Church* and *Kirk* have been added to village names, as with Church Brampton (Nth), Church Enstone (O), Church Lawford (Wa), Kirkharle (Nb), Kirkheaton (WRY), and Kirk Langley (Db). An unusual affix is found in Stowe Nine Churches (Nth), named from the fact that the lord of the manor of Stowe had the right of presentation to nine churches.

Some places are named from the saint to whom the parish church was dedicated without the addition of a word meaning 'church', and occasionally the saint's name is in the possessive case as with the self-explanatory St. Albans (Hrt) and St. Helens (La, Wt). Some are from the names of less known saints, especially those of Welsh or Cornish origin like Austol in St. Austell, Brioc in St. Breock, Cleder in St. Clether, Dyfrig in St Devereux, Ia in St. Ives in Cornwall, and Gwennarth in St. Weonards (He). In Cornwall, too, there is a considerable group consisting simply of the saint-name without an initial St., as with Cornelly St. Cornelius, Illogan St. Illogan, Mawgan, St. Maugan and Zennor St. Senara. Mevagissey apparently contains the names of two saints St. Mew (and) St. Ida, while Perranzabuloe in the same county means 'St. Peran in the sand' with -zabuloe the modern form of a medieval Latin affix *in sabulo* 'in the sand'. Incidentally, the place has in fact been buried at least once in the past. Outside Cornwall the saint's name is used alone in Botolphs (Sx) St. Botolph, Ippollitts (Hrt) St. Hippolytus, and Sellack (He) St. Suluc.

The patron saint of France has given his name to St. Denys (Ha) and St. Giles, the French form of the Latin St. Egidus, has given St. Giles on the Heath (D). Several other places are named from Anglo-Saxon saints -St. Bees (Cu) from Bega, a virgin saint mentioned by Bede, St. Neot (Co) and St. Neots (Hu) from Neot, said to have been buried at Eynesbury in Cambridgeshire and translated to the nearby St. Neots in the late 10th century, and St. Osyth (Ess), from the daughter of an under-king of Surrey, who founded a nunnery here.

The name of the saint to whom the church is dedicated has sometimes been prefixed to an old village name. The earlier name of Germansweek (D) was simply *Wike, Wyke* from OE wīc, probably in the sense of 'dairy-farm'. To this by at least the 15th century was added the name of St. Germanus of Auxerre to whom the local church is dedicated. St. Mary Cray and St. Paul's Cray are obvious enough and so too are Ayot St. Lawrence and Ayot St. Peter (Hrt), Chalfont St. Giles and Chalfont St. Peter (Bk) and Deeping St. James and Deeping St. Nicholas (L), in which the saints' names have been added to the village-name. Papworth St. Agnes (C), however, is misleading and St. Agnes must be due to popular etymology, for Agnes is the name of a 12th century holder of the manor of Papworth and not derived from a saint at all. In a few names St. has been lost, so we have modern forms like Alton Pancras (Do), Stoke Gabriel (D), and Margaret Roding (Ess), from the dedications of the churches to St. Pancras, St. Gabriel, and St. Margaret respectively.

The French loan-word *chapel* occurs in only a few place-names like Chapel en le Frith (Db), discussed elsewhere, Chapel St. Leonards, (L) from its dedication, and Whitechapel (Mx), which is presumably to be compared with Whitchurch. The Northern French form was *capel* which has given Capel (K, Sr), as well as Capel St. Andrew and Capel St. Mary (Sf). Like *church*, *chapel* has occasionally been added to an older village-name as in Chapel Ascote (Wa), Chapel Brampton (Nth), and Chapel Chorlton (St).

We have seen in a previous chapter the occurrence of *temple* prefixed to older names and that this denoted a place which belonged to the Knights Templar. In addition there are a couple of names derived directly from ME *temple* – Temple in Cornwall, where they had a house, and Templeton (Brk, D) 'manor of the Templars', at both of which they held estates. The Devonshire Templeton, incidentally, is first recorded in the simplex form *Temple*. Most interesting of the names associated with the Knights Templar is Baldock (Hrt), a place founded by them in the 12th century. The name is derived from Old French *Baldac* 'Baghdad' and was no doubt so named because of the associations of the Templars with the Arabian city during the Crusades.

The usual word for a hospital in Middle English is *spitel* which has given numbers of minor names and field-names in Spittle and Spital but which is very rare in place-names. Indeed, Spital on the Street (L) is the only one to appear in place-name dictionaries. No similar name of Anglo-Saxon origin is known for certain, but it has been suggested that Cotterstock (Nth) means literally 'sick house place', i.e. 'hospital' though this is by no means certain.

Another French loan-word, ME *ermitage* 'hermitage' is the source of Armitage (St), where a hermitage is recorded from the 13th century. The Old English word for a hermitage was *ānsetl*, literally 'dwelling for one', 'lonely dwelling', and this is the first element in Ansley (Wa) and Anslow (St), both of which mean 'glade with a hermitage'. One or two place-names are derived from ME *ermite* 'hermit' as for example Armathwaite (Cu) 'hermit's clearing', where a house of Benedictine nuns was established in the 12th century, while the Scandinavian word *papi* 'hermit' occurs in Papcastle (earlier *Papecastre*) in the same county, 'the Roman fort inhabited by a hermit', the Romano-British name of the fort being *Derventio*, from the river on which it stands.

We have already seen something of the origin and development of *cross* in an earlier chapter. Here belong other examples of its occurrence in place-names such as the common Scandinavian compound Crosby 'village with a cross', which must be the meaning also of Croston (La) in which the second element is OE *tūn*. Other Scandinavian compounds include Crossthwaite (NRY), Crosthwaite (Cu, We), and Crostwick (Nf), each meaning 'clearing with a cross', and Crossrigg (We) 'ridge with a cross'. As the second element it is found in Hoar Cross (St) 'grey cross' and Twycross (Lei) 'double cross', which may well have been a cross with four arms. Rey Cross (NRY) seems to mean 'cross on the cairn' marking the boundary between Yorkshire and Westmorland. Minor names derived from wayside crosses, some being boundary marks, are reasonably common, in particular Lady or Lady's Cross, dedicated to Our Lady, and Stump Cross denoting a cross which had lost its head.

The usual Old English word for a cross, *rōd*, modern *rood*, is rare in place-names, but is found in Radstone (Nth) and Rudston (ERY), literally 'rood stone', and the stone from which Rudston is named still stands in the village church-yard. *Rood* is also prefixed once to an old name, Rood Ashton (W). Another Old English word for a cross is *mǣl*, the first element of a group of names such as Malden (Sr), Maldon (Ess), and Meldon (Nb) 'hill marked with a cross'. This word is the second element of the Old English compound *cristelmǣl* 'cross' the source of Christian Malford (W) 'ford with a cross', Christleton (Ch) 'village with a cross', and Kismeldon (D) 'hill with a cross'. The modern form of Christian Malford is completely misleading and must be the result of popular etymology. It is recorded in 1374 as *Cristine Malford*, in the reign of Elizabeth I as *Christen Malford* and in 1611 as *Christon Malford al. Christian Malford*.

We noted at the beginning of this chapter the lost name Halstow 'place with holy associations' and *holy* is often used with Christian reference in a number of place-names; the best known instance is probably Holy Island (Nb), on which the priory of Lindisfarne was situated. In spite of its present-day spelling Hallington, also in Northumberland, means 'holy valley'. But *holy* is particularly widespread, in various forms, in the names of springs such as Halliwell (La), Halwell and Halwill (both D), Holwell (O) and the common Holywell. The meaning of all these names, 'holy well', is also that of Hallikeld (NRY) which has a Scandinavian word for 'spring' as second element. It should be noted that OE *hālig* 'holy' also had a pagan connotation, but no place-name is known where this must necessarily be the case.

The names of various ecclesiastics occur in place-names, sometimes where they lived but more often denoting land and property belonging to them. The commonest is *priest*, OE *prēost*, which as we saw in the first chapter when combined with OE *tūn* is the source of the common Preston 'manor of the priests' and incidentally identical with Purston (Nth, WRY). Prescot (La, O) means 'priests' cottage'. Prestwich (Ch, Gl) and Prestwick (Nb) 'priests' farm' and Prestbury (Ch, Gl), like Preston, 'priests' manor'. *Monk*, OE *munuc*, has given Monkton 'monks' manor' in at least six counties and each must have been the property of a monastery though the allusion in most is not clear. We saw examples of the use of Monk as an affix in an earlier chapter, but Buckland Monachorum in Devon is worthy of note here, for the Latin genitive plural frequently found in medieval references to the place has survived as a suffix to the present day. In this case we do know that the reference is to the monks of the Cistercian abbey founded here in 1278.

Canon, ME *canoun*, is only found very occasionally in place-names such as Canonbury (Mx) 'manor of the canons', those of St. Bartolomew's, London. It is equally rare as an affix, but it does occur in Canons Ashby (Nth) from the Priory of Augustinian canons and in Whitchurch Canonicorum (Do), from the Latin genitive plural and so comparable to Buckland Monachorum. It is 'of the canons' because the manor belonged to the canons of Salisbury.

The use of *abbot*, OE *abbod*, as an affix has already been noted, but it has also given rise to a few place-names. Abbotsbury (Do) is 'manor belonging to the abbot', in this case the abbot of Glastonbury. The name is first recorded in 946 and though there was a monastery here, it has been pointed out that it was not founded until about 1026. Abbotstone in Itchen Stoke (Ha) and Abson (Gl) each also mean 'abbot's manor' and it has been noted that Itchen Stoke was held before the time of Domesday Book by Romsey Abbey, while Abson was held before the Norman Conquest by Glastonbury Abbey.

In the absence of direct evidence it is difficult to decide whether place-names in Nun- are derived from the Old English personal name Nunna or OE *nunne* 'nun'. It seems at present there are in fact no major names containing the latter, though as we saw in Chapter Nine there is a small number in which Nun has been prefixed to an older name. Similarly, there do not appear to be any place-names derived from OE *myncen* also 'nun', though there are at least two in which the word appears as an affix – Minchin Buckland (So) where there was a priory of the Sisters of St. John of Jerusalem and Minchinbarrow in the same county, from the priory of Benedictine nuns there.

ME *ancre* could mean either 'anchorite' or 'anchoress', but the meaning of Ankerwyke (Bk) is clearly 'anchoresses' dwelling', since it was formerly a priory of Benedictine nuns.

We have already noted the use of Lady, referring to the Virgin Mary, in Lady or Lady's Cross and it is this word which occurs in Lady Halton (Sa) from the dedication of the village church. The same word is found also in White Ladies Aston (Wo), so-named because Aston was held by nuns of the Cistercian order, as was Brewood Black Ladies (St) by a priory of Benedictine nuns.

There is also a group of village-names dinstinguished by the addition of the name of the religious house which at one time held land there. This is the case with Acaster Selby (WRY) from Selby Abbey, Hartley Wintney (Ha) from Wintney Priory, Morton Tinmouth (Du) from Tynemouth Priory, and St. Paul's Walden (Hrt) and Wickham St. Paul's (Ess) from St. Paul's Cathedral, London. Newton Longville (Bk), Offord Cluny (Hu), and Weedon Beck (Nth), however, were possessed by French foundations, the church of St. Faith of Langueville by the mid 12th century, the abbey of Cluny already in 1086, and the abbey of Bec-Hellouin in Normandy also by the mid 12th century respectively.

Where *bishop*, OE *biscop*, occurs in place-names the reference is usually to the fact that the place belonged to a particular see, usually the one in which the village is situated. Bishopstone (Bk, He, Sx, W), Bishopton (Du, WRY), Bishton (Gl, Sa, St), and Bushton (W), as well as Bispham (La) and Bushbury (St) all mean 'bishop's manor' and most of these are thought to be comparatively late formations. This must certainly have been the case with Biscathorpe (L) for this is a Scandinavian compound of *biskup* and *þorp* 'dependant, outlying settlement'. Bishopstone, in Stone, (Bk) is the most interesting of these names for it was probably that part of the manor of Stone held by Odo, Bishop of Bayeux in the reign of William the Conqueror. It has been pointed out that if this is so it is a remarkable example of a place-name created by a very brief tenure of an estate.

twelve

Place-names illustrating social and legal customs

Judging from the extant codes of law, the main division in Anglo-Saxon society below the king was between the freeman and the serf. Both classes were subdivided, in the one case into freemen of noble birth and ordinary peasant cultivators, in the other into various classes of serfs. Here the reason for the differences in uncertain. Ignoring the serfs, the Laws of King Alfred divide society into three main classes: those of noble birth with more than five hides of land, those of noble birth with less than five hides of land, and the freemen not of noble birth. These distinctions are peculiar to the Wessex of King Alfred in the late 9th century, but similar ones with local variations appear in other Anglo-Saxon kingdoms. An interesting group of place-names reflects these early divisions of society.

The obvious place to begin is with the numerous names containing the word *king*, in Old English *cyning*, *cyng*. This is often combined with *tūn*, in all probability with the sense 'manor', as in Kingston, a name found in at least fifteen counties, the most northerly being Staffordshire. Identical with Kingston is Kingstone (Brk, He, St). In addition there is a group derived from *cyning* without the possessive -*es*, Keinton (So), Kenton (St), Kineton (Wa), and Kington (Gl, W). With others it is difficult to decide whether the first element is *cyning* or the related word OE *cȳne* 'royal. Kennington (K), Kenton (Nb), Kineton (Gl), Kington (Do, He), and Kyneton (Gl) seem to be derived from the latter and mean 'royal estate'. However, it must be emphasized that it is really impossible to decide between the two words in some of these names. It will be recognized of course that it is the similarity of form between *cyning*, *cyng* and *cȳne* which inevitably led to confusion, so that doubts about the correct etymology are hardly surprising. Moreover the precise significance of 'king's manor' and 'royal manor' is uncertain. The earliest of these groups to be recorded in Anglo-Saxon documents is Kingston on Thames in 838, and what evidence is available to date suggests that they all belong to a later rather than earlier period in Anglo-Saxon England. Further, less than twenty of the names derived from *cyning* or *cȳne* have royal associations during their recorded history, though clearly each must have been a royal manor or estate at the time the names were given. A good deal of research has already been completed on the Kingstons but more remains to be done before we can define their meaning and significance much more exactly.

The problem is not eased by the fact that in a few names the Danish word *konungr*, corresponding to *cyning*, has apparently replaced the English word. So, instead of Kingston, we have Congerston (Lei) and Coniston (ERY, La, WRY) and instead of Kington, Conington (C, Hu). Moreover, it is at least highly likely that in two Lincolnshire place-names, Conesby and Coningsby, both Danish compounds meaning 'king's estate, manor', an original OE *Cyningestūn* has been completely Scandinavianized to *Konungsbȳ*. This would seem to be the most likely interpretation on historical grounds in view of the royal associations of the names.

The Old English word is also found with other second elements. A word for 'hill' occurs in Kingsdon (So) and Kingsdown (K), for 'wood or glade' in Kingsley (Ch, Ha, St), for 'bridge' in Kingsbridge (D), for 'ford' in Kingsford (Wa), for 'stone' in Kingstone (So) and for 'wood' in Kingswood (Gl, Sr, Wa). *Cȳne* is found once with *stān* in Kingston on Soar (Nt) 'royal stone', though the editors of *The Place-Names of Nottinghamshire* comment cryptically "No such stone is known here now".

Later, *King* occurs as an affix in the names of some places held by the crown like King's Cliffe (Nth), Kings Newnham (Wa), King's Walden (Hrt), and Areley Kings (Wo). In medieval sources this is often translated as Latin *Regis*, the genitive singular, and this survives in Bartley Regis (Ha), Grafton Regis (Nth), and Newton Regis (Wa).

Special consideration should be given to a discussion of Kingston upon Hull, popularly referred to as simply Hull. The earlier names of the place were *Wyke*, presumably in some such sense as 'dairy-farm', and Hull, itself derived from the river of that name. The etymology, and so the meaning, of Hull is quite uncertain, though the most plausible suggestion is that it is a river-name of pre-English origin. The explanation of Kingston is given in *The Place-Names of the East Riding of*

Yorkshire, where it is noted that in 1292 Edwald I exchanged with the monks of the Cistercian Abbey of Meaux lands which the king held in Wawne (ERY) and Wilsby (L) for the purpose of securing the port. The place was then officially called 'the king's town'. Then in 1382 Richard II made a grant to the mayor and people of Kingston upon Hull "to have a port below the said town formerly called *Sayercryk* and now called *Hull*", *Sayer* here being apparently a ME personal name.

Old English *cwēn*, modern *queen*, unlike *cyning*, is rare in English place-names, though it may well occur in Quainton (Bk) and Quinton (Gl, Nth, Wo) 'queen's manor'. However, there can be no doubt that ME *quene* is the first element of Quinbury (Hrt) and Queenborough (K), since documentary evidence shows that they were named in honour of Maud, wife of King Stephen, and Philippa, wife of Edward III respectively. Queen survives at least once as an affix in Queen Charlton (So) after the manor had been given to Catherine Parr by Henry VIII.

A few places seem to have been named from Old English words meaning 'prince, such as *fengel* in Finglesham (K) 'prince's homestead', and *æðeling*, perhaps in Athelington (Sf) and Allington (Do, L, W) 'manor belonging to the princes', more certainly in Athelney (So) 'princes' island of land', and Adlingfleet (WRY) 'prince's water-channel'.

The rank of *aldormann*, modern *alderman*, was that next to the king and members of the royal family. Its meaning is 'nobleman of the highest rank' and the word is found in Aldermanbury (Mx) 'alderman's manor', the likely meaning also of Aldermaston (Brk) and Alderminster (Wo). This modern form of the Worcestershire name completely belies its origin for it is a name in *tūn*, the editors of the Worcestershire survey commenting "Later the name underwent a curious corruption". During the 10th century, because of the influence of the Danish *jarl* 'nobleman, earl', *aldormann* was replaced as a title by OE *eorl*, originally merely 'nobleman'. This *may* occur in Arleston (Db) and Earlstone (Ha) 'estate, manor', but there was also an Old English personal name Eorl and this is perhaps more likely to be the first element of these two names. After the norman Conquest *earl* was the usual title for the great magnates and as such it is found as an affix to older names like Earl Framingham (Nf) from the Earls of Norfolk, Earls Heaton (WRY) from the Earls of Warren and Surrey, Plympton Erle (D) from the Earls of Devon, and Winterbourne Earls (W) from the Earls of Salisbury. The usual term in the 9th and 10th century for a member of the lesser nobility was *þegn*, modern *thane*, but the original meaning of this word was 'servant'. In Thenford (Nth) 'thanes' ford' it is really impossible to say in which sense it is used, though as we shall see terms for servants are in fact rare in place-names.

The usual term for a free peasant below the rank of noble was OE *ceorl*, modern *churl*, which occurs frequently in Charlton, as well as Charleton (D) and Chorlton (Ch, La, St) 'village of the free peasants'. In Carleton and Carlton, both fairly common names in Scandinavianized districts, however, the English word has been replaced by the corresponding Old Danish word *karl* 'a freeman of the lower class', and this word is perhaps the first element of Carlby (L) 'village of the free peasants'. Alternatively, Carlby may rather contain the personal name Karl, a byname formed from *karl* itself. *Ceorl* is also found in Chorley (Ch, La, St) 'wood, glade', as well as the self-explanatory Charlecote (Wa), Charlcote (W), Charlcott (Sa), as well as Charlwood (Sr). Only occasionally do we find a word for servant in English place-names, but OE *gōp* is likely in Gopsall (Lei) 'hill' and *esne* in Isombridge (Sa) 'bridge of the servants'.

Two Old English words call for special mention – *cild*, modern *child*, and *cniht*, modern *knight*. The former is apparently used in various senses in place-names and in Childwall (La) and Chilwell (Nt) the meaning is quite uncertain, though the second element in both is *wella* 'a spring'. In the common Chilton 'farm, village, estate', and Chilhampton (W) the genitive plual *cilda* is compounded with a word for a habitation and the sense is thought to be 'young noblemen', for it has been suggested that the word referred to the younger sons of a family to whom an estate had been given as a joint possession. The meaning of the word in Chilcote (Lei, Nth), like that in Childwall is really unknown. On the other hand, it would appear that individual possession is indicated by Chilson (O) and Chilston (K) where the first element is the genitive singular of *cild*. However, the young men who gave their name to Childwick (Hrt) were in all probability oblates of the abbey of St. Albans, who according to medieval records of the abbey, obtained milk from the place. A meaning 'dairy farm of the oblates' would seem eminently satisfactory. Occasionally, *Child* was later affixed to an older name as in Chilfrome (Do) and Child's Ercall (Sa) in some sense now uncertain.

OE *cniht* similarly means 'youth' so that Knightsbridge (Mx) is presumably 'bridge where young men meet'. The word also meant 'servant', 'retainer of a lord' and either sense is possible in the common Knighton 'village, estate', Knightcote (Wa) 'cottage', Knightley (St) 'wood, glade', and Knightwick (Wo), 'dairy-farm'. The later sense of *knight* 'a man raised to honourable military rank by the king' does not occur until the 12th century and so is not really to be reckoned with in place-names.

Some examples of Scandinavian terms for various ranks of society have already been noted. Others which occur occasionally in place-names include *hold*, an officer of high rank in the Danelaw, in Holderness (ERY) 'headland of the hold'; *dreng*, a free tenant, probably in Dringhoe (ERY) 'hill', Dringhouses (WRY) self-explanatory, and Droiton (St) 'village, estate'; and *leysingi* 'freeman' perhaps in Lazenby (NRY) and Lazonby (Cu) 'farm', though the first element of these two names may rather be the personal name Leysingi, formed from the noun. Similarly, the first element of Bonby (L) and Bomby (We) 'farm, village' could represent either *bondi* 'peasant' or the personal name Bondi.

Official titles too are only rarely found in place-names, but OE *dōmere* 'judge' is the first element of Damerham (Ha) 'enclosure', *tollere* 'tax-gatherer' of Tollerton (NRY) 'village, manor', and *gerēfa* 'reeve, bailiff' of Reaveley (Nb) 'wood, glade'. *Sheriff*, literally 'shire-reeve' is the source of Shrewton (W) and Shurton (So) 'manor' and of Screveton (Nt), but here the form of the name has been partially Scandinavianized with initial Sc- for English Sh-. It is also found as an affix in Sheriff Hales (Sa) from the Sheriff of Shropshire who held the manor in 1086 and Sheriff Hutton (NRY) from a sheriff of York, Bertram de Bulmer who died in 1166.

Anglo-Saxon law recognized two main categories of land tenure. *Folcland* 'folk-land' was held according to folk-right or customary law and from it the king drew certain food-rents and customary services. This has given Faulkland (So) and Falkland in minor names and field-names. *Bōcland* 'book land' was granted by royal book or charter, usually with freedom from some of the customary services and is the source of the common Buckland, a name so far only noted in Hertfordshire and Lincolnshire outside the South of England.

We have already seen that two of the three divisions of free society in King Alfred's Wessex were men of noble birth with more than five hides of land and those with less than five hides. Sir Frank Stenton long ago pointed out that the *hide*, OE *hīd*, formed the basis of social organization everywhere in Anglo-Saxon England except Kent. *Hide* denoted the amount of land which would support a household, a free family and its dependants and as we saw in an earlier chapter it seems to have been on an average 120 acres. This word occurs in place-names in the simplex form Hyde (Bd, Ch, Ha, Mx), which Ekwall believed should be translated 'homestead consisting of one hide'. When it occurs as the second element of a compound it sometimes appears in the modern form as -field or -head. Occasionally it is compounded with a numeral as in the Wiltshire Toyd 'two hides', Fifield Bavant 'five hides', assessed as five hides in Domesday Book, and Tinhead 'ten hides'. Fifield is paralleled by Fifield (O), and Tinhead by the affix in Stoke*teignhead* and Combe*inteignhead* (D), the name of an area containing thirteen manors, and, as the editors of *The Place-Names of Devon* point out, whose total hidage amounted to about ten. This area became known as the 'Ten Hide', and so we find early spellings like *Stok in Tynyde* in 1285 and *Cumbe in Tenhide* in 1227. The development to *Teign*head is simply explained through the influence of the nearby R. Teign. Two further examples may be added, Nynehead (So) 'nine hides', and the affix in Piddle*trenthide* (Do) 'thirty hides', a manor actually assessed as thirty hides in Domesday Book.

The names of some places reflect the fact that they were charged with the payment of some particular tax. Galton (Do) and Yeldham (Ess) were respectively a farm and a homestead each having as first element OE *gafol* and *geld*, both meaning 'tax'. Pennington (Ha, La) and Penton (Ha), where first element is OE *pening*, modern *penny*, apparently mean 'estate subject to a penny rent', and Galhampton (So), Galmington (D, So), Galmpton and Gammaton (both D) 'estate of the rent- or tribute-paying peasants', from the genitive plural of OE *gafolmann* and *tūn*.

The first element of others indicates that their ownership had at one time or another been in dispute as must have been the case at Threapland (Cu, WRY) 'disputed land', Threapwood (Ch) and Threepwood (Nb) 'disputed wood', from *þrēap* 'dispute quarrel'. This is also the meaning of Callingwood (St) which is a French-English hybrid name. On the other hand, Warley (Ess) may perhaps have a first element OE *wǣr*, 'agreement, covenant' and so mean 'agreement wood or glade' which would indicate the settlement of such a dispute. Other names denote places which were communally owned as with Manton (Nt, R, W) referring to a farm, estate or manor which was communally owned, since the first element here is OE *mǣne*. Both Manea (C) and Maney (Wa) were islands of land or raised pieces of land in marsh which were similarly owned, while Mangreen (Nf), Manley (Ch, D), and Meanwood (WRY) were respectively a grassy place, a wood or glade, and a wood held communally, each being derived from *mǣne*. Some similar statement of ownership or possession seems to be indicated by Almondbury (WRY) presumably 'fortified place belonging to the community' for the first element is the ODan word *almenn* 'all men'.

Words for different types of criminals are not infrequent in minor names. OE *sceaða* 'thief, criminal' occurs in Scadbury Park (K), a name which presumably denoted a disused fortification frequented by thieves; *sǣtere* and *scēacere* 'robber' are found repectively in Satterleigh (D) and the Lancashire Shackerley and Shakerley, each meaning 'robbers' wood'. *Flēming* 'fugitive' is thought to occur in Fleam Dyke (C), a post-Roman earthwork and so is comparable with Wrekendike (Du), which has *wrecca*, modern *wretch*, 'fugitive' as first element. OE *wearg* 'felon' is compounded with *hyll* in Wreighill (Nb), the name probably meaning 'hill where criminals are executed' and with *burna* in Warnborough (Ha) 'stream where felons are drowned', while Worgret (Do) and Warter (ERY) have *rōd* 'cross' and *trēow* 'tree' as respective second elements, denoting 'gallows where criminals are executed'. *Gallows* itself is especially frequent in minor names and lost medieval field-names, but Gawber (WRY) 'gallows hill' is an example of the occurrence of the word in the name of a more important place. *Gawber* and *Gawtre(e)* are in fact spellings commonly found in lost names of the 16th and 17th centuries, the latter clearly meaning 'gallows tree'. Here too probably belongs Dethick (Db) literally 'death oak', no doubt an oak-tree on which criminals were hanged. On the other hand Flamstead (Hrt) means 'place of flight', for fugitives and perhaps also criminals, and it has been pointed out that later a condition of the tenure of the manor was that protection should be given to travellers. It would seem, therefore, that something of the original meaning of the place-name was still alive in the Middle Ages.

Examples have already been given of names denoting meeting-places connected with local government, especially those which became the names of hundreds and wapentakes. Similar names are not uncommon, though often we have no idea what kind of a meeting was held at the particular place. This is so with Matlock (Db), literally 'speech oak-tree', derived from OE *mæðel* 'speech', hence 'oak at which a meeting is held' and Matlask (Nf), literally 'speech ash-tree', and so 'ash-tree at which a meeting is held'. It is worth noting that the -ask spelling here is a Scandinavianized form of OE *æsc*, modern *ash*. Similar names for meeting-places include Spellow (La) literally 'speech mound', and Spellow is also commonly found in minor names. Like Spellbrook (Hrt) 'speech brook', which must have been a brook where meetings were held, they are derived from OE *spell* 'speech', while Spetchley (Wo) 'speech glade', one of the meeting-places of the hundred of Oswaldlow, is from OE *spēc*, modern *speech*. Another meeting-place of the same hundred was probably Stoulton, literally 'seat farm, village', from OE *stōl* 'stool, seat', modern *stool*. It has been suggested that here it was the seat of the judge or speaker at the hundred court and if so the place-name would mean 'village with or near the speaker's seat'. A comparable name would be Mottistone (Wt) 'speaker's stone', from OE *mōtere* 'a speaker at an assembly', the stone being a large menhir which still stands on the hill above the modern village.

Runnymede (Sr) is apparently an old meeting-place which may be the reason why the meeting between King John and the Barons, at which Magna Carta was sealed, took place there. Its present-day form means 'meadow at *Runy*', and *Runy* originally meant 'island where a council is held', from OE *rūn* 'secret, mystery, council', which has given modern *rune*, the term for the ancient Germanic alphabet.

OE and ODan *þing* 'meeting, assembly' each occur as the first element of several names. The English word is found in Thinghill (He) 'hill', Tingrith (Bd) 'stream', in Finedon (Nth) 'valley', and Fingest (Bk) 'wooded hill'. In the last two names F- for Th- is a late dialectal development. The Scandinavian word is found more particularly in the compounds *þingvǫllr* 'assembly field'. The first is the source of Fingay Hill (NRY), perhaps the meeting place of the whole Riding, and the second has given Thingwall (Ch, La) and Dingbell Hill (Nb), as well as Tynwald, the site of the court of the Isle of Man.

thirteen

English settlement-names

The names dealt with here are those of settlements. These are often called habitative names, those of places where men and women lived, and they include in them a word denoting a habitation. This contrasts with 'nature names', those of natural or artificial features of the landscape, many of which, of course, became the names of villages. The four principal elements from which they are derived normally survive today as ham, ton, wick, and worth and, though the last two occur as simplex names, they occur chiefly as the final element of compounds. The first element in these names may be a personal name, a term indicating personal or group ownership, a word descriptive of situation, size, shape and so on, or a term for a bird or animal, or for a crop, plant or tree. There are literally thousands of names of this type and only a selection of them can be included here.

We have already seen in an earlier chapter that OE *hām*, modern *home*, 'homestead' is believed on good grounds to belong to the early periods of Anglo-Saxon settlement in Britain. A further piece of corroborative evidence is that it is the commonest of all habitative place-name elements in the earliest recorded English names 670-731. Attention has been drawn in Chapter Five to its occurrence in compounds in which the first element is the genitive plural of Old English group-names like Nottingham and Waddingham. Similarly, it will have been noted that place-names derived from the compound *wīchām*, like Wickham and Wykeham, must have belonged to a very early stratum of name-giving in Anglo-Saxon England. It has further been shown that names in -ham are rare in the west of the country, that is in districts settled at a later date.

OE *hām* occurs frequently with a personal name as first element and a selection of these is given at the end of this chapter. In the following examples only the meaning of the first will be given, that of *hām* being understood to be 'homestead' or as has been more recently suggested 'village', a natural development of *hām*. The first element is often descriptive of situation as in the self-explanatory Northam (D), Norham (Nb), Southam (Gl, Wa), Eastham (Ch, Wo), and Middleham (Du, NRY); of size in Mitcham and Mickleham, both in Surrey, 'big' and Medmenham (Bk) 'middle-sized'. In should be noted that some of these names as well as some of those which follow may be derived from OE *hamm* 'land hemmed in by water or marsh; river-meadow; cultivated plot on the edge of woodland or moor', since it is often difficult in some place-names to distinguish for certain between hām and hamm. The latter will be discussed further in a later chapter.

Some were named from a nearby river like Cockerham and Irlam (both La), Measham (Lei, formerly Db) and Trentham (St) from the Cocker, Irwell, Mease, and Trent respectively, while Burnham (Ess, Nf) and Fleetham (Nb) both mean 'village on the stream'. From other natural features there are Barham (Hu, Sf), Downham (C, Ess, Nf), Dunham (Ch, Nf, Nt), and Clapham (Bd, Sr, Sx) all with words meaning 'hill', Dalham (Sf) 'valley', Sulham (Brk) 'narrow valley, gully', Saham (Nf) 'lake', and Seaham (Du) 'sea'.

A number of 'homesteads' or 'villages' were named from the animals kept there – goats at Gotham (Nt), horses at Horsham (Nf, Sx), cattle at Neatham (Ha), sheep at Shipham (So), and a stud or herd of horses at Studham (Bd).

Others are named from the crops or other plants which grew there – beans at Banham (Nf), bent-grass at Bentham (Gl, WRY), clover at Claverham (So), fern at Fareham (Ha) and Farnham (Bk, Do, Ess, Sf, WRY), and grass at Gresham (Nf). Names from trees appear to be rare, but beech-trees grew at Bookham (Sr), elms at Elmham (Nf, Sf), and maples at Mapledurham (Ha, O).

It has been suggested that except in such names as Newham (Nb) and the common Newnham and Nuneham (O) 'new homestead, village' OE *hām* probably ceased to be a living place-name element fairly early in the Anglo-Saxon period. Like Newnham is the common Needham, which was probably named from the poor land there.

There are no simplex place-names derived from *hām* for all those with a modern form Ham are from *hamm*. There are, however, two compound words with *hām* as first element, *hāmstede* literally 'site of a homestead' and *hāmtūn* again literally 'home farm' which have given rise to a number of names. Hampstead (Bk, Mx), Hamstead (St, Wt), Hempstead (Ess), as well as Hemel Hemstead (Hrt) where Hemel is an old district-name meaning 'broken country', are all derived from *hāmstede*. From *hāmtūn* we have Hampton (Gl, O), Hampton Lovett (Wo), and Highampton (D) and Littlehampton (Sx) as well as the selfexplanatory Bridgehampton (So), Brookhampton (Wa, Wo), Fenhampton (He), Netherhampton (W), and Shorthampton (O). As will have been noticed only a literal meaning has been given, for it is clear that both compounds must have had very precise meanings which we do not at present know. Clearly, careful and detailed research is needed into both groups of names to determine their full significance.

The commonest element in English place-names is OE *tūn*, modern *town*, and cognate with German *Zaun* 'hedge', and 'fence, hedge' is the sense in Primitive Germanic. There is, however, no certain example of this meaning in our place-names. Here, it seems to have meant 'farmstead', which developed a meaning 'village', then 'manor, estate'. This word is very rare in our earliest recorded documents to 731 and there are in fact only six examples. Indeed I have suggested that place-names derived from *tūn* were, for the most part, not being formed in numbers much before the end of the 7th century. It is almost impossible to suggest the meaning of *tūn* in individual names, but it was traditional in the volumes of the English Place-Names Society to translate it as 'farm', sometimes 'farm, village'. Recently, it has been suggested that the correct translation is often 'estate' and this is probably the most accurate. For example, this might seem logical in names in which *tūn* has been added to an earlier topographical name as is the case with Claverton (So), where the first part is identical with Clatford (Ha) 'ford where burdock grows' and Milverton (Wa) with Milver- identical with the common Milford 'mill ford'.

It is perhaps safer to assume a meaning 'village' or 'estate' when the first element is a personal name. The number of such compounds is very large; for example, there are over 230 in Devonshire alone, of which some 60 are said to have been given after the Norman Conquest; on the other hand only a single example of such a compound has been noted in Surrey. Occasionally, the same name is repeated in different counties, so that Wessington (Db), Wistanton (Ch) and Wiston (Sx) all mean 'Wīgstān's estate'. A selection of names of this type will be found at the end of this chapter, but here a small and interesting group may be noted, which the references in Domesday Book suggest is each named from the holder of the estate in the time of Edward the Confessor, 1042-66. This includes Alston (D) 'Alwine', Blackmanstone (K) 'Blæcmann', Osmaston by Derby (Db) 'Osmund', Shearston (So) 'Sigeræd', and Affington (Do) 'Ælfrūn', the last a lady. It is very likely indeed that these names were 11th century formations.

For the rest, an attempt will be made to give a representative selection of examples in meaningful groups, like those derived from terms for groups of people. Bickerton (Ch, He, Nb, WRY) is named from bee-keepers, Sapperton (Db, Gl, L, Sx) from soap-makers, Shepperton (Mx) from shepherds, Smeaton (NRY, WRY) and Smeeton (Lei) from smiths, Tuckerton (So) from tuckers, i.e. cloth-fullers, as well as the self-explanatory Fisherton (D, W), Potterton (WRY), and Salterton (W).

The first element frequently denotes the situation of the village or estate as in the common Norton, Sutton, Easton, and most of the Astons as well as Weston and Middleton. Netherton (Nb, Wo) and Overton (Ch, Db, Ha, R, Sa, W) are respectively 'higher' and 'lower' than some neighbouring place. Otherton (St, Wo) does literally mean 'the other estate', perhaps in relation to some earlier settlement. The first element in Heaton (La, Nb, WRY) means 'high', while Hampton (Ch, Sa), Hampton in Arden (Wa), Great Hampton (Wo) and Wolverhampton (St, with Wolver- added later from the name of a lady, OE Wulfrūn), Heanton (D), Hinton (Brk, Gl, Ha, So) are all derived from OE *Hēantūne* 'at the high village or estate'. Langton is found in many counties and like Lanton (Nb), Launton (O), Longton (La, St), and Longtown (Cu) has a first element meaning 'long', compared with Scampton (L) in which it is ON *skammr* 'short'. Mickleton (Gl, NRY) and Storeton (Ch) both denote large estates, as does Middleton on the Hill (He), the modern form of which is completely misleading. Alton (Db, Lei) were 'old' in contrast to the common and self-explanatory Newton, identical with which is Niton (Wt). Most of the Newingtons, however, represent an OE dative form *æt Nīwantūne*, 'at the new *tūn*', and the -n- of the inflectional form survives also in Naunton (Gl, Wo) and Newnton (W).

The first element refers to the nature of the soil in a number of names – clay in Clayton (La, St, Sx, WRY), gravel in Girton (C, Nt), and sand in Sancton (ERY), Santon (Cu, L, Nf), and sandy or chalky ground in Manton (L).

Many are named from the river near which they are situated, as is the case with Charwelton (Nth, Cherwell), Crediton (D, Creedy), Glympton (O, Glyme), Itchington (Wa, Itchen), Linton (Nb, Lyne),

Lonton (NRY, Lune), and Tamerton (D, Tamar). Even more have as first element a word meaning 'river' or 'brook'. This is the case with Beighton (Db), Brockton (Sa), Brunton (Nb), Eaton (Bk, Brk, He, Nt, O, W), Eaton Socon (Bd), Water Eaton (St), as well as Fletton (Hu) and Flitton (Bd). Mitton (La, Wo, WRY) and Myton (NRY, Wa) were 'near the river confluence', while Alton (Ha), Alton Pancras (Do), and the Wiltshire Alton Barnes and Alton Priors were 'near the source of the river'. Eaton (Ch, Db, Lei), Church Eaton (St), Eaton Bray (Bd), and Eton (Bk) are all derived from OE *ēg* 'island', commonly used in place-names for a piece of raised ground in a wet area. This word will be discussed in a little more detail in a later chapter.

Marten (W), Merton (D, Nf, O), and the common Martin and Marton have as first element OE *mere* 'pond' and this compound has been the subject of an in-depth study by Ann Cole. She has shown that the pools varied in size, that some were natural, others man-made, that at least half are on major travel routes and that they seem to have denoted places of some importance, though most today are only small villages. Their earlier importance lay in the products of the pools, providing a ready water-supply, fish, wildfowl, as well as reeds and withies. In other words these products were not only an important feature of the local economy but performed a special function as places where travellers could expect water and refreshment. It may be pointed out that it is now thought that some of the other compounds in *tūn* with a topographical term similarly had a special function arising out of their situation.

A number of place-names indicate that the *tūn* was in a valley, like the common Compton, Dalton, and Denton, as well as such examples as Clotton (Ch), Claughton (NRY) 'clough', Corton (Do, So) 'gap, pass', Dorton (Bk) 'pass', Hopton in several counties 'valley' and Yatton (He, W) again 'gap'. Considerable research has taken place in the last decade into the vocabulary of topographical names and the meanings of the words which form the second element of such place-names will be discussed in the next three chapters. Suffice it to say here that it has been shown that Old English had a vast topographical vocabulary in which there were few synonyms, each of the words for valley, for example, denoting different and specific shapes of valleys.

OE *halh* 'nook' has a variety of meanings in place-names, and Halloughton (Nt) and the common Haughton as well as Holton (So) may be translated here as 'nook village, estate'. The nature of the nook, however varies considerably, as has recently been pointed out, from small valley, shallow recess, land between rivers or in a river-bend, recess in a hill, and island of slightly raised ground (in marsh). Only local topography can determine between these. This word is found also in the north in Haighton, Halton, and Westhoughton, all in Lancashire and Haughton (Du, La, Nb). Since *halh* is the source of northern dialect *haugh* 'flat land by a river, water-meadow', this sense must be considered in these names.

The first element of some names in *tūn* is a word for hill, as in Hilton (Db, Hu, NRY, St), and Hulton (La, St), Downton (He, Sa, W), and Dunton (Ess, Lei, Nf, Wa), as well as Clapton and Clopton, found in many counties, 'hill, hillock', the common Clifton 'cliff, slope', Hoghton (La), Hooton (Ch, WRY) and Hutton, in many counties', 'heel, hill-spur', Neston (W) 'ness, headland' and Shelton and Shilton, both occurring several times, 'shelf, ledge'. As with words for valleys some of the words for 'hill' will be discussed in a little more detail in a subsequent chapter.

Other names derived from terms for natural features include Morton and Moreton, both fairly frequent, and Murton (Du, Nb, NRY) 'moor or marsh' and Slaton (Bk, D, Nth) 'slippery place'. Woodton (Nf), the common Wootton and Wotton all mean 'village, estate near a wood', while the well-recorded Grafton was 'near a grove'.

The settlement was sometimes named from a neighbouring building such as a 'mill' in Millington (Ch, WRY) and Milton (Cu, Db, Nt, St), or a church with a 'steeple' in Steepleton (Do).

Judging from the first elements of place-names in *tūn* many such names must have been noted for the animals kept there. Perhaps in these names the meaning is 'farm, village', so that Shepton (So) and Shipton (Do, Gl, Ha, O, Sa) may be translated 'farm, village where sheep are kept'. The reference is to rams in Rampton (C, Nt), to cattle in Natton (Gl), Netton (W) and Notton (Do, W), to calves in Calton (D, St, WRY) Cawton (NRY), Cawton (Ha), Kelton (Cu) as well as Calverton (Bk, Nt) from the genitive plural, to boars in Everton (Bd, La, Nt), to hounds in Hunton (Ha), to ducks in Doughton (Gl, Nf) and perhaps to mules in Moulton (Ch, L, NRY, Nth, Sf), though here the first element may be a personal name OE *Mūla* or ON *Múli*. Two other names in which the meaning may be 'farm' are Butterton (near Newcastle St), one noted from its butter, and Honiton (near South Molton D) for its honey. Occasionally the first element is the name of a wild animal or bird as in

Darton (WRY), which has been translated 'deer park or enclosure', Foxton (C, Lei, NRY) where foxes must have been common, Dufton (We) presumably where doves were kept, and Storrington (Sx) where storks were common.

Again, 'farm, village' even 'settlement' seem reasonable translations of *tūn* in place-names indicative of the crops grown there. The commonest of these is Barton where barley and more generally corn was grown. This is certainly suggested by a reference in an Anglo-Saxon charter dated 945 where an unidentified Barton is glossed by Latin *villa frumentaria* 'corn farm'. There is also evidence that it later denoted an outlying grange where crops were stored. It would appear that most of the Bartons were names given in the later Anglo-Saxon period. For example, in a charter for Barrow upon Humber (L) dated 971, it can be shown that the bounds of the estate given there include those of the modern parish of Barton upon Humber. There is, however, no mention of Barton at all. One can only presume, therefore, that Barton itself is a late 10th or 11th century formation.

In addition to barley or corn, flax was grown at Flaxton (NRY) and also probably at Linton (C, Db, ERY, He), hay at Hayton (Cu, ERY, Nt, Sa) and rye at Royton (La), Ruyton (Sa) and Ryton (Du, Sa, Wa). Garston (Ha, Hrt) was specially noted for its grass and this name has been translated 'meadow' or 'grass enclosure'; coarse grass grew well at Faxton (Nth), clover at Claverton (Ch), while Foddington (So) and Grassington (WRY) must have been noted for their grazing.

The names of plants form a distinctive group, too, especially broom in the common Brampton, Branton (WRY), Brompton (ERY, Mx, NRY, Sa), leeks in Latton (Ess, W), Laughton (Lei, Sx WRY) and Leighton (Bd, Ch, Hu, La, Sa). Bent-grass grew at Beeston (Nf, Nt, WRY), wild-saffron at Crafton (Bk), fern at Farrington (So), brooklime at Lemmington (Nb), rushes at Sefton (La), thistles at Thistleton (R), and woad at Watton (Hrt).

Many place-names in *tūn* have as first element the name of a tree and some of these are self-explanatory, like Ashton (Ch, Gl, La, So, W), Elmton (Db), Mappleton (Db, ERY), Treeton (WRY) and the common Thornton. Less obvious are Acton (Ch, He, Mx, Sa, St), Aighton (La) and Aughton (ERY, La, WRY) 'oak', Allerton (La, WRY), Ellerton (ERY, NRY), Ollerton (Ch, Nt), Orleton (He, Wo) and Owlerton (WRY) 'alder', and Saighton (Ch) and Salton (NRY) 'sallow'. Pirton (Hrt, Wo), Puriton (So), Purton (Gl, W) and Pyrton (O) all mean 'village, estate where peartrees grow'; while the common Appleton seems to mean 'village, estate where apple-trees grow'. The problem with the Appletons, however, is that Old English *æppeltūn* is recorded with the sense 'orchard' and this may have been the meaning of some of these names.

Somerton (L, Nf, O, So) and Winterton (Nf), identical with which is Winderton (Wa), clearly indicate the seasonal uses of these places and here 'farm' seems an eminently likely translation of OE *tūn*. However, the meaning of Dray- in the common Drayton is uncertain. The first element is certainly OE *dræg*, modern *dray* 'cart', but the word seems to have had an early meaning 'drag, portage'. So, besides a sense 'cart', we have to reckon with 'portage where boats are dragged overland or dragged up from water' and 'tract where sleds can be dragged'. Local topography will sometimes indicate which is meant.

We saw earlier in this chapter that though we can recognize the etymology of the compound *hāmtūn*, which gives modern Hampton, we can do no more than give a literal translation. It was pointed out there that it is clear that *hāmtūn* must have had a precise meaning which eludes us. This is the case, too, with OE *wīctūn*, the source of names like Market Weighton (ERY), Wighton (Nf), Witton (Ch, Wa, Wo), and Wyton (Hu). Other possible senses of *wīc* will be noted later, but in Witton, both in Cheshire and Worcestershire, *wīc* presumably refers to an industrial centre – more specifically a salt-production centre – since each is near a salt-town, Droitwich and Northwich respectively. In these, a meaning 'village, estate near a salt-production centre' seems eminently plausible.

A further group of names in *-tūn* consists of a personal name followed by a connecting particle *-ing-*, as in Paddington (Mx), in Old English *Pad(d)ingtūn*. Names of this type are to be distinguished from those like Hoddington (Ha) from OE *Hod(d)ingatūn* 'village, estate of the Hod(d)ingas (people of Hod(d)a)'. Here the first element is the genitive plural of a group-name. These will have some early spellings in *-ingeton*, whereas those like Paddington have no such forms. They have only *-ington*. The interpretation of such names has been disputed, but that consistently followed by the editors of the English Place-Name Society's volumes is that *-ing-* here is a connective particle indicating some sort of association between the person named and the village or estate. Paddington would, by this token, be taken to mean 'village, estate associated with or called after Pad(d)a'. This formation is very common and examples are given at the end of this chapter.

OE *tūn* is not recorded at all as a simplex place-name and it is also very rare indeed as a first element. It occurs in Towneley (La) 'wood, glade belonging to the village' and in this case the village is Burnley. Elsewhere, it forms part of two compounds. One is *tūnstall*, a word not recorded in independent use in Old English but found in place-names as early as Domesday Book, 1086. Its literal meaning is 'site of a farm' and it is found today as Tunstall in at least nine counties, as well as Dunstall in Lincolnshire and Staffordshire. The second of these words is *tūnstede* 'farmstead' and this has given Tunstead (Db, La, Nf). Whereas Tunstall occurs in minor names and field-names distributed fairly widely, Tunstead on the other hand occurs only rarely in such names.

Recent research has shown that OE *wīc* had several meanings in place-names. In Chapter Three, we saw that names derived from the compound *wīchām* have a direct connection with small Roman settlements. When it occurs as a second element, it is now clear that it denoted a trading centre in names like Aldwych (Ln) 'old', Fordwich (K) 'by a ford', Dunwich (Sf) from an earlier Celtic name of uncertain etymology, and Ipswich (Sf) from an OE personal name Gip and Sandwich (K) 'sand'. A similar meaning seems likely for Kepwick (NRY), where the first element is a partially Scandinavianized form of OE *cēap* 'trade, market'.

In parts of the West Midlands a further specialized development from 'trading centre' to 'salt-production centre' is certain in Leftwich, from an Old English feminine personal name Lēoftæt, Middlewich 'middle', Nantwich 'famous' and Northwich 'north', all in Cheshire, and in Worcestershire is Droitwich 'dirty, muddy'. All were centres of the salt-industry.

A similarly specialized meaning 'dairy farm' seems to have developed and this, indeed, may be the commonest sense of the word in place-names. It would certainly suit such names as Bulwich (Nth), Calwich (St), Oxwich (Nf), Shapwick (Do, So), and Shopwyke (Sx), as well as the common Hardwick or Hardwicke, where the first element denotes farm animals – bulls, calves, oxen, sheep, and a herd of livestock respectively. Similarly, we have the common Butterwick noted for butter, Casewick (L), Cheswick (Nb), and Chiswick (Ess, Mx) for cheese. Spitchwick (D) produced bacon and Woolwich (K) wool, while Bewick (ERY, Nb) must have been noted for bees and Barwick (Nf, So, WRY) and the common Berwick for barley. Perhaps Barwick, Borwick (La), and and Berwick are to be compared with Barton and had the senses 'grange' or 'outlying farm where crops are stored'.

Sometimes the *wick* was named from a personal name and a selection of these is given at the end of the chapter. From this usage it is clear that *wīc* was still being used to form new place-names in the post-Conquest period. For example, neither Battleswick in Colchester (Ess) named from the *Bataille* family nor Stilesweek in Tavistock (D), from the *Stoyls*, could have been named before the 13th century.

Wick occurs in other compounds such as the common Southwick, Eastwick (Hrt, Sr, Sx), and Astwick (Bd, Nth), as well as Westwick in at least five counties and Hewick (WRY) 'high'. Aldwick (Sx) and Haultwick (Hrt) are comparable to Aldwych, while Greenwich (K) and Greenwick (ERY) are self-explanatory. Occasionally the *wick* is named from a river as with the Northumberland Alnwick and Lowick on the Aln and Low, but there is also Flitwick (Bd) 'near a stream'. Gratwich (St) is 'on gravelly ground', Papplewick (Nt) 'in a pebbly place', and Standerwick (So) 'on stony ground'.

Particularly interesting is the fact that *wīc* has sometimes been added to an older name as in Eton Wick (Bd), Hackney Wick (Mx), and Writtle Wick (Ess). None of these has been recorded before the 13th century and so are perhaps comparable to Battleswick and Stilesweek above.

The basic sense of OE *worð* seems to have been 'enclosure', but at an early date this had developed to 'enclosed settlement' the likely meaning in place-names derived from it. This is the meaning in place-names in which the first element is a personal name, and about three-quarters of the names in -worth are in fact compounded with such a name. For example 15 out of 23 surviving examples in Surrey are from a masculine name; in Berkshire the relative numbers are eight or nine out of 13, in Derbyshire eight out of 12, and in Hertfordshire seven out of 11. These seem typical of the counties so far suveyed in detail. Examples of the personal names compounded with -worth are given at the end of the chapter.

Where the first element is an appellative, those in Longworth and Southworth (both La) are self-explanatory; Heworth (Du, NRY) is 'high worth' and Rowarth (Db) 'worth on rough ground'; the adjective in Littleworth, in Great Farringdon, (Brk) has been added later to a simplex Worth, which has survived to the present day in Worth (Ch, Do, K, Sx). Stanworth (La) was on stony ground, Greatworth (Nth) in a gravelly area, and Edgeworth (Gl, La) on an edge or hillside, though a personal name is possible here. Tamworth (St) was named from the river Tame on which it stands.

Lindsworth in King's Norton (Wo) is named from lime-trees, and nettles and reeds grew respectively at Nettleworth in Warsop (Nt) and Redworth (Du). Five other names Ashworth 'ash-tree', Dilworth 'dill', Hollingworth (also Ch) 'holly', and two Farnworths 'fern' are in Lancashire. Here names in -worth are relatively common, but the proportion containing a personal name seems to be well below the average, as it is also in Cheshire. In the Place-Name Society's survey for the West Riding of Yorkshire it is pointed out that *worð* is as relatively common there as in Lancashire, but the distribution is uneven. There is only a single example in the whole of the East and North Ridings, but 53 examples in the West. Of these, however, no less than 44 are in districts south of the R. Aire, thus connecting the southern part of the West Riding with the Midlands. The proportion of examples with a personal name as first element is lower than the average, 32 out of 53.

OE *worð* is not recorded at all in pre-731 documents. Only four examples of the word have been found in genuine 8th century Anglo-Saxon charters and they do not become numerous there before the 10th century. A full-scale study of *worð* is needed, but at the moment it seems reasonable to suggest that this word was being used in the formation of place-names during the 7th century, as is suggested by such names as Bobbingworth (Ess) 'the enclosed settlement of the Bubbingas (Bubba's people)', Callingworth, in Bingley, (WRY) 'of the Cūlingas (the people of Cūla)', and Worlingworth (Sf) 'of the Wilheringas (Wilhere's people)' as well as Abinger (Sr) 'of the Abbingas (the people of Abba)'.

The evidence suggests that it did not become common till the late Anglo-Saxon period, but it also demonstrates that it continued to be used as a name-forming element long after the Norman Conquest. Its distribution, too, deserves detailed research and all that can be said at present is that *worð* is common, for example, in Surrey and Sussex, and is represented in most eastern and south-eastern counties, as well as Lancashire, Northumberland, and the West Riding of Yorkshire, but is rarely found in the West Midlands and in the South-west.

In the West Midlands and South-west its place is taken by derivatives, with similar meanings, *worðig* and *worðign*. The first of these is confined mainly to the South-west, especially to Devon. Early spellings in both *-worth* and *-worthy*, however, occur for the same name, so that it is sometimes difficult to be absolutely certain which is the original form.

The simplex form survives as Worthy (D, Gl, Ha, W) and among the more interesting examples (all in Devon, except where noted) are Smallworthy 'narrow', Yalworthy 'old', and Wringworthy (also Co) which may mean 'enclosed settlement with a press, i.e. for cheese or cider'. The first element is an Old English personal name in Elworthy (So) 'Ella', Halsworthy and Holsworthy 'Heald', Hockworthy 'Hocca' and Wembworthy 'Wemba'. It is clear, however, that *worthy* was still in living use after the Norman Conquest, for Ditsworthy seems to be from a Middle English personal name or surname *Durke* and Gulsworthy from a family called *Golle*. Neither of these place-names has been recorded before the middle of the 14th century. A further point to note is that most of the names quoted above are those of small places, though a good number are the names of parishes.

Place-names derived from *worðign* are characteristic of the West Midlands, but they are also found in Devon. As a simplex name it usually survives in the form Worthen as in Devon and Shropshire, but occasionally as Worden of which there are at least five examples in Devon itself. In compound names its usual present-day spelling is -wardine, but this is not exclusively the case as in Harden (St) 'high', Marden (He) which seems to have meant 'enclosed settlement belonging to Maund' (some three miles away), Northenden (Ch) 'north' and Brockworth (Gl) 'brook', in which the original ending *worðign* had been replaced by *worth* itself, already in the early 13th century. The Herefordshire Leintwardine and Lugwardine are named from a lost river-name Lent and the R. Lugg respectively, while Wrockwardine (Sa) means 'enclosed settlement by The Wrekin'. The English Place-Name Survey volume for Shropshire points out that the modern form in *-wardine* appears as early as the later 13th century and the precise spelling first in 1616.

In a number of names the first element is an Old English personal name – Bēda in Bedwardine (Wo), Bēdel in Belswardyne (Sa), Ella in Ellerdine (Sa), and Pēoda in Pedwardine (He). No example of the type of formation in which the first element is a Middle English personal name or surname, like Ditsworthy above, has so far been noted, though the word has been found in surnames like Richard *atte Worthyne* as late as the 14th century. Indeed it remained in living use until at least the early 18th century in dialect as *worthine*, recorded from Herefordshire in the sense 'division of land'.

Place-Names in *-hām* compounded with an Old English personal name include: Biddenham (Bd) Bȳda, Bloxham (O) and Bloxholm (L)

Blocc, Bluntisham (Hu) Blunt, Cadnam (Ha) and Cadenham (W) Cada, Chippenham (C) Cippa, Dagenham (Ess) Dæcca, Edenham (L) Ēada, Egham (Sr) Ecga, Epsom (Sr) Ebbi, Hailsham (Sx) Hægel, Haversham (Bk) Hæfer, Loudham (St) and Lowdham (Nt) Hlūda, Masham (NRY) Mæssa, Oakham (R) Occa, Pickenham (Nf) Pīca, Puttenham (Hrt, Sr) Putta, Rodmersham (K) Hrōðmǣr, Tatham (La) Tāta, Tickenham (So) Tica, Wappenham (Nth) Wæppa, all *masculine* names; and Alpraham (Ch) Alhburg and Wilbraham (C) Wilburg, both feminine.

Place-Names in *tūn*, of which the first element is an Old English personal name: Acton (Sf) and Acton Turville (Gl) Acca, Alfriston (Sx) Ælfrīc, Chapel Allerton (So) Ælfweard, Amaston (Sa) and Ambaston (Db) Ēanbald, Atherstone on Stour and Edstone (both Wa) Ēadrīc, Bacton (He, Nf, St) Bacca, Barmpton (Du) Beornmund, Barnston (Ess) and Barnstone (Nt) Beorn, Bayton (Wo) Bæga or the feminine Bēage, Breaston (Db) Brægd, Cayton (NRY) Cæga, Durweston (Do) Dēorwine, Edmonton (Mx) Ēadhelm, Edwalton (Nt) Ēadwald, Hadstone (Nb) Hæddi, Harmston (L) Heremōd, Hexton (Hrt) Hēahstān, Hoxton (Mx) Hōc, Kilmeston (Ha) Cēnhelm, Kimbolton (He, Hu) Cynebald, Kinvaston (St) Cynewald, Lullingstone (K) Lulling, Lupton (We) Hluppa, Picton (Ch, NRY) Pīca, Selmeston (Sx) Sigehelm, Simpson (Bk) Sigewine, Tilton (Lei) Tila, Wigginton (Hrt, O) and Wigton (Cu) Wicga, Wilbarston (Nth) Wilbeorht, Woolverstone (Sf) Wulfhere and Wyboston (Bd) Wīgbald, all *masculine* names.

Abberton (Ess) and Edburton (Sx) Ēadburg, Aylton (He) Æðelgifu, Chellington (Bd) Cēolwynn, Knayton (NRY), Kneeton (Nt) and Kniveton (Db) Cēngifu, Leverton (Brk) Lēofwaru, Sevington (K) Sgifu, Wollerton (Sa) Wulfrūn and Wolterton (Nf) Wulfūryð, all *feminine names*.

Further examples of the Paddington type, 'village, estate associated with or called after Pad(d)a', include the following. Only the personal name which occurs as first element is given and a translation 'village, estate associated with or called after' is to be supplied in each case: Aldington (Wo) Ealda, Avington (Brk, Ha) Afa, Bavington (Nb) Babba, Bovington (Do) Bōfa, Bridlington (ERY) Berhtel, Cockington (D) Cocc(a), Coddington (Ch, Db, He, Nt) Codda or Cotta, Covington (Hu) Cofa, Diddington (Hu) and Doddington (C, K, L, Nb, Nth) Dudda, Eckington (Db, Wo) Ecca or Ecci, Evington (Gl) Ge(o)fa, Folkington (Sx) Folc(a), Hullavington (W) Hūnlāf, Kensington (Mx) Cynesige, Killington (We) Cylla, Kirklington (NRY, Nt) and Kirtlington (O)

Cyrtla, Lillington (Wa) Lylla, Luddington (Wa) Luda, Pilkington (La) Pīleca, Puckington (So) Pūca, Snoddington (Ha) Snodd, Waddington (L, WRY) Wada, Wallington (Hrt) Wændel, Wennington (Ess) Wynna, Workington (Cu) Weorc or Wyrc and Paignton (D) Pǣga. The usual early 19th century spelling of the last was Paington and the modern form is said to have been adopted by the Railway Company after 1850. All the personal names in this list are *masculine*.

Place-names derived from *wīc*, with a personal name as first element: Baswich (St) Beorcol, Canwick (L) Cana, Chadwich (Wo) and Chadwick (Wa) Ceadel, Earswick (NRY) Æðelrīc, Elwick (Nb) Ella, Elswick (La, Nb) Æðelsige, Heckmondwike (WRY) Hēahmund, Ipswich (Sf) Gip, Orgarswick (K) Ordgār, Pattiswick (Ess) Patti, Postwick (Nf) Possa, Winwick (Hu, Nth) Wina, Wistanswick (Sa) Wīgstān, all Old English masculine names; and Goodwick (Bd) Gōdgifu, a feminine name. Beswick (ERY) Besi and Renwick (Cu) Hrafn, in each case probably a masculine Scandinavian personal name.

A representative selection of the large group of place-names composed of an Old English personal name and *worð* probably in the sense 'enclosed settlement' comprises: Ainsworth (La) Ægen, Badgeworth (Gl) Bæcga, Badsworth (WRY) Bæddi, Bedworth (Wa) Bēda, Betchworth (Sr) Becci, Blidworth (Nt) Blīða, Brinkworth (W) Brynca, Broxworth (Nth) Bricel or Brihtel, Chatsworth (Db) Ceatt, Culworth (Nth) Cūla, Elworth (Ch, Do) Ella, Fittleworth (Sx) Fitela, Hansworth (St) Hūn, Harmondsworth (Mx) Heremōd, Hunstanworth (Du) Hūnstān, Idsworth (Ha) Iddi, Ingworth (Nf) Inga, Inworth (Ess) Ina, Kensworth (Bd) Cægin, Kibworth (Lei) Cybba, Ludworth (Ch, Du) Luda, Lulworth (Do) Lulla, Marsworth (Bk) Mæssa, Mereworth (K) Mǣra, Molesworth (Hu) Mūl, Papworth (C) Pappa, Pebworth (Gl) Peobba, Pickworth (L, R) Pīca, Rickmansworth (Hrt) Rīcmær, Tetsworth (O) Ttel, Wadsworth (WRY) Wada, Whitworth (Du, La) Hwīta, Wirksworth (Db) Weorc or Wyrc, all *masculine* names, and Kenilworth (Wa) from the *feminine* Cynehild.

fourteen

Roads and ways

The only metalled roads in England before the construction of turnpikes were built by the Romans. The most important of these are Akeman Street, Ermine Street, Fosse Way, Ryknield Street, and Watling Street. There were other prehistoric trackways, however, the most important being Icknield Way.

In Roman Britain there was a network of roads with eight radiating from London, the centre of the system. Others intersected and linked with the main roads and today many such roads are still being discovered. Some utilized in part older trackways like the Icknield Way, but of course most were laid out by the Romans themselves for purposes of military and civil government.

We do not know whether the Romans gave names to the roads they built and if they did certainly none has survived. Most of the names by which they are known today are Old English in origin. Nonetheless their importance is attested by the fact that, under William the Conqueror at latest, the special privilege of the King's Peace protected travellers on Ermine Street, Fosse Way, Watling Street, and Icknield Way. No doubt it was at least in part due to this fact and because of the importance of these roads that their names were applied to others which had nothing to do with them. This practice is not due to modern antiquarians, as has sometimes been supposed, for such transferred names are recorded as early as the 13th century. Some of these have not survived like *Ykelingstrete* found in a Lincoln charter of 1277, *Ykeling* being paralleled by a similar spelling for Icknield Way recorded in a Berkshire document. This must have been a transferred use of Icknield Street, an alternative form of Icknield Way, referring to Ermine Street as it crossed the fields north of Lincoln.

The word *street* occurs in four of the six road-names mentioned above and is derived from OE *strēt* (*strǣt*), itself borrowed from Latin *strata*, and meaning 'paved road, Roman road'. Indeed, its normal meaning in place-names is 'paved way', very often 'Roman road'. In the form Stret-, Strat- it frequently occurs as the first element of place-names, as we shall see later.

Akeman Street, the most important east-west road in the South Midlands, is today the name of the branch road from the Fosse Way at Cirencester which continues the Bath-Cirencester road to Alchester and Tring. Originally it probably joined Watling Street at St. Albans. In Anglo-Saxon times, however, the road from Bath to Cirencester was not called Fosse Way as it is today. The name Akeman Street suggests that the entire road through the South Midlands to Bath was earlier called by that name, since its meaning is probably 'Acemann's Roman road' and it can hardly be coincidence that the earlier Anglo-Saxon name for Bath itself was *Acemannes ceaster*, that is 'Acemann's Roman fort'. It seems likely, therefore, that Bath and the important road running from it were named from the same man. An originally local name has become that of the road along its entire length. As with other Roman roads, the name Akeman Street was applied to an independent road, that from Cambridge to Ely and Denver (Nf).

Like Akeman Street, Ricknield Street was not one of the privileged roads and in fact its name was transferred from that of Icknield Way. It is certainly known as Icknield Street, at least from the late 12th century, the form Ricknield being first used by Ranulf Higden (d. 1364). Higden described it as running from St. David's in Wales to York by way of Worcester, Birmingham, and Lichfield, but today it is considered to be a branch from Fosse Way at Bourton on the Water, through Alcester, Birmingham, Wall, Little Chester, and Chesterfield to Templeborough, near Rotherham. The change in the name from Icknield to Ricknield is probably due to metanalysis. In the ME phrase *at ther Icknilde strete* the final *-r* of the oblique case of the definite article *ther* has been mistakenly assumed to belong to the following syllable, so *at ther Icknilde strete* became *at the Ricknilde strete*. Locally south of Bidford (Wa) Ricknield Street is known as Buckle Street 'Burghild's Roman road', perhaps named from Burghild, a daughter of Cenwulf, king of Mercia 796-821. Another stretch of the same road in Warwickshire is called Haydon Way, literally 'head way', i.e. chief way.

The four privileged roads were Ermine Street, Watling Street, Fosse Way, and Icknield Way, as we have seen. Ermine Street runs from London to the Humber near Winteringham, through Braughing,

Chesterton and Lincoln. North of the Humber it continues from the Roman fort at Brough to York, though this section is no longer called Ermine Street. In Old English it is *Earninga stræt* 'Roman road of the Earningas (Earn's people)' and these people also gave their name to Arrington (C) 'village, estate of the Earningas', which is itself situated on Ermine Street. The name must originally have been used locally, but by the time of the Norman Conquest it had been extended to the whole length of the road. Ermine Street has also given its name to another quite independent Roman road, that from Silchester to Gloucester, variously spelt Ermin Street and Irmine Street.

Watling Street is the name of the main road from Dover to London, through Canterbury and Rochester. From London it runs to Wroxeter, by way of St. Albans, Towcester, High Cross, and Wall. It may follow the line of an older route from the South Coast towards Wheathampstead, near St. Albans, the centre of an important British tribe, the Catuvellauni. Like Ermine Street, Watling Street was originally simply a local name for the road in the neighbourhood of St. Albans. It appears in Old English as *Wæclinga stræt* and *Wætlinga stræt* and though the latter has given the modern name, *Wæclinga stræt* is closer to the original one. The reason for this assumption is that the Anglo-Saxon name of St. Albans was *Wæclingaceaster* 'Roman fort of the Wæclingas (Wacol's people)' and it is clear that Watling Street is named from the same folk-group. Again, like Ermine Street, the name was extended to the whole road. The original Watling Street has also given its name to another Roman road, which runs north and south through Wroxeter from Chester in the north to Monmouth in the south. This particular extension of the name was perhaps inevitable, since Watling Street itself apparently terminated at Wroxeter. The name has also been applied to roads which had no connection at all with it. That from York to Corbridge is called Watling Street, especially in the North Riding of Yorkshire, and so too are parts of Roman roads between Manchester and Ribchester and between Ribchester and Poulton le Fylde in Lancashire.

The terminus of Fosse Way in the south-west is not known for certain but is thought to have been near Axmouth in Devon. It went by way of Ilchester, Bath, Cirencester, High Cross and Leicester to Lincoln, where it joined Ermine Street. In all the early sources it is referred to simply as *Fosse*, occasionally as Fosse *Street*, the modern name appearing first in the 15th century. The name seems to be derived ultimately from Latin *fossa* 'ditch', presumably a reference to a prominent ditch on one or both sides of the road. It is thought that the ditch or ditches may have been defensive and that Fosse Way may have been a frontier line protected by forts.

The fourth of the privileged roads was the prehistoric trackway Icknield Street, which connected the Wash with Salisbury Plain. It seems to have run from near Hunstanton by way of Newmarket, Dunstable, the Thames at Streatley, and then south-west into Dorset. The meaning of Icknield is unknown but is almost certainly pre-English. The name has been associated with the Celtic tribe the Iceni, which had its capital at Caister St. Edmund in Norfolk, the *Venta Icinorum* of the *Antonine Itinerary*. Unfortunately, the evidence is insufficient to establish a direct connection between the tribal name and the road-name. As we have already seen, the name Icknield Way was given to another road now called Ricknield Street, a feature of each of the most important old roads in England.

Wool Street is the name of part of a Roman road in Cambridgeshire, sometimes called Via Devana. The meaning of the former is 'wolves' road', presumably because it was particularly frequented by wolves. Via Devana is not a genuine Latin name for it was invented by an 18th-century Professor of Geology in the University of Cambridge, who believed that the road thought to run from Colchester to Cambridge and Godmanchester (Hu) led ultimately to Chester, the Romano-British Deva. Via Gellia (Db), however, is completely misleading for it was constructed in 1791-92 between Cromford and Grangemill in the parish of Brassington by Philip *Gell* whose family lived at Hopton nearby and who invented the name. Its Latin appearance even deceived the Ordnance Survey, for on the old 1 in OS map it is printed in type reserved for Roman road names.

Other names for short stretches of Roman roads are Devil's Causeway, Devil being commonly used of ancient sites or roads; Maiden Way, a name *perhaps* comparable with Lover's Lane; and Peddars Way, in East Anglia, 'pedlar's road'. Hare Street has been noted, for example, twice in Hertfordshire, three times in Essex, and four times in Wiltshire, while Hare Lane in Gloucestershire was earlier Hare Street. It means literally 'army road', i.e a road wide enough for an army to march along, and so 'highway'.

Stane Street, from Canterbury to Lympne (K) and again from Halesworth to Woodton (Nf), and Stane Street from London to

Chichester (Sx) and from Braughing (Hrt) to Colchester, both mean 'stone, i.e. paved, road'. Stane Street, however, is not a genuine old form, but an antiquarian reintroduction. Had it been in continuous use it would have given Stone or Stan in Modern English. On the other hand, Stane would have been the regular development in the North, and the Roman road from Manchester to Wigan must have been earlier known as Stany Street 'stony road', for Stanystreet on that road survives as the name of a place in Worsley in Lancashire. A parallel to Stane Street is Stanegate, the name of the road from Corbridge to Carvoran and on to Carlisle, for it too means 'stone road'. The second element of this name is ON *gata* 'road', a word also used of Roman roads in Derbyshire; Batham Gate 'road to the baths' led from Brough to Buxton, the latter the site of a Roman bath and identified with *Aqua Arnemeze* in the *Ravenna Cosmography*, while Doctor's Gate is the name of the road from Brough to Melandra, near Glossop. It is first recorded on a Plan dated 1627 as *Docto Talbotes gate* (sic); the identity of the Doctor himself has unfortunately never been discovered.

High Street, in the sense 'important road' is used of Roman roads, too, as is the self-explanatory King's Street. But in the past it appears that Roman roads were simply referred to as Street or The Street. Few of them actually retain this form of the name today, but some have given rise to the names of villages on or near them. Streat (Sx) and the more common Street, found in several counties, are examples of this, though Strete Raleigh (D) is probably named from an ancient trackway and not a Roman road. Street has also been used as an affix in names like Barton le Street (NRY), Chester le Street (Du), Thorpe le Street (ERY), and Spital in the Street (L), all situated on Roman roads.

Many place-names in England have been named from Roman roads on which or near which they are situated. They usually, but not always, survive today with a first element Strat- or Stret-. So, for example, a ford carrying such a road has given the common Stratford and Stretford, but also Startforth (NRY) and Strefford (Sa). A farmstead, village or estate near a Roman road is called Stratton or Stretton, as well as Sturton (L, Nb, Nt, WRY), while Stratton (So) and Stretton (Wa) have been further distinguished as 'on the Fosse' and 'under the Fosse' respectively, with reference of course to Fosse Way. OE *hām* 'homestead, village, estate' is the second element of Streatham (Sr) and Stretham (C) and OE *lēah* 'clearing, glade' occurs in Streatley (Bd, Brk), Streetly (C, Wa) as well as Strelley (Nt). Other places named from

Roman roads include Stratfield (Brk, Ha) and Stradsett (Nf) with second elements meaning 'open land' and 'place'.

Field-names in Street, like Street Field and Street Close, can be of considerable importance, for their presence is often, though not always, an indication of a Roman road close to them. On occasion they occur where no such road has been identified on the ground. One such stretch of road from Chesterfield to Templeborough was known only over part of its length. The presence of such field-names as Street Fields and Streetgate in Eckington (Db) are on the likely route of the road. Subsequent to the publication of these names local historians have found further examples of relevant field-names and have been able to identify on the ground additional stretches of the same road. The importance, in this connection, of similar field-names, even ones recorded only in documents of the 18th and 19th centuries, has only been recognized fully in more recent years, and already they have proved a useful source of information. Wherever a Street Field or Street Close has been found, and no Roman road or for that matter prehistoric trackway is known, it is well worth the local historian or archaeologist checking on the ground.

One particular stretch of Roman road, the continuation of the London-Silchester road to Old Sarum in Wiltshire, is called Port Way. This is a name found in many parts of England where it usually refers to an old trackway. Some of these are in fact pre-historic in date such as those in Derbyshire and Devon, for example, which are still called, in places, Port Way. The literal meaning of the name is 'road leading to a town or market', though it is rarely possible today to know which town or market is meant.

The four commonest names for roads and tracks of post-Roman origin are Broad Way, Hollow Way, Ridge Way, and Salt Way. The meaning of *way* in such names varies from 'road' to 'small track'. Salt Way is particularly common in Worcestershire and it has been shown that there were formerly a dozen tracks of this name leading from the neighbourhood of Droitwich. Some still survive in that county, but the former existence of others is indicated by modern farms with this name. Salt Way is found in counties other than Worcestershire both where salt-works were to be found and elsewhere, and it indicates a track used by pack horses to transport the salt. In the Danelaw the more usual name seems to have been the fairly common Saltergate 'salt-merchants' road', in which the first element is the occupational name *Salter*. This name also occurs in place-names such as Salterford (Nt) and Salterforth (WRY) 'salt-merchants' ford' and Salters Bridge (St) 'salt-merchants' bridge', fords and a bridge on routes formerly used by salt-merchants.

Broad Way, Hollow Way, and Ridge Way are common and are found in many counties and numerous villages and also farms have been named from them. Bradway (Db) and Broadway (So, Wo) mean 'broad road', Holloway (Db, Mx, Sr, W) 'road running in a hollow' or 'sunken road', while Ridgeway (Db, K) and Rudgeway (St) mean 'way along a ridge'. Some of the Ridge Ways certainly take their names from ancient trackways, a notable example being Ridge Way (Brk-W).

Way, OE *weg*, is of course common in minor names, but not in village-names, except for the compounds just discussed and it has been estimated that there are only about 25 major names with a second element *weg*. Among these are Barkway (Hrt) apparently 'way along which birch-trees grow', Halsway (So) 'way through the pass', Redway (Wt) and Roundway (W) 'cleared way', and Radway (Wa) and Rodway (So) 'way suitable for riding', identical with modern *roadway*. Stantway (Gl) as well as Stanway (Ess, Gl, He, Sa) and Stowey (So) all mean 'stone way'. Only two names in -way certainly have an Old English personal name as first element, Garmondsway (Du) from Gārmund, and Hanwell (O), earlier *Haneway*, from Hana. Clearly ways named after a person were unusual.

The use of Scandinavian *gata* 'way, road' in compounds is common in the North and North Midlands, where it seems to take the place of *way*. It appears to have given rise to only two major names, Galgate (La) thought to mean 'road to Galloway', a reference to Scottish drovers, though this is quite uncertain since the name is recorded only in late sources, and Harrogate (WRY) perhaps 'road to the cairn'. It is also found in a number of minor names like Holgate 'road running in a hollow', 'sunken road' and so comparable with Holloway, Dorket (Nt), earlier *Dalegate*, 'road running in the valley' and Clappersgate (We) 'road to the bridge', in which the first element survives in dialect as *clapper* 'rough bridge'. *Gate* has also been prefixed to two village-names, Gate Fulford (ERY), and Gate Helmsley (NRY), in each case from their situations on a Roman road.

Modern *lane*, OE *lane*, *lanu*, is common everywhere in minor names and street-names, but is extremely rare in place-names. There are, however, one or two interesting examples particularly Laneham (Nt), which is derived from the dative plural and means literally 'at the lanes', as we saw in Chapter Two. The editors of *The Place-Names of Nottinghamshire* commented that several tracks and roads meet here, but in a more recent study, Dr Margaret Gelling noted that it is "no more clearly a road-junction than are its neighbours". She considers that *lane* may have a specialized sense in this name like the Scottish dialect sense of the word 'hollow course of a large rivulet in meadow-land; a brook whose movement is scarcely perceptible; the smooth, slowly moving part of a river'. Markland (La) is a second interesting example, since its current spelling is completely misleading. Its meaning is 'boundary lane', not 'boundary land', as might be supposed.

Path, OE *pæð*, too, is uncommon in place-names, but it has given rise to at least half a dozen village-names. Gappah (D) was a path for goats and Horsepath (O) for horses, as the modern form would suggest. In the North, a dialect variant *peth* is found in Urpeth (Du), the first element of which means 'wild cattle' and in Morpeth (Nb) literally 'murder path', clearly one of evil repute. In three names we have to do with a personal name, Old English in origin in Brancepeth (Du) and Hudspeth (Nb) from Brant and Hodd respectively, but Scandinavian in Gamelspath, also in Northumberland, from Gamel. In this example the dialectal form has been replaced by Standard English *path*.

OE *stīg* and ON *stígr* 'path, narrow road' both survive in a few place-names normally as *sty* and as such can be easily confused with *sty* 'pen'. Linguistically they are related to a verb meaning 'to climb' and so, at least sometimes denote a road which climbs a hill, as in Bransty (Cu) 'steep path' and Bringsty (He), literally 'brink path', the road itself following the edge of a hill. The first element is probably a bird-name in Corpusty (Nf), ON *korpr* 'raven', the word raven itself appearing in Ravensty (La). It is certainly possible that *raven* in this name is from ON *hrafn*, rather than the English equivalent, and if this is so then both Corpusty and Ravensty could well be Scandinavian compounds. As with *path*, at least two names in -sty are named from individuals, a Hardwulf in Hardisty (WRY) and þorfinnr in Thorfinsty (La), the first being of English origin, the second Scandinavian.

One derivative of *stīg*, *ānstīg* or *ānstiga*, has been the subject of a close study. It was thought to mean 'a single-file path up a hill', since the word literally means 'one path', but the topography of only one example, Anstey (D), fits this definition, as Dr Margaret Gelling has pointed out. There are six more instances of this compound in major place-names, Anstey (Ha, Hrt, Lei) and Ansty (Do, W, Wa) and three in minor names. After close examination of the sites of each, Dr Gelling concluded that *ānstīg* denoted "a short stretch of road used by at least four roads which converged on it at either end". Furthermore, she discovered that the topography of the sites does not support the view that the road itself was narrow or that single-file traffic was involved. It appears, therefore, that the Anstys and Ansteys have some such developed meaning as she suggests.

Gang, which survives in dialect in the sense 'way, track, cattle-walk' has the same form in both Old English and Scandinavian. It is no doubt the English word which is the source in Blackgang (Chine) (Wt), while the Scandinavian word is likely in the North and North-east Midlands, as in Summergangs (ERY) 'ways which could only be used in summer'. This last is repeated in minor names in Lincolnshire. It is also the probable source of Outgang 'way out', usually the way out to the common fields of a village, a name occurring as far north as Cumberland and as far south as Derbyshire and Nottinghamshire.

OE *drāf* 'herd, drove' is used in Fenland dialect of 'a road along which cattle and the like are driven'. As such it is found both in minor names and in field-names in Cambridgeshire and Lincolnshire, as in Parson Drove (C) and Dog Drove (L), though it is not confined to these counties. Similarly ME *wente* also survives in dialect as *went* 'path, way'. It often appears with the numeral *four* in such names as Four Want Ways (Hrt), The Four Wents (Ess) and Fourwents (Sr), where it denotes cross-roads. OE *lǣt* 'a junction of roads' has given Radlett (Hrt) 'road junction', a place situated at an old cross-road on Watling Street. This word survives in dialect also as 'a water-channel' and this is the meaning required for Longleat (W) 'long water-course'.

There are also a few names containing the word *mile*, OE *mīl*, as for example Milemead (D), literally 'a mile distance', situated about a mile from Tavistock. Similarly Mile End (Ess, Mx) means 'end of a mile'; the Essex place is about one mile from Colchester, while the more famous Mile End in Middlesex is about one mile from Aldgate on the old London-Colchester road.

fifteen

Rivers, river-crossings, and marshland

In this and the following two chapters we shall discuss place-names which describe topographical features both natural and artificial. A great deal of research has been done in this field over the past twelve years and the results of this research published in an outstanding book, *Place-Names in the Landscape*, and also in a series of learned articles. Further work is in progress and field-work will enable us to be even more precise about the meanings of topographical terms, as we saw in the discussion of OE *wæsse* in the opening chapter. Already we know that Old English had an extensive vocabulary in this area, but what we did not recognize fully was that there are very few synonyms. Nor did we appreciate fully that this vocabulary is "a subtle code which can be deciphered by relating names to their surroundings". Most of the words for physical features denoted different shapes of hills and valleys, different type of marsh, different aspects of streams. An attempt will be made here to pinpoint some current findings, and in this I am dependent upon the published work of Margaret Gelling and Ann Cole.

In addition to those names still used of rivers and streams, there are many others which, though originally river-names, survive only as the names of villages and towns. No distinction will be made here between the two types and only names of English or Scandinavian origin will be considered.

Many such names are simply adjectives, or more often derivatives of adjectives, descriptive of the particular river, as with Blyth (Nb, Nt, Sf) 'pleasant, cheerful', i.e. 'gentle or pleasant river'. Others of similar origin are Brun (La) 'brown', Rede (Nb) 'red' and Skerne (Du) 'clear'. Belah (We), a mountain stream is apparently derived from an adjective meaning 'roaring'. Cave (ERY) and Tale (D) both mean 'swift', Stour (C-Ess, K, O-Wa, St-Wo, W-Ha) apparently 'strong' and Tove (Nth) 'slow'. Hamble (Ha), Waver (Cu), Weaver (Ch), Wantsum (K), Wensum (Nf), and Worf (Sa) each means 'winding one', with which can be compared Manifold (St) literally 'with many folds', hence 'winding'. Loud (La), Lud (L), from which Louth (L) is named, as well as Lyd (D), Lyde (He, So) mean 'loud river', Writtle (Ess) is 'babbling one', while Idle (Nt-L) is apparently from OE *īdel* 'idle'. Sid (D) is 'broad one' and Meden (Nt) and Medina (Wt) 'middle one'; the first is the middle of three streams, the Medina with a latinized spelling, flowing through the middle of the Isle of Wight. From Scandinavian adjectives are derived Bain (L, NRY) probably 'short', Blean (NRY) and Bleng (Cu) 'dark', Gaunless (Du) 'useless' and Skell (WRY) 'resounding'.

Other river-names are derivatives of nouns or verbs. From nouns are derived Greet (Nt) 'gravel', Mease (Lei-St) and Meese (St-Sa) 'moss', Piddle (Do, from which Affluddle, Tolpuddle etc. are named) 'marsh' and Sheaf (WRY) 'boundary', and from verbs Lymm (Ch) perhaps 'resounding', Smite (Lei-Nt, Wa, Wo) perhaps 'dirty' and Swale (K, NRY) 'rushing'. One or two comparable names of Scandinavian origin include Sprint (We) 'bounding stream', a derivative of a verb meaning 'jump, spirt', appropriate enough for a mountain stream, and Wreak (Lei) probably 'twisted' i.e. 'winding river'.

A few Old English river-names are formed in a similar way, but with the addition of the suffix *-ing* meaning 'place, 'stream', including Guiting (Gl) 'running stream', Leeming (NRY) perhaps 'gleaming river', Wantage (Brk), earlier *Waneting*, 'intermittent stream', that is one of varying volume of water, and Wenning (WRY-La) 'dark river'.

Another type is that formed from the name of a nearby village or town and called back-formation. Some of these developed in the early Modern English period as their forms indicate – Chelmer (Ess) from Chelmsford, earlier *Chelmersford*, and Wandle (Sr) from Wandsworth, earlier *Wandelsworth*. Other examples of river-names the result of back-formation include Alde (Sf) from Aldeburgh, Arun (Sx) from Arundel, Lark (Sf-C) Lackford, Plym (D) Plympton, Tas (Nf) Tasburgh and Yare (Wt) from Yarmouth. Here we may note Isis (O), first noted as *Isa* and *Ise* in the 14th century. It has been suggested that *Ise* is from Tam*ise* (i.e. Thames), a name at that time thought to be a compound derived from Thame, one of the streams at the head of the Thames, and a hypothetical name *Ise*. Isis is presumably simply a latinized form of *Ise*.

The largest groups of river-names of English origin are those derived from OE *brōc* and *burna*, modern *brook* and *burn*. It was thought that *burna* was common in the early Anglo-Saxon period and that it was later replaced by *brōc*. The simplex Bourne, for example, is fairly common, while there is only Brook (K, Wt) and Brooke (Nf, R). Eastbourne and Westbourne (Sx) were also originally simplex names, *Bourne*, to which the distinguishing East- and West- were added. However, it has recently been shown that both words are used for streams of considerable size, though not for major rivers, and that the difference in usage has rather to do with physical features of the streams. It appears that those derived from *burna* are in chalk country or have gravel beds, with clear water and submerged water plants. *Brōc*, on the other hand, seems to have been the word used of muddy streams with sediment-laden water.

Both *brook* and *burn* are the source of many compound names, and sometimes each is found with the same first element, but more often with a similar meaning. The first element describes the water in Colburn (NRY) and Colebrook (D) 'cool', Saltburn (NRY) 'salt', Sherborne (Do, Gl, Ha), Sherbourne (Wa), Sherburn (Du, ERY, WRY), Shirburn (O) and Shirebrook (Db) 'clear', as well as several which denote a muddy or dirty stream like Fulbrook (Bk, O, Wa), Harborne (St), Sharnbrook (Bd), Shernborne (Nf) and Skidbrook (L). In others it refers to the bed -Cheselbourne (Do) 'gravel', Claybrooke (Lei) 'clay', Sambourn (Wa) and Sambrook (Sa) 'sand', and Stainburn (Cu) and Stambourne (Ess) 'stone', while the first element in Whitbourne (He) is 'white', probably a reference to efflorescences of lime, which Mrs Cole noted in the banks of the stream. Some denote the course or speed of the stream, hence perhaps 'gushing' in Gisburn (WRY), 'raging' in Webburn (D) and 'winding' in Woburn (Bd, Sr, W), Wombourn (St) and Wambrook (So), as well as Cringlebrook (La) and Wrangbrook (WRY). A few are named from natural features such as a 'valley' in Combrook (Wa), a 'fen or marsh' in Morborne (Hu), a 'meadow' in Umborne (D) and Wimborne (Do). Holborn (Mx) and Holbrook (Db, Do) may belong here also, for the meaning is likely to be 'stream running in a hollow', though an alternative meaning may be 'deep brook' as in Daybrook (Nt). Millbrook (Bd, Ha), Milborne (Do, So) and Milburn (We) each mean 'stream with a mill', as does the fairly common Cuttle Brook. A further group of names of identical meaning included Marlbrook (Sa), Meersbrook (WRY), Tachbrook (Wa), and Tyburn (Mx), each meaning 'brook forming a boundary'. Drybrook (Gl) and Dryburn (Cu, Nb) were so-named because they soon became dry, while Winterborne (Do),

Winterbourne (Brk, Gl, Sx, W) and Winterburn (WRY) must have flowed only in winter. Honeybourne (Gl, Wo) may denote a stream running through rich land or may simply indicate that honey was found along its banks.

In some cases the brook and burn were named from an animal or birds, no doubt found near or on them, as in Hartburn (Du, Nb), Hindburn (La), Lambourn (Brk), Otterbourne (Ha), Otterburn (Nb, WRY), Roeburn (La), all self-explanatory, as well as Gadbrook (Sr) 'goat', Shipbourne (K) 'sheep', Tichborne (Ha) 'kid'; Cranborne (Do), Cranbourne (Ha), Cranbrook (K) and Cornbrook (La) 'crane or heron', Enborne (Brk), 'duck', Gosbrook (St) and Gusborne (K) 'goose', and Kidbrook (K) and Kidbrooke (Sx) 'kite'. One or two were noted for their fish – Fishbourne (Sx, Wt), Fishburn (Du), and Roachburn (Cu), and there is also Auburn (L) 'eel'.

The first element of a further group denotes the kind of vegetation which grew there. So, there is Ashbourne (Db), Ashburn (Sx), Rushbrooke (Sf), Sedgebrook (L), as well as Fairbourne (K) and Fairburn (WRY) 'fern', Golborne (Ch, La) 'marsh-marigold', Radbourn (Wa), Redbourn (Hrt), Redbourne (L), and Rodbourne (W) 'reeds'.

In some cases the stream was named from the man who presumably owned the land through which it flowed – Bedburn (Du) *Bēda*, Chatburn (La) *Ceatta*, Cottesbrooke (Nth) *Cott*, Leybourne (K) *Lylla*, Lilbourne (Nth) and Lilburn (Nb) *Lilla*, Ockbrook (Db) and Ogbourne (W) *Occa*, Tedburn (D) *Tetta* and Tilbrook (Hu) *Tila*. A small number are from group-names as with Bolingbroke (L), Hassenbrook (Ess), Hollingbourne (K), and Pangbourne (Brk) named from 'the people of' *Bula*, *Hassa*, *Hōla*, and *Pǣga* respectively, as well as Sittingbourne (K) 'stream of the *Sīdingas*', where *Sīdingas* seems to mean 'dwellers on the slope'. One further name may be noted here, Marylebone (Mx), earlier called Tyburn. In the 15th century the name was changed to *Maryburn* 'stream of St. Mary', from the dedication of a new church there. Then in the 17th century, a medial -le- was inserted, perhaps as has been suggested on the analogy of a name like St. Mary le Bow. The modern form has developed from this, with the substitution of -bone for -borne.

Though brook and burn are the commonest terms found in English stream-names, what has been called 'the standard word' for a river in Old English is *ēa*. It seems to have been used of a waterway larger than a brook or burn, and of course most of these had individual names of their own. So, *ēa* which survives in dialect as *ea* in Lancashire, *eau* in a pseudo-French form in Lincolnshire, and as *yeo* in Devonshire, is rare in English river-names. It has survived, however, in Freshney (L) 'fresh river', Mersey (Ch-La) 'boundary river', Pevensey (Sx) 'Pefen's river', Waveney (Sf/Nf) 'river flowing through a quaking bog', Romney (K) the first element of which is quite uncertain, as well as Hipper (Db) 'river where osiers grow', with the loss of the final syllable. It is much more common in the compound *Ēatūn*, as in Eton (Bk) and most of the Eatons, as well as Yeaton (Sa), which have recently been translated as 'river settlement'. It has been suggested that this is not a simple geographical statement, but denoted a place which performed some special local function in relation to the river.

OE *riŏ* 'small stream' does not seem to occur with certainty in place-names north of Warwickshire, where it has given Shottery, probably 'small stream of the Scots'. It appears in a variety of forms as second element – -ed, -reth, -rith and -ry, as in Hendred (Brk) 'wild birds', Rawreth (Ess) 'heron', Shepreth (C) 'sheep'; Fingrith (Ess) may have been a small stream shaped like a finger, while Sawtry (Hu) means 'salt stream', Childrey (Brk) 'small stream rising from a spring', and Coldrey (Ha) 'charcoal stream'. It has been pointed out that not far away from Coldrey is Isnage 'iron wooded hill', so the charcoal was probably used for iron-smelting. In at least a couple of instances the first element is a personal name, Ceawa in Chaureth (Ess) and Mæŏelgār in Meagre (Hu). In one example, Ryde (Wt), the simplex form survives.

Another word found chiefly, but not exclusively, in stream-names in the South and South Midlands is OE *lacu* 'small stream, watercourse', modern dialect *lake*, the source of Lake (W), the self-explanatory Darklake (D), Fishlake (WRY), Fenlake (Bd) and Venlake (D), the last having dialectal initial V- for F-. Charlock (Nth) is 'cold stream' and Shiplake (O) and Shiplate (So) 'small stream where sheep are found'. Medlock (La) 'meadow stream' is apparently the only surviving river-name derived from *lacu*. It is a tributary of the R. Irwell, whereas, it has been pointed that some of the examples quoted above are side-channels of rivers. It would appear that *lacu* was used not only in the specialized sense of 'side-channel', but, on occasion, of a tributary proper.

Other Old English words occur occasionally in the name of streams; *læcc*, modern dialect *latch*, *letch*, is used in the North and North West Midlands of a 'stream-flowing through boggy ground', where we find it in Blacklache (La) 'black boggy stream', Cranage (Ch) 'where crows are found', Shocklach (Ch) 'haunted by goblins', and Shurlach (Ch) 'with scurf on the surface'. Leech (Gl) seems to be the only modern river-name derived from *læcc* and this has given name to Eastleach and Westleach on its banks; and *wisce* 'marshy meadow', used of a river presumably in the sense of 'marshy river', is found in Erewash (Db/Nt) 'wandering marshy river'.

The two most important Scandinavian terms for 'river, stream' are *á*, equivalent to OE *ēa*, and *bekkr*. The first means 'river' and though less frequent than *bekkr* has given rise to several river-names in the North -Brathay (We-La) 'broad river', Greta (Cu), Greeta (WRY-La) 'rocky river' and Rawthey (WRY-We) 'trout river'. *Bekkr* 'stream', on the other hand, is very common in minor names and field-names both in the East Midlands and the North, though its distribution is patchy. The *beck* is sometimes named with reference to the water or bed, as in Fulbeck (L, Nt) 'foul', Skirbeck (L) 'clear', Drybeck (Cu, We), and Holbeck (ERY, Nt, WRY), the last comparable to Holbrook and Holburn. Routenbeck (Cu) means 'roaring stream', Welbeck (Nt) presumably 'stream rising in a spring', while Troutbeck (Cu, We) is self-explanatory. Birkbeck (We), Ellerbeck (La, NRY), and Maplebeck (Nt) are named from trees growing nearby, the birch, alder and maple respectively.

In local names OE *wella* is used both of a stream and a spring, though in most cases it no doubt denotes the latter. The modern form is *well*, but a dialectal variant *wall* is found in the West Midlands. A meaning stream is likely for some names like Cromwell (Nt) and Irwell (La) both 'winding stream', Irwell in fact being the name of a river. Since, however, it is sometimes impossible to decide in which sense this very common element was used it is more convenient to take all the examples together. It will sometimes be clear, of course, from the meaning that it denotes a spring, as in Tywell and Sywell, both in Northamptonshire, from the numerals 'two' and 'seven' respectively.

It has been pointed out that the largest group of village-names derived from well describes the physical nature of the spring – 'black, dark' in Blackwell (Db, Du, Wo), 'bright' in Brightwell (Brk, O) 'cold' in Caldwell (NRY), Cauldwell (Bd, Nt), Chadwell (Bk, Ess, Hrt, Lei) and Caldwall (Wo), 'loud' in Ludwell (Db, Nth, O, W), 'red' in Radwell (Bd, Hrt), 'shallow' in Shadwell (Gl, Mx), 'white, clear' in the common Whitwell, each with an adjective as first element. Others similarly descriptive of the spring, but with a noun as first element, are 'chalk' in

Cawkwell (L), 'pebbles' in Shiglewell (K), 'boundary' in Shadwell (Nf), and 'stone' in Stanwell (Mx) and Stowell (Gl, So, W). There is also a large group, including Carswell (Brk), Caswell (Do, Nth), Causewell (Hrt), Crasswall (He), Cresswell (Db, Nb, St), and Kerswell (D), denoting a spring or a stream where cress grows. Still others are named from wild animals or birds which frequented them – Cornwell (O) and Cranwell (L) 'cranes', Hartwell (Ek, Nth, St) 'harts', Roel (Gl) 'roe-deer', Snailwell (C) 'snails' and Tathwell (L) 'toads'.

A comparatively large number of *well*s were named from indivi-uals. So, Badeca gave his name to Bakewell (Db), Brand to Brauncewell (L), Cāfhere to Caverswall (St), Doggod to Dowdeswell (Gl), Eoppa to Epwell (O), Heresa to Harswell (ERY), Hūdel to Hudswell (NRY), Offa to Offwell (D), and Wocga to Ogwell (D). Hardwell (Brk) means 'trea-sure spring', and since Hardwell is near the site of a Romano-British villa, it has been suggested that the reference may well be to a find of Roman coins, though it could have been a spring into which coins were thrown. Some springs are associated with religious beliefs, like the self-explanatory Holywell (Hu, K, Nb), identical with which are Halwell (D) and Holwell (Do, O), while Maidwell (Nth) 'maidens' spring' and Bridwell (D) probably 'brides' spring' are perhaps to be associated with fertility rites.

OE *celde* 'spring' is rarely found in place-names, but it does sur-vive in two names in Kent – Bapchild and Honeychild, derived from the Old English personal names Bacca and Hūna respectively. The corre-sponding Scandinavian *kelda* is rather more frequent in minor names than in the names of villages, but it is found in the hybrid Hallikeld (NRY) 'holy spring' and in Scandinavian compounds in Threlkeld (Cu) 'thralls' spring' and Trinkeld (La) 'þrandi's spring'.

It had been believed that OE *flēot* in the majority of place-names meant 'estuary, inlet, creek' and indeed there are names where this must be the case. However, more recently it has been shown that in inland names the meaning is 'small stream'. This is the case in Hunslet (WRY) 'Hūn's small stream' and it is perfectly possible in names in Lincolnshire such as Saltfleet 'salt', Surfleet 'sour', and Wainfleet 'waggon', denoting a stream which could be crossed by a wagon. A meaning 'small stream' has been assumed for Byfleet (Sr) usually trans-lated as an elliptical name meaning '(place) by the stream'. However, as a result of a survey of this and minor names of identical form, it has been suggested that OE *bīfleet* was a compound appellative describing a topographical feature in the sense of a piece of land cut off by the changing course of a stream, a sense recorded later in dialect. In a number of names 'estuary etc.' is presumably the sense, but in others 'small stream' is clearly to be considered. This is certainly an area where local knowledge has much to contribute.

Ewell (K, Sr), Ewelme (O), Ewen (Gl), and Toller Whelme (Do) each means 'source of the river', the last two those of the Thames and *Toller* (now the R. Hooke) respectively. With these can be compared Dove Head (Db) and Ribble Head (La), as well as other names in which *head* is used in the same sense. On the other hand, Wearmouth (Du), Weymouth (Do and Yarmouth (Nf) are named from the estuaries of the Wear, Wey and Yare. Emmott (La) is 'junction of the rivers or streams', as also are Meeth (D) and Mytham Bridge (Db). OE *twisla* 'fork of a river, junction of streams' is found in the Lancashire Entwistle and Oswaldtwistle, presumably from the men who owned the land there, Enna and ōswald.

Hythe (K), as well as Greenhithe (K), is derived from OE *hȳð* 'landing-place on a river'. Both Earith (Hu) and Erith (K) have as first element a word meaning 'gravel', while at least three – Bolney (O), Lambeth (Sr), and Rotherhithe (Sr) were presumably landing-places for bulls, lambs, and cattle respectively. Knaith (L) was situated in a 'river bend' and Stockwith (on both sides of the Trent, L, Nt) was apparently made of tree-trunks. Putney (Sr) is probably named from an Anglo-Saxon, Putta, and Stepney (Mx) from Stybba, though alternative etymologies have been suggested for these. Maidenhead (Brk) is certainly 'maidens' landing-place', though the significance of *maidens* here can only be a matter of speculation. Another Old English word with a similar meaning, *stæð*, has given Stathe (So) and from the dative plural Statham (Ch) 'at the landing-places', as well as Bickerstaffe (La) 'of the beekeepers'. Croxteth and Toxteth, both in Lancashire, however, are derived from the corresponding Scandinavian word and each has a personal name as first element, Crōc or Krókr and Tóki respectively, and both may well be Scandinavian compounds.

OE *ēgland*, modern *island*, rarely occurs in place-names, but the first part of this compound, *ēg*, is common. It, too, means 'island' in some names, like Mersea (Ess) 'island of the pool' but it usually refers to a *patch* of slightly raised land in marsh or the like. It is also the commonest of all Old English terms recorded in documents up to 731 and so presumably must have been common in early Anglo-Saxon England.

Indeed, it has been suggested that *ēg* was more commonly used before that date than afterwards; further that the sites of villages with *ēg* are often the likeliest places for colonists to choose, and also that some of our early monasteries were founded on such 'island' sites – Bardney (L), Bermondsey (Sr), Chertsey (Sr), and Partney (L), each of which has a personal element as first element – Barda, Beornmund, Cerot, and Parta.

A detailed study of the topographical characteristics of names derived from *ēg* has been made. It has been demonstrated that besides the sense of a patch of raised ground in marsh, it also seems to denote in north Derbyshire and further north 'a hill jutting into flat land' and 'a patch of good land in moors'. The regional distribution of names in *ēg* has also been shown to be by no means as widespread as had been thought and that this is not entirely dictated by topography. It is not easy to summarize the evidence or the conclusions reached in this study and for this readers will have to turn to Dr Gelling's analysis in *Place-Names in the Landscape*.

OE *ēg* is found in the common simplex name Eye, as well as in the dative plural in Eyam (Db). The most striking feature of compounds with this word, however, is that almost half have a personal name as first element. Because of this, it has been suggested that *ēg* is a topographical element which has a quasi-habitative meaning, a characteristic it probably shares with *ford*, a word discussed later in this chapter. Among the many Old English personal names in such compounds are Abba in Abney (Db), Beornrǣd in Bardsea (La) and Bardsey (WRY), Beaduric in Battersea (Sr), Blanca in Blankney (L), Citta in Chitty (K), Haca in Hackney (Mx), Hemele in Gate Helmsley (NRY), Lida in Lydney (Gl), Olla in Olney (Bk), Rūm in Romsey (Hu), and Wittel in Whittlesey (C). All these are masculine names, but Adeney (So) is from the feminine Ēadwynn.

Others have the name of an animal or bird as in the self-explanatory Harty (K), Horsey (Nf, So), Oxney (K, Nth), Chickney (Ess) as well as Chalvey (Bk) 'calf' and Quy (C) 'cow'. Dorney (Bk), which is almost surrounded by water, is 'island of land where humble-bees are found'. Pease grew at Pusey (Brk), rushes at Bunny (Nt), and wild-garlic at Ramsey (Ess, Hu). The first element of Thorney (C, Mx, Sf, So, Sx) is self-explanatory; the 'island' at Sidney (Sr) was 'wide' and at Quaveney (C) a 'quaking bog'. The corresponding ON *ey* certainly occurs in a Scandinavian compound in Lundy Island (D) 'puffin island', but it does not seem to have been used in inland place-names.

The common Scandinavian term for an 'island', however, is *holmr*, and like *ēg* it frequently denotes a raised piece of land in marsh. It also refers sometimes to a 'water-meadow' and is found in a rare sense 'island promontory', the most obvious instance of which is Durham 'hill island promontory'. *Holmr* is by far the commonest Scandinavian topographical term in English place-names. The word, itself, seems to have been taken over into English in the late Old English period and clearly became part of the local dialect vocabulary in parts of eastern England, such as Yorkshire and Lincolnshire, where it is well-represented in minor names and in field-names. As noted above the sense is 'island of land in marsh' in many names; striking examples are Holme near Newark and Holme Pierrepont near Nottingham, in Nottinghamshire, as well as in other examples of the common Holme, and also as Hulme. The first element in compound names occasionally denotes animals which grazed there – Oxenholme (We), Tupholme (L), and Studholme (Cu), where it was a 'herd of horses'. 'Bracken' grew at Brackenholme (ERY), 'oats' at Haverholme (L), and 'pease' at Peaseholme (La). Broadholme (Nt) is, however, a misleading name, for the first element is the Scandinavian personal name Broddi; a similar personal name Ketill occurs in Kettleshulme (Ch), but Wulfstān in Wolstenholme (La) is Old English in origin. Conisholme (L) is named after a 'king', while Oldham (La) is as misleading as Broadholme, for it is in fact a holme-name meaning 'old island promontory' with that rare sense we noted in Durham.

OE *pōl* 'pool' is a fairly common element in English place-names, but in coastal names also means 'harbour', as in such obvious instances as Poole in Dorset, Hartlepool (Du) 'hart island harbour' as well as Skippool (La) where there was formerly a harbour for 'ships'. 'Tidal creek' is also a sense to be reckoned with, especially in Liverpool (La), the first element of which refers to 'thick or muddy water'. Other examples of this word seem to denote pools in a river or stream or a junction of two streams, some since dried up, and here local expertize is needed to define the usage precisely. Among such names are Cople (Bd) and Hampole (WRY), each of which may mean 'pool where cocks are found', Otterpool (K) and Claypole (L), both self-explanatory, and Wimpole (C) from the personal name Wina.

Three studies of OE *mere* 'pond, lake' have appeared in recent years and these have shown that the word was used of natural ponds and lakes, man-made ponds, and to a lesser extent seasonally flooded valleys or marshlands. Clearly size does not enter into the equation and *meres* could vary from that of a duck-pond in southern counties to that of the extensive lakes of north Shropshire, Cheshire and the Lake District. A considerable number of villages have taken their names from such *meres*, including such simplex examples as Maer (St), Meare (So), and Mere (Ch, L, W). Among the numerous compounds containing this word are Ringmer (Sx) 'circular pond', Tangmere (Sx) 'shaped like a pair of tongs', and Holmer (Bk, He) 'in a hollow'. Many have as first element the term for an animal or bird – Boulmer (Nb) 'bull', Catmore (Brk) 'wild cat', Ilmer (Bk) 'leech', Woolmer (Ha) 'wolf', Anmer (Nf) 'duck', Bridgemere (Ch) 'bird', Cranmere (Sa) 'crane', Cromer (Hrt), Nf) 'crow', while Frogmore (D, Do, Hrt) was noted for frogs, Almer (Do) and Elmer (Sx) for eels and Pickmere (Ch) for pike. The reference in other names is to the vegetation there – Redmere (C) 'reeds', Rushmere (Sf) 'rushes' and Grasmere (We) 'grass', whether a reference to its grassy shores or in the lake itself. Only rarely is the pond named from a person, but Badlesmere (K), Ellesmere (Sa), and Patmore (Hrt) are from the Old English personal names Bæddel, Elli, and Patta respectively.

OE *mere* is also the first element of a group of some thirty names comprising the common Marton, Martin (Ha, L, La, K, Nt, Wo), and Merton (D, K, Nf, O, Sr), all meaning 'village with a pond'. These have been the subject of detailed research, which has shown that although few of them are today places of importance, many were such at the time of Domesday Book. Some of these villages had man-made ponds, but over one-third are beside natural meres *and* Roman roads; none has been found to be on a pre-historic routeway. It has been suggested that the settlements founded at these sites served as watering places for travellers. It is likely enough that most of these ponds would provide fish and wildfowl, as well as reeds and rushes, so that their importance in earlier times arose from their products; in other words, they had economic importance, as well as providing rest and refreshment for travellers. The decline in importance of many of the Martons, Martins and Mertons, it has been further suggested, is probably to be attributed to the natural and gradual development of new routes, so the *mere-tūn*s declined in importance and today remain mostly as small villages. It is interesting to note that since the study was published, the presence of Roman roads beside two other of the Martons has been demonstrated; clearly, here again, is an area where detailed local knowledge could make an important contribution to place-name studies.

Ford OE *ford*, is one of the commonest topographical place-name elements as indeed we might expect, in view of its importance to new settlers in any area. It is also well-represented in English documents recorded before 731 and it is likely to have been used to form place-names from an early stage in the Anglo-Saxon settlement of Britain. Further, most names in -ford must have had a local significance and it has been pertinently said they can only reflect routes by which villagers communicated with their neighbours. It is hardly surprising, therefore, that a large number were named from some early owner, who presumably also owned the land there. So, Aylesford (K) is named from Ægel, Basford (Nt) from Basa, Chelmsford (Ess) from Cēolmǣr, Doxford (Nb) from Docc, Elford (Nb, St) from Ella, Ickford (Bk) from Ica, Stortford (Hrt) from Steorta, and Wilsford (L, W) from Wifel, all the names of men, while Alford (So) is from a lady called Aldḡyð. Occasionally, however, the ford was named from a group of people as in Hemingford (Hu) 'Hemma's people' and Shillingford (O) 'Sciella's people'. Consequently, Dr Margaret Gelling has suggested that *ford* has "a quasi-habitative sense" and was understood to mean 'settlement near a ford'". This interpetation is perhaps supported by the fact that over 550 names in *ford* have become those of villages, even towns and the local significance of most fords is attested by the fact that Ford has survived as a village name in at least six counties.

In compound names, the first element only rarely refers to the river the ford crosses, but this is the case in Brentford (Mx), Dartford (K), and Lydford (D) across the Brent, Darent, and Lyd respectively, while Yafforth (NRY) has been taken to mean 'river ford', though this hardly seems meaningful. Others refer to the road or way the ford carries as is the case in Farforth (L), Styford (Nb), Wayford (So), and Wentford (Sf). In the common Stratford, Strefford (Sa), and Stretford (He, La), as well as Trafford (La) it is a 'Roman road', while the Ditch-in Ditchford (Wa, Wo), literally 'dyke ford', refers to Fosse Way, which crosses the stream here.

The common Barford and also Barforth (NRY) mean 'barley ford', presumably one used particularly when the barley harvest was taken in, comparable to which Heyford (Nth, O) 'hay ford'. Others were named from the vegetation there – broom at Bramford (Sf) and Brampford (D), chag at Chagford (D), and burdock at Clatford (Ha). It was thought that marsh-marigolds grew at Guildford (Sr), but it has recently been shown that the first element probably refers to golden sand on the bed of the ford. The sites of some fords were no doubt marked by a prominent tree or trees as at Ashford (D, Db, Sa), Boxford (Sf) and Oakford (D), as well as Pyrford (Sr) 'pear-tree', Salford (Bd, La) 'sallow' and Widford (Ess, Hrt, O) 'withy'.

A considerable number are from the animals which used them or were found near them, for example Catford (K), Catforth (La) 'wild cats', Gateford (Nt), Gateforth (WRY) 'goats', Nafford (Wo) and Rutherford (NRY) both 'cattle', Rochford (Ess, Wo) 'raches', i.e. hunting dogs, Shefford (Nb, Brk), Shifford (O) 'sheep', Swinford (Brk, Lei, Wo), Kingswinford (St) 'swine', as well as the self-explanatory Hartford (Ch, Nb), Hartforth (NRY), Horsford (Nf), Horsforth (WRY). Others are from birds, as with Carnforth (La), Cranford (Mx, Nth) and Cransford (Sf) 'cranes or herons', Gosford (D, O, Wa) and Gosforth (Cu, Nb) 'geese', Ketford (Gl) 'kites' and the self-explanatory Buntingford (Hrt).

It has been shown that the commonest words compounded with *ford* are descriptive of the ford itself. It was 'long' at the common Langford and Longford, 'broad' at the almost as common Bradford, 'wide' at Romford (Ess), 'deep' at Defford (Wo), Deptford (K, W) and Diptford (D) and 'shallow' at Shadforth (Du), Shalford (Ess, Sr), and Shelford (Nt). The water was 'clear' at Sherford (D), 'slaggy', i.e. muddy, at Slaggyford (Nb) and 'foul' at Fulford, a name found in at least six counties. The way across was 'rough' at Rufford (La, Nt) and Rufforth (WRY), covered with 'cinders' at Cinderford (Gl), and with 'loose stones' at Clatterford (Wt). There was 'chalk' at Chalford (Gl, O) and 'stones' at Stainforth (WRY), Stamford (L, Mx, Nb), Stamford Bridge (ERY), Stowford (W), and the common Stanford; and either the bottom or the water was 'red' at Radford (D, Nt, Wa, Wo) and Retford (Nt). Somerford (Ch, Gl, St, W) was clearly a ford only passable in summer and Efford (Co, D, Ha) at ebb-tide.

The ford at Maidford (Nth) was specially associated in some way with 'maidens', those at Lattiford (So) and Latherford (St) with 'beggars' and that at Glamford Brigg (L) and Glandford (Nf) with 'merriment'. Freeford (St), as the name seems to suggest, was presumably free from toll, while Tetford (L) and Thetford (C, Nf) denote a 'public ford'.

Other terms for 'ford' occur only very occasionally. OE *wæd* is the source of Wade (Sf), Biggleswade (Bd) 'Biccel's ford' and Iwade (K) 'yew-tree ford' and it has been suggested that this word went out of use as a place-name forming element at an early date. The cognate

Scandinavian noun is *vað* and is found rather more frequently as in Waithe (L) and Wath (NRY, WRY). In compounds it often survives as -with, hence Brawith (NRY) 'broad', Langwith (ERY, Db, Nt) 'long', Sandwith (Cu) 'sand', Stenwith (L) 'stone' and twice in Lincolnshire as -worth in Langworth, identical with Langwith above. Like Brawith and Stenwith, Winderwath (We) is a Scandinavian compound, for the first element is the Old Norse personal name Vinand. So too is Solway (Firth) (Cu) probably meaning 'ford marked by a pillar or post', which would then be Lochmaben Stone, a large granite boulder which stood at the Scottish end of the ford.

As one might expect, *bridge*, OE *brycg*, occurs less frequently in major place-names than *ford*, since the bridge, later, took the place of the ford. The usual modern form is *bridge*, but *brigg* is not unusual in some districts due to the influence of Scandinavian *bryggja*, which, however, originally meant 'jetty, quay', as in Brigg (L), earlier *Glanford Brigg*. Though the usual meaning is 'bridge', occasionally it refers to a causeway or a raised track through marshland, as in Bridgend (L). In some cases the bridge was apparently built or owned by an individual as in a number of names with a personal name as first element such as Abridge (Ess) Æffa, Curbridge (O), Creoda and Harbridge (Ha) Hearda. Others were named from the rivers they crossed – Bainbridge (NRY), Doveridge, earlier *Dovebridge*, (Db), Stourbridge (Wo), and Weybridge (Sr). A number refer to the shape of the bridge or to the material from which it was constructed – the self-explanatory Stonebridge (Nx) and Stanbridge (Bd, Do, Ha, Sx), and Woodbridge (D, Sf), as well as Stockbridge (Do, Ha, La, WRY) 'bridge made of logs', Felbrigg (Nf), Thelbridge (D), Elbridge, earlier *Thelbridge*, (K, Sx) and Shide Bridge (Wt) all meaning 'plank bridge'. Ironbridge (Ess) is a misleading name, however, for it means 'ewes' bridge' and so belongs to the same group as Bulbridge (W) and Cowbridge (Ess, W) named from the animals using it. Ivybridge (D) must have been covered with ivy; Botolph Bridge (Hu) is named from the dedication of the nearby church of Orton to St. Botolph, patron saint of wayfarers; and Wakebridge (Db) probably means 'bridge where the wake or annual festival is held'. Pennybridge is common in later names for a bridge with a penny toll and an early example is Pennybridge, near Wadhurst, (Sx), first noted in 1438. Grampound (Co) and Grandpont in Oxford are French names meaning 'great bridge', but the latter was originally a 'causeway' and not a bridge in the usual modern sense of the word. We have already noted that *bridge* occasionally denoted a causeway and it has been suggested that Ricebridge (Sr) and Risebridge (Du, Ess), names found elsewhere especially in field-names, represent an OE appellative *hrīsbrycg* 'brush-wood causeway' and are not *ad hoc* place-name formations. The name occurs so comparatively frequently that this seems to be a sensible suggestion.

The term for 'marshland' most common in place-names is *marsh* itself, OE *mersc*, as in Marsh (Bk, Sa), Saltmarsh (He), and Wildmarsh (Mx). Stodmarsh (K) was named from a 'stud or herd of horses' and Killamarsh (Db) from the personal name Cynewald. Marston is so common, as well as Merton (K, Sx, Wt) and Morston (Nf), meaning 'marsh village' that it has been proposed that such villages served a specialized function in the exploitation of the marsh from which they are named.

Fen, OE *fenn*, is found frequently in later *Fen*land names, where it is often added to a river- or village-name, as in the Cambridgeshire Ouse Fen and Wisbech High Fen. When it occurs in the south-west, it often survives in a dialect form Venn (D, Do). It is also the source of a number of place-names with a personal name as first element – Gedda in Edvin Loach (He), Mǣrhard in Mason (Nb), Mūl in Mousen (Nb), and Hrōða in Ratfyn (W) – as well as others like Fulfen (Ess, St) 'foul marsh' and Redfern (Wa) perhaps 'winding marsh'. Fenton, found in at least seven counties, 'fen village' has been compared to Marston and thought to have a similar specific function in relation to the fen as Marston to the marsh.

Slough (Bk), from OE *slōh*, has its obvious meaning and a deriv-ative of the same word has given Slaughter (Gl) 'muddy place'. Strood (K), Stroud (Gl), and Stroud Green (Mx) come from OE *strōd* 'marshy land overgrown with brushwood' and is the second element of Gostrode (Sr) 'marshy land where geese are found'. OE *wisce* probably means 'marshy meadow' and is the source of Cranwich (Sf) and Glydwish (Sx), frequented by cranes and kite respectively, and of Dulwich (Gl, Sr) 'where dill grows'.

In those areas settled by Scandinavians ON *kjarr* 'brushwood' is used later of a 'marsh' especially one overgrown by brushwood. It sur-vives in dialects as *carr*, and also as *alder-carr* 'a piece of bog-, fen-land overgrown with alder trees', with which can be compared Aldercar (Db, Nt) and Ellerker (ERY) literally 'marshy land where alders grow'. 'Reeds' and 'willows' grew at Redcar (NRY) and Selker (Cu) respec-tively, while Trencar (NRY) was 'frequented by cranes' and Altcar (La) was named from the R. Alt. It is very common in minor names and field-names, especially in Lincolnshire. ON *mýrr*, modern *mire*, though well-represented in field-names is otherwise uncommon, but is found in Knavesmire in York (ERY) 'Knǫrr's marshy ground'. A unique name of Scandinavian origin, Thirsk (NRY), may be included here, for it is apparently derived from ON *þresk* 'fen'.

sixteen

Hills and valleys

A very large number of names referring to particular hills and valleys are the names of villages but, because they were in origin those of natural features of the landscape, they are considered here along with those which are still only used of a hill or valley. In the following discussions, as in the last chapter, of necessity I have relied heavily on the work of Margaret Gelling and for detailed analyses of many of the terms the reader must consult her *Place-Names in the Landscape*.

Hill, OE *hyll*, is, of course, common in place-names and in that form is found in most counties. Occasionally, however, Hull occurs in the west and south-west of England. Names in *hyll* are not recorded at all in pre-731 sources, but as has been pointed out this word is so widely distributed throughout the country that it was probably used to form place-names through the whole of the Old English period. It describes natural hills, but Dr Gelling notes that it does not seem to denote one that is low-lying or one above 1000 ft, with at least one very notable exception. This is the tautological compound Pendle (La) noted in Chapter Three.

Hill survives as a simplex name in at least six counties as well as Hill and Moor (Wo), first recorded simply as *Hyll* in 1046-53 and then as *More et Hylle* in Domesday Book, indicating as the editors of *The Place-Names of Worcestershire* point out "the contrast between the 'hill' and the low-lying 'moor' or swamp". Hull, on the other hand, apparently only survives as a village-name in Bishops Hull (So).

The word is common as the second element of a compound, with the first element sometimes denoting the shape as in Coppull (La) 'with a peak' and Cropwell (Nt) 'with a crop or hump', or the steepness in Stapenhill (St), as well as Shottle (Db) 'hill with a steep slope'. Windhill (WRY) and Windle (La) mean 'windy hill' and Snodhill (He) may be 'snowy hill', Wardle (Ch, La) and Warthill (NRY) 'watch hill', i.e. a look-out hill, the meaning also of the common minor name Toothill, Tothill, Tottle, and Tuttle. The first element is an adjective 'green' in Grindle (Sa), 'grey' in Hernhill (K), 'white' in Whittle (La, Nb) and Whitle (Db); it is 'clean' in Clennell (Nb), perhaps denoting one free from weeds or the like, 'barren' in the common Hungerhill and 'uncultivated' in Wildhill (Hrt). In others it refers to the crops which grew there as with Wheathill, as well as 'barley' in Bearl (Nb), 'oats' in Haverhill (Sf), 'pease' in Pishill (O), 'rye' in Ryhill (ERY, WRY), Ryal (Nb) and Ryle (Nb), while 'broom' grew at Broomhill, frequently occurring as a minor name, and 'woad' at Odell (Bd). Those in which the first element is a tree-name are usually self-explanatory, hence Ashill (So), Birchill and Thornhill (both in most counties), as are those derived from the name of an animal or bird – Catshill (Wo), Harthill (Ch, Db, WRY), Hawkhill (Nb), though less obvious are Coole (Ch) and Keele (St) 'cows', Gledhill (WRY) 'kite', and note also Beal (Nb) 'bee hill'. Many of the names containing *hill* which later became the names of villages have a personal name as first element, including Hengest in Hinxhill (K), Ocga in Ogle (Nb), Pohha in Poughill (Co, D), Snodd in Snodshill (W), Tāta in Tatenhill (St), Wyrma in Wormhill (Db), and a group-name 'Sunna's people' in Sunninghill (Brk). It has been usual to interpret Poughill (Co, D) as 'Pohha's hill', but a possible alternative meaning is certainly 'pouch-shaped hill'.

However, though *hill* is common in village-names, the commonest of all the terms for this physical feature is OE *dūn*, modern *down*, with almost twice as many surviving examples. A full study of *dūn* has revealed that "it *usually* [my italics] denotes a low eminence (characteristically between 200 and 500 ft) with a good area of flattish summit which offers an excellent settlement-site". Three further points may be made. Firstly, it had been considered that *dūn* was one of a small handful of words borrowed from Celtic into West Germanic. This view is no longer held by Celticists and we can be certain that *dūn* is indeed an Old English word and therefore cannot be used as evidence for Celtic influence or survival. Secondly, place-names containing this word are recorded in pre-731 sources and so it must have been used as a place-name forming element in the earliest periods of Anglo-Saxon settlement here. This seems to be supported by the fact that places with names derived from *dūn* are often those of some importance in the Anglo-Saxon period. Thirdly, we saw in the last chapter that it has been suggested that names derived from *ēg* and *ford* could well have what has been called a "quasi-habitative significance". Dr Gelling believes the same to be true of some of the names in -don. So, for example Chelmorton in Derbyshire, 'Ceolmǣr's hill', with the common interchange of -don and -ton, was understood to mean 'settlement at Chelmorton'.

OE *dūn* is uncommon as a simplex name and when it occurs it is usually distinguished in some way as in East Down and West Down (D). It is frequently compounded with a personal name — Æbba, or the feminine Æbbe, in Abingdon (Brk), Bealda in Baldon (O), Cærda in Charndon (BK), Cissa in Chessington (Sr), Ealāc in Elkstone (St) and Ilkeston (Db), Wærma in Warndon (Wo), Winebeald in Wimbledon (Sr).

Some hills in -don are named from the animals found there, as in the case of Cauldon (St), Chaldon (Do, Sr) 'calves', Everdon (Nth) 'boars', Horton (Gl) 'harts', and Swindon (St, W), Swinden (Gl) 'swine'; others from the crops or plants growing there, 'hay' at Haydon (Do, So, W), 'rye' at Raydon and Reydon (both Sf), 'wheat' at Whaddon (Bk, C, Gl), 'clover' at Claverdon (Wa), 'broom' at Brandon, found in several counties, and Bromden (Sa), 'fern' at Faringdon (Brk, Do, Nth, Wa), while Black Heddon (Nb) means 'heather-covered hill'. The first element denotes the colour of the hill in Fallowdon (Nb) 'fallow, yellow', Fawdon (Nb) 'multi-coloured', Grendon (Bk, D, Nth, Wa), Grindon (Du, Nb, St) 'green', Blackdown (Do, Wa) indentical with which is Blagdon (D, Do, So); or the type of surface or soil in Clandon (Sr) 'clean', perhaps free from weeds, Rowden (He) 'rough', Smithdown (La) 'smooth', Standen (Wt), Standon (Hrt, Sr) and Stondon (Bd, Ess) 'stone' ie. stony, as well as the self-explanatory Claydon (Bk, O) and Sandon (Brk, Ess, Hrt, St). Headon (Nt), Hendon (Mx), and High Down (Sx) all mean 'high hill' and Shenington (O) is 'beautiful hill'.

There is also a group of names including Hambledon (Do, Ha, Sr), Hambleton (NRY, R), Hemeldon (La), Humbledon (Du) and Hammerton (Db), as well as a number of minor names and lost fieldnames, meaning literally 'maimed, mutilated hill'. The characteristic feature of these is that the hill-top is irregularly shaped or has a rough profile. There are sufficient instances of this compound to suggest that Old English *hamoldūn* was an appellative and not an ad hoc place-name formation. Others are similarly named from their shape such as Bowden (D, Db) 'like a bow', Neasden (Mx) 'like a nose' and Edgton (Sa) 'having an edge'. Weldon (Nth) is 'hill with a spring' and Laindon

(Ess) 'near the *Lea*', a lost stream-name identical with the R. Lea in the same county. Warden is a common name meaning 'look-out hill', Burden (WRY), Great Burdon (Du), and Burradon (Nb) 'hill with a fortification', and Boldon (Du) 'hill with a dwelling'.

Modern English *cliff*, OE *clif*, is common enough in place-names and the topography of the places so-called make it clear that it could refer to a river-bank as well as a steep escarpment or hill-slope. Readers with local knowledge will know to which of these broad categories an individual name belongs. A third possible meaning 'small hill of bluff' has been suggested and this is certainly possible in some cases noted by Dr Gelling. As a simplex name it survives in the common Cliff and Cliffe but also as Clive (Ch, Sa). Among the many compounds is the self-explanatory Redcliff, a name found frequently, identical with which is Radcliffe (La, Nt), Radclive (Bk), Ratcliff (Mx), and Ratcliffe (Lei, Nt). Briercliffe (La) was named from 'briars', Catsley (Do) and Gatley (Ch) from 'wild-cats' and 'goats' respectively, and Arncliffe (WRY) from 'eagles'. Occasionally the *cliff* was named from a near-by river as with Avoncliff (W), while Wycliffe (NRY) may be 'cliff in a river bend' and Scarcliffe (Db) 'cliff with a gap or pass'. A personal name, however, occurs only occasionally as the first element, but there is Alstān in Austcliff (Wo), Headda in Hatcliffe (L), and Hocga in Hockliffe (Bd).

OE *beorg* 'hill, mound', the source of Modern English *barrow* 'tumulus', sometimes denotes a burial-mound, especially in southern England where it has been shown to be normally the term used for a pre-historic burial-mound and sometimes for a similar tumulus in which intrusive Anglo-Saxon burials have been made. Examples of names of this kind have been given in Chapter Four. In the sense 'hill' or 'mound', it has given Barrow (R) and Barugh (NRY, WRY) from the singular of the word, and from the plural the Westmorland Barras and Barwise. *Beorg* survives as -barrow, -berry, -borough, -bury, or -ber as the second element of compounds each of which is illustrated in the following examples, most referring to natural features of the landscape. The first element may be the name of a tree as in Mappleborough (Wa), Thornborough (Bk), and Limber (L) 'lime-tree hill'; a crop in the Leicestershire Market Harborough 'oats' and Whatborough 'wheat'; or some other plant in Brackenborough (L) and Farmborough (So), Farnborough (Brk, Ha, K, Wa) 'fern'. Occasionally it is a bird, as in Finborough (Sf), Finburgh (Wa) 'wood-pecker', and Kaber (We) 'jack-daw'. The first element of Grandborough (Bk, Wa) means 'green',

Whitbarrow (Cu) 'white', and Mickleborough (Nt) 'big'; in others it denotes the type of soil, hence 'gravel' in Chiselborough (So), 'shingle' in Singleborough (Bk), 'stone' in Stanborough (Hrt), while the *cockle* in Cocklebury (W), identical with which is Cockleberry (NRY), perhaps refers to the fossils in the stones there. It should be noted here that in Scandinavian there was an ON *berg*, cognate to OE *beorg*. It is impossible to distinguish between these two words in medieval spellings, but it is highly probable that *berg* is to be presumed in some names in eastern and northern England particularly in names when it is combined with another Old Norse element. Of the names quoted above Brackenborough (L) and Kaber (We) are very likely to belong here, as are Aigburth (La) and Aikber (NRY) the first element of which is certainly ON *eik* 'oak'.

Like OE *beorg*, OE *hlāw* was used both of a tumulus and a natural hill. Examples of its use in the sense 'burial-mound' have been given in Chapter Ten, but it should be added that this has been shown to be its commonest usage certainly in southern England, but also for example in Derbyshire. Further, it has similarly been demonstrated that *hlāw* was the word normally used by the Anglo-Saxons for their own tumuli. The meaning, however, seems certainly to be 'hill' in such names as Horelaw (La) 'grey hill', Callow 'cold', Grindlow 'green', Shardlow 'with a gap', and Wardlow 'look-out' all in Derbyshire. In Northumberland, the first element of Heatherslow means 'stag' and in Cushat Law 'wood-pigeon', while in Durham Kellow is 'calf hill', and Moorsley perhaps 'hill of the moor'. In both these counties *hlāw* seems frequently to be used in the names of natural hills.

In Chapter Four we saw how ON *haugr* 'hill, (burial-)mound' was used in the latter sense in some wapentake-names. It occurs sometimes in major place-names of a hill as in Blacko (La) 'dark hill', Scallow (Cu) 'bare hill' and Ulpha (Cu) 'wolf hill', as well as Clitheroe (La) 'hill with loose stones', the reference no doubt being to the loose limestone of the prominent hill there.

In Old English *hōh* means 'a heel' and so is used in place-names in a transferred topographical sense of a spur or a sharply projecting piece of land. Its geographical distribution, of course, is dictated by topography. In place-names it survives in minor names in a simplex form commonly as Hoe, Hoo and Hooe, but the -h- is sometimes lost when it occurs as the second element of a compound. The first element is often a personal name – Ega in Aynho (Nth), Bill in Belsay (Nb), Fleca probably in Flecknoe (Wa), Wata in Watnall (Nt), and Wifa in

Wivenhoe (Ess). In a few it is a group-name, 'Ifa's people' in Ivinghoe (BK), 'Pydda's people' in Piddinghoe (Sx), as well as 'dwellers on the R. Beane' in Bengeo (Hrt). Other examples of *hōh* include Langenhoe (Ess) 'long' and Sharpenhoe (Bd) 'sharp', Sharrow (WRY) 'boundary' and Wellow (L) 'spring'.

Rudge is a common dialectal form of OE *hrycg*, which appears in the standard language as *ridge*, but Rigg from the corresponding Scandinavian word occurs in the East Midlands and the North of the country. Among the many places named from a 'ridge' are Ridge (Hrt) and Rudge (Gl, Sa), as well as numerous compounds like Brantridge (Sx) 'steep', identical in meaning with Stickeridge (D), Rowridge (Wt) 'rough', and the self-explanatory Brownridge (Nb) and Longridge (La). Ditteridge (W) means 'ridge near the dyke', apparently a reference to Fosse Way, and Melkridge (Nb) 'milk ridge', presumably one which had pasturage giving plenty of milk. 'Eagles' were to be seen at Eridge (Sx) and 'hawks' at Hawkridge (Brk, So) and Hawridge (Bk), while Totteridge (Hrt) and Waldridge (Bk) were named from men called Tāta and Wealda respectively. The Scandinavian word is the source of Castlerigg (Cu) 'ridge with a castle', Crossrigg (We) 'with a cross', and Wheyrigg (Cu) 'with a sheepfold', as well as Lambrigg and Whelprigg (both We) where 'lambs' and 'whelps' were found, and Haverigg (Cu) and Loughrigg (We) where 'oats' and 'leeks' grew.

OE *ofer* is a word which does not occur independently in Old English texts, but which has been adduced from a number of place-names containing such a word. Judging from the topography of these, it appears to have meant 'flat-topped ridge'. Dr Gelling has shown that the sites of settlements with names in -over "show a remarkable consistency" and that the shape of the end of the ridge is distinctive – the curve is gentle and convex "like the end of an upturned canoe". Names containing this word include Over (C, Ch) and Littleover and Mickleover (Db), both named from the same ridge, with prefixes meaning 'little' and 'big' added later. Southover (Sx) is however an original and self-explanatory compound. Other compounds include Heanor (Db), Hennor (He) 'high ridge', Longnor (St) 'long ridge' and Hadzor (Wo), Tittensor (St) and Wentnor (Sa) the first elements of which are the personal names Headd, Titta, and Wonta or Wenta respectively. Calver (Db) means 'calf ridge' while Ashover (Db), Birchover (Db) and Bircher (He), Haselor (Wa) and Haselour (St), and Okeover (St) were named from the ash, birch, hazel and oak. The distribution pattern of

names in -over indicates that, apart from occasional instances for
example in Sussex and Somerset, it is found predominantly in the
Midlands. Further, such names are often found along routeways, often
marking significant points along them. The full historical significance
of this has still to be fully worked out, but already patterns have been
noted and these can hardly be the result of chance.

A full study of OE *ōra* by Ann Cole has shown that it, like *ofer*,
dcnotes a flat-topped hill, "which when seen from a distance, has a long
flat top terminating at one or both ends with a curved shoulder". Again
like *ofer*, it has a profile "more like an upturned canoe". It was a term
originally applied to a natural feature and must have been a landmark.
Many are found beside Roman or pre-Roman routeways, but also near
ancient ports and in some cases in iron or salt working areas.
Furthermore, it has very much a southern provenance and though the
two words denote similar shaped hills, there is little overlap in the distribution patterns of names in *ōra* and in *ofer*. Indeed *ōra* does not seem
to occur north of Herefordshire, and it is found in greatest numbers in
districts where very early Anglo-Saxon settlement is thought to have
taken place. It is found not only inland but also near the south coast, and
Mrs Cole has suggested that some of the latter must have been seen (and
named) from the sea or shore. In view of its occurrence in areas of early
Anglo-Saxon settlement here, its general proximity to Roman roads and
ancient ports, it is not surprising that it has been suggested that OE *ōra*
is a loan-word from Latin *ora*. If it was an English borrowing in this
country it would then be comparable to such words as *camp*, *funta*, and
port discussed in Chapter Three.

OE *ōra* 'flat-topped hill' is the source of Oare (Brk, K, W), Ore
(Sx), and Bognor and Itchenor (both Sx) and Lewknor (O) from the personal names Bucge (feminine), Icca, and Lēofeca respectively. The first
element in Pershore (Wo) means 'oziers', that in Wardour (W) 'watch',
presumably denoting a look-out hill, and that in Windsor (Brk, Do, Wa)
and Winsor (D, Ha) 'windlass', but what the significance of *windlass* is
here has not yet been satisfactorily explained.

For the most part OE *scelf* denotes a broad, level shelf of land, or
one which is only very gently sloping and as such occurs in such simplex
names as Shelf (Db, WRY) and Shelve (Sa). It is also the first element of
Shelton (Bd, Nf, Nt, Sa, St) and the partially Scandinavianized Skelton
(Cu, ERY, NRY WRY). As the second element, it is found in Bashall
(WRY) 'on a ridge' and with a personal name Hūn, Mann, and Tibba, in

Hunshelf (WRY), Minshull (Ch), and Tibshelf (Db). The corresponding Scandinavian word, however, has given Raskelf (NRY) 'roe-deer', Hinderskelfe (NRY) from the feminine name Hildr, and Ulleskelf (WRY) from the masculine Úlf, all three being Danish compound place-names.

Ness (Ch, Sa, NRY) and Naze, common in minor names, are derived from OE *næss*, *ness*, modern *ness*, which was used not only of a promontory or headland, but also for projecting pieces of high land, "promontories of dry ground jutting into fen". It occurs in compound names such as Foulness (Ess) 'birds', Sharpness (Gl) and Sharp Ness (K) 'sharp, pointed', Sheerness (K) 'bright', and Totnes (D) and Wrabness (Ess) both from personal names, Totta and Wrabba. The cognate Scandinavian word *nes* will of course give similar early forms to the English one, but it is certainly found in Ashness (Cu) 'where ash-trees grow', and Skegness (L) the first element of which is the Danish personal name Skeggi.

Tor, OE *torr*, 'rock, rocky peak, hill' is a Celtic loan-word into English and is almost entirely restricted in early names to the South-west of the country. It is, however, not uncommon in Derbyshire, though usually in names first recorded after 1500. The names containing this element are still often those of natural features or of very small places, as in the following examples – Black Tor (D), Pig Tor (Db), as well as Scobitor (D), Vobster (So), and Worminster (So) from the personal names Sceobba, Fobb, and Wyrm as first element. In Mam Tor (Db), *tor* was added, apparently in the 17th century, to a Celtic hill-name meaning 'breast-like hill'.

Other Old English words occur much less frequently in place-names denoting a hill; *cnoll*, modern *knoll*, in the sense 'a small hill, more or less rounded in form' has given Knole (K, So), and Knowle (Do, Wa) as well as Bigknowle (Sx), Chetnole (Do), and Edge Knoll each from a personal name Bibba, Ceatta, and Ēadin respectively. Similarly *copp*, modern *cop*, 'summit, hill-top' is rare in major names, but is the source of the Lancashire Copp, as well as Pickup 'with a point', and Warcop (We) 'look-out'. *Cop* is the second element of OE *setcopp* and this has given Sidcup, (K) as well as similar minor names and field-names in several counties. Its meaning is uncertain but may be 'seat-shaped hill' or 'flat-topped hill', since at least two examples in which it survives as the name of a physical feature have distinctively flat profiles. A similar meaning seems certain for Sadberge (Du) and Sedbergh (WRY) from ON *setberg*, for this describes the hills exactly.

OE *hlið* is rare in major names, though it is certainly the second element of Adgarley (La) 'Ēadgār's slope', but the cognate Old Norse word *hlíð* is found more often as in Lyth (We), and Lythe (La, NRY), twice meaning 'slope with a spring' in Kellet (La), and Kelleth (We), as well as with a Scandinavian personal name Hagne in Hanlith (WRY). Ireleth (La) is particularly interesting since it means 'Irishmen's slope', a further piece of evidence for the presence of Irish settlers in north-west England. It should be noted, however, that from a recent examination of places with names derived from *hlið*, Dr Gelling has concluded that the word did not simply refer to a hill-slope, but had a more specialized meaning of 'concave hill-slope'.

Other Scandinavian words for various types of hills and the like have given rise to place-names in the north-west, like *brekkr* 'slope', a term associated with Norwegian rather than Danish settlement here. It is commonest in Lancashire where we find Breck, Norbreck, and Norbrick 'north', Warbreck 'with a cairn', and Swarbrick from the Scandinavian personal name Svartr. In Westmorland is Haverbrack 'slope on which oats grow'. It has been pointed out that ON *fell* 'hill, mountain' rarely survives as a settlement-name, as it does in Whinfell (Cu, We) 'where whin grows', rather it gives rise to names of topographical features – Mell Fell and Sca Fell (both Cu) in which *Fell* has been added to an old hill-name, apparently meaning 'bare hill' and 'bald hill' respectively.

In some hill-names an ordinary word is used in a transferred topographical sense, as in the case of *edge*, OE *ecg*. It has been shown that this denotes an escarpment, the edge of a hill, or rock scars. It occurs in such names as Alderley Edge (Ch) and Lincoln Edge (L), and in Lancashire and the West Midlands, where Edge is a common minor name. It has given the self-explanatory Brownedge (La), Harnage (Sa), and also Stanedge (Db, La) both 'stony', Heage (Db) 'high', and Hathersage (Db) 'Hæfer's edge', and Liversedge (WRY) 'Lēofhere's edge'.

Like OE *ecg*, OE *hēafod* 'head' is used in place-names in a transferred topographical sense of a projecting piece of land. Dr Gelling points out that it is used of features "varying in height from a few feet above fenland to the elevation of considerable hills" though "examples predominate in which it refers to hills of less than 500 ft, and that the choice of this word was "probably dictated by the shape of the feature". Examples in which *head* is compounded with a term for an animal in the genitive singular have been discussed in Chapter Ten and this is the

largest single category of head-names. Other names formed from
hēafod include Birkenhead (Ch) 'birch-covered', Thicket (ERY) 'thick,
dense', presumably a reference to vegetation there, and the
Westmorland Arnside and Burnside from the personal names Arnwulf
and Brūnwulf respectively. Minehead (So) is an interesting example for
the first element is the Primitive Welsh word *mönith* 'mountain, hill', as
too is Mamhead (D), another hybrid name, for *mam* is derived from
Primitive Welsh *mamm* 'breast-like hill', a word we have already noted
as occurring in Mam Tor (Db).

The Scandinavian cognate *hǫfuð*, of OE *hēafod*, is the source
of a few names in the north-west such as Sellet (La) 'with a shieling'
and Whitehaven (Cu) 'white headland', to which *haven* was added.
The 'white headland' has been identified by a local antiquarian with
"a great rock or quarry of white hard stone", the rock being known as
'white headland'.

OE *bile* 'bill, beak' has also been used in place-names occasionally in a transferred topographical sense of something resembling a bill,
and this has given Amble (Nb) 'Anna's headland, promontory', while in
Portland Bill (Do) it has been added to an older name Portland, discussed in Chapter Three. Other Old English words have been used in
similar ways. OE *hēap*, modern *heap*, denotes a hill in Heap (La), but
Shap (We), which ultimately goes back to the same word, is thought to
refer to a heap of stones from the ruins of an important megalithic mon-
ument, a stone circle. Hett (Du) is derived from OE *hætt*, modern *hat*,
here used of a hill; OE *stīgrāp*, modern *stirrup*, is the source of Styrrup
(Nt), from a hill with the fancied shape of a stirrup, while *stigel* 'stile'
has given dialect *steel* 'ridge', the sense apparently required for Steel
(Nb). Preen (Sa) is derived from OE *prēon* 'brooch', presumably used
again in some transferred topographical sense, perhaps of the ridge
there. Clegg (La) is from ON *kleggi* 'haystack', used here of a hill with
the supposed profile of a haystack.

A word commonly used in a similar way is OE *sīde*, modern *side*,
used of long hill-slopes, as in the common Brownside, Birkenside (Nb)
'birch-covered', Whernside (WRY) 'where millstones are quarried', and
a group including Facit (La), Fawcett (We), Fawside (Du), and Phoside
(Db) each meaning 'variegated, multi-coloured hill-slope'.

Of the numerous place-name elements denoting a valley, *valley*
itself is very rare and *vale*, also a French loan-word into English, is
infrequent. Noteworthy, however, are Merevale (Wa) 'pleasant valley',

and the North Riding Jervaulx and Rievaulx 'valley of the R. Ure' and 'valley of the R. Rye' respectively, the last apparently according to one scholar a French 'translation' of the English *Ryedale*. *Dale* on the other hand is common enough, particularly in Scandinavianized areas of the country, and sporadically elsewhere. OE *dæl*, modern *dale* meant 'pit, hollow' and the general view today is that it was really only in general use with the sense 'valley' due to the influence of the cognate Scandinavian word *dalr* which did mean 'valley'. It would appear, therefore, that it was only in late Old English, for the most part, that *dæl* denoted a 'valley'. The usual English word for this topographical feature was *denu*, modern *dene*, as we shall see later. The widespread use of dale in later minor names and field-names must, it would seem, ultimately be the result of Scandinavian influence. Suffice it to say here that in major place-names the occurrence of *dæl* 'valley' is rare indeed and south of the Thames it is not found at all. In Devon, for example Dalwood is not recorded before 1175 and is probably of post-Conquest origin, while the other *dale*-name in Devonshire is Dymsdale, in Alwington, first recorded in 1371. The editors of *The Place-Names of Devon* comment "As the element *dale* is otherwise unknown in Devon the name can hardly be of local origin". Indeed, there can be little doubt that Dymsdale is derived from the topographical surname *Dymmyngesdale*, that of a miner or miners from Derbyshire or Staffordshire impressed into work in the royal stannaries in the southwest, for which there is evidence certainly from 1295. A John *Dymmyngesdale* is actually mentioned in the 1371 document noted above. The surname, itself, is doubtless derived from a place-name such as Dimin Dale in Taddington (Db) or Dimsdale (St), but unfortunately the first element has not yet been fully explained. *Dale* is found most frequently to the north of the R. Mersey and R. Humber but it also occurs as far south as Northamptonshire. Even in the north, however, it is comparatively rare in Durham and Northumberland, where Scandinavian influence is much less than in Yorkshire, and it has been plausibly suggested that the degree of Scandinavian influence is crucial in the use of *dale* in the formation of place-names. Further, because of "its wide currency as a term for 'valley' it often replaced the more usual OE word *denu*". This has happened in the self-explanatory Deepdale (Nth), Oxendale (La) 'where oxen are found', Saxondale (Nt) 'valley of the Saxons', and Stavordale (So), the first element of which may mean 'stake'.

Dale has been added to a number of river-names like Airedale (WRY), Eskdale (Cu), Lonsdale (Lune, La), Ribblesdale (La), Swaledale (NRY), and Wharfedale (WRY). It is named from animals in Cowdale (Db) and Kiddal (WRY) 'cows', Grisdale (We) 'young pigs', and Withersdale (Sf) 'wether-sheep', from plants in Farndale (NRY) 'fern', Matterdale (Cu) 'madder', and Mosedale (Cu) 'moss', from a cross in Crossdale (Cu), a church in Kirkdale (La, NRY), and from a fortification in Borrowdale (Cu, We). In the north-west the first element is sometimes a Scandinavian personal name as in Bannisdale (We) from Bannandr, Bleasdale (La) from Blesi, and Skelmersdale (La) from Skelmer, while Patric, an Irish name, is the first element of Patterdale (We).

OE *denu* has been referred to as "the standard OE term for a main valley" and as such is widespread in this country. We have seen how it has sometimes been replaced by *dale* and in at least one name, Longdendale (Db), the latter has been added to an original *Langdene* 'long valley'. Indeed, it has been shown that most valleys derived from *denu* are long and sinuous, and Ann Cole notes that "denu is mostly used of long, narrow valleys with two moderately steep sides and a gentle gradient along most of their length". As a simplex place-name it survives as the common Dean, as well as Deane (Ha), Deene (Nth), and as Dene in minor names. Eastdean and Westdean in Sussex were originally simplex names later distinguished by East- and West-. Indeed, Dean is the usual modern form of *denu* in Sussex. Compound names derived from *denu* are common, and though the modern form is usually -den, there is also -don and even -ton. In some cases the first element denotes the nature of the ground, 'gravel' in Chisledon (W), 'dirt, mud' in Horden (Du), 'mud' in Sladen (La); or the shape, 'like a sack' in Ballidon (Db), 'like a trough' in Trawden (La); others are named from a natural feature such as a 'brook' in Brogden (WRY), while Marden (Nb), Marden Ash (Ess), and Marsden (La) all mean 'boundary valley'. The first element is an adjective in Blagdon (Nb) 'black', Bradden (Nth) 'broad', Dibden (Ha, K) and Dipton (Du, Nb) 'deep', Holden (La, WRY) 'hollow', Marden Park (Sr), Meriden (Wa) and Merriden (Sr) 'pleasant', Shalden (Ha) 'shallow' and Sudden (La) 'south'. Occasionally *denu* has been added to an older name now lost, as in Todmorden (WRY), in which Todmor- may mean 'Totta's boundary'. A large number, however, are named from a person -Bæssel in Basildon (Brk), a lady called Bucge in Buckden (Hu), Ceadd in Chaddesden (Db), Citta in Chidden (Ha), Ecga in Egdean (Ess), Helma in Helmdon

(Nth), and Walsa in Walsden (La), or from a group of people as in Essendon (Hrt) 'Ēsla's people' and Rottingdean (Sx) 'Rōta's people'. Others are from the animals found there, 'wild-cats' in Catton (Nb), 'foxes' in Foxton (Du, Nb), 'sheep' in Shipden (Nf) and Skibeden (WRY), 'swine' in Swinden (WRY), and 'wether-sheep' in Wetherden (Sf). Barden (WRY) was a valley where barley grew, Hebden (WRY) where hips were found, while others were named from the trees which grew there, 'hazels' in Hesleden (Du), 'sallows' in Sawdon (NRY) and 'yews' in Yewdon (Bk).

OE *cumb*, modern *coomb*, has also been subject to detailed study, from which Mrs Cole has concluded that this word was used of valleys shorter and broader than those we have just considered. They are also bowl-shaped or trough-shaped with three fairly steeply rising sides. Dr Gelling has pointed out that such valleys provide sheltered sites for settlement but are "too secluded for economic growth or administrative importance". Place-names derived from *cumb* are particularly common in major names in the south-west, excluding Cornwall, so that it would appear that there it seems to have been the "standard" word used for a valley. In Devon, for instance, it is the second most common element found in place-names. Presumably it must have been used in a more general sense of valley than in other parts of the country. It has given the common Comb, Combe, Coomb, and Coombe, as well as Cowm (La), and Culm Davy (D). In compounds the first element is sometimes an adjective meaning 'hidden' in Darncombe (NRY), 'hollow' in Holcombe (at least six counties) and Hollacombe (D), 'shallow' in Shalcombe (Wt) and 'wide, broad' in Whitcombe (Do), Widcombe (D, So), Widdecombe (D), Witcomb (W), Witcombe (Gl), and Wydcombe (Wt). Ashcombe (D), Thorncombe (Do), and Withycombe (D, So), identical with the Devonshire Widdicombe, were named from the particular tree growing there, as was Appuldurcomb (Wt) 'apple-tree' and Boxcombe (W) 'box-tree'. Wheat grew at Whatcombe (Do). As was the case with *denu*, the *coomb* was often named from an early owner with a personal name of Old English origin – Ielfrēd, a dialectal variant of Ælfrēd, in Ilfracombe (D), Babba in Babbacombe (D), Ceawa in Chalcombe (Nth), Titta in Tidcombe (W), and Wifel in Wiveliscombe (So). In Devon, the personal name is of Celtic origin occasionally as with Branoc in Branscombe and Caradoc in Croscombe. Indeed, it has for long been assumed that *cumb* itself was borrowed from Primitive Welsh into Old English, but more recently it has been argued that it may well have been a native English word. No certainty is possible.

OE *hop* survives in northern dialect as *hope* denoting a small enclosed valley, especially one overhanging or branching from the main valley. In Old English, however, the word is only recorded with reference to marsh retreats, and a sense 'enclosed land in marsh or moor' certainly fits the topography of a few place-names. However, 'secluded valley', in particular, is the meaning required in most place-names. It is possible, but uncertain, that here we have to do with two different words with similar forms. A full study has certainly shown that *hop* is used in the great majority of place-names of a *secluded* valley. Because they are varied shapes it has been plausibly argued that shape is not the determining factor; rather it is the notion of seclusion. It is the source of the common Hope and of compounds such as Longhope (Nb) 'long', Ryehope (Du) 'rugged', and with a personal name as first element Alsop (Db) Ælli, Eccup (WRY) Ecca, Glossop (Db) Glott, Worksop (Nt) Weorce or Wyrc. Stanhope (Du) and Stanshope (St) probably both mean 'stony secluded valley'; Bacup (La) is apparently 'secluded valley below the back or ridge', and Pontop (Du) 'of Pont Burn'. Swinhope, an isolated example in Lincolnshire is named from 'swine', and the West Riding Oxenholme from 'oxen'. Ash-trees grew at Ashop (Db), broom at Broomhope (Nb), and cress at Kershop (Cu). It will be noted that many of these names are in the northern part of the country, but there are also examples in Shropshire – the self-explanatory Easthope, Middlehope, and Westhope, as well as Presthop 'priests' secluded valley' and Wilderhop 'Wilðryð's secluded valley'.

In those parts of the north occupied by Norwegian settlers *gil* 'ravine, deep narrow valley with a stream' is common, especially in minor names. There is Howgill (WRY) 'hollow ravine', Skell Gill (WRY) from the R. Skell, and a few with a personal name as first element like Ēadmær in Admergil (WRY), Gerard in Garrigill (Cu), probably Skakari in Scargill (NRY). Several are from terms for animals or birds – foxes in Reagill (We), horses in Rosgill (We), and geese in Gaisgill (We) and Gazegill (WRY). Occasionally this word was later used of swallow-holes as in Gaping Ghyll near Ingleborough (WRY), the spelling *ghyll* which sometimes occurs being a pseudo-archaism apparently due to its use by the poet Wordsworth.

Other elements occur much less frequently than most discussed so far. OE *botm*, *boðm* 'valley bottom' is found in the North and North

Midlands particularly where Bottom and Bothom are common minor and field-names. Broadbottom (Ch), Longbottom (WRY), and Ramsbottom (L) are self-explanatory. Another word appearing chiefly in the North is *clōh*, modern *clough*, 'deep valley', as in Meerclough 'boundary clough', and Loveclough from the personal name Lufu, both in Lancashire. On the other hand, *cinu*, modern *chine*, 'ravine' is especially to be found along the South coast and in the Isle of Wight, where there is Blackgang Chine, Linstone Chine, and Shanklin Chine. OE *corf* 'gap, pass' seems, however, to be restricted to the West and South-west as in Corfe (Do, So), Corve (Wt), as well as Corve (Sa), now the name of a river.

Like *gil*, ON *slakki* 'shallow valley' occurs principally in areas settled by men of Norwegian stock and has given Slack (Cu, La, WRY) and the self-explantory Castle Slack and Dead Man's Slack in Cumberland. Perhaps surprisingly it has been noted in field-names occasionally in Nottinghamshire and rather more so in north-east Lincolnshire.

As was the case with terms denoting hills, several words are similarly used in a transferred topographical sense for a valley. Modern *gate*, OE *geat*, sometimes means 'gap in hill, deep ravine' as in the famous Symond's Yat (He) and Ayot (Hu), from the personal names Sigemund and Ægra respectively, and in the compound *windgeat*, which has given Windgate (Du), Wingates (Nb), Winnats (Db), and the affix in Compton Wyniates (Wa). A similar development of meaning to 'pass, gap' has occurred in the place-name use of *dor* 'large door, gate' in Dore (WRY) and of *duru*, modern *door* in the second element of Lodore (Cu) 'low pass', the lower gap into Borrowdale. OE *cēodor*, a derivative of *cēod* 'pouch, bag', and denoting a 'gorge', is no doubt the source of Cheddar (So), while Beedon (Brk) appears to be from OE *byden* 'tub, butt', which was evidently used of the steep narrow valley above which the village stands. With this can be compared the use of *tub*, presumably in a similar sense in Buttertubs Pass (WRY). Chettle (Do) is from OE *cetel* 'kettle' with a transferred usage of 'deep valley surrounded by hills'; Chew (La) is apparently from *cēo* 'gill of a fish', which like ON *gil*, is used of a 'narrow valley'; while Bowling (WRY) is probably formed from *bolla* 'bowl' and the suffix -*ing*, meaning 'place in a bowl', a reference to a bowl-shaped hollow or depression there. Similarly OE or ON *hals* 'neck' occasionally denotes a pass through hills as in Hawes (NRY) and in several Cumberland names such as

Buttermere Hause and Esk Hause; in other names, however, it is used of a neck of land between valleys, the sense required by the topography of Halse (D, So). Here too may be noted one or two place-names derived from OE *trōg*, modern *trough*, as in Trough (La, NRY, WRY), Trow (W), and The Trough of Bowland (WRY-La), in each used of a 'valley like a trough'.

seventeen

Woods, clearings, and open land

Numerous words for *wood*, both English and Scandinavian, occur in place-names. *Wood* itself is common and has been rightly described as being probably the most colourless OE term for a collection of trees. Few of the names derived from OE *wudu*, modern *wood*, are those of important places. The word, however, occurs frequently compounded with OE *tūn* in the common Wootton, as well as Wooton (Bk, Gl, Sr) and it has been suggested that such a name meaning 'village, estate in or by a wood' might well have economic significance, these places per-haps having a special function in relation to the wood and its products. Woodham (Du) is derived from the dative plural of *wudu* 'at the woods'. Of the compounds of this word those named from the cardinal points of the compass are frequently found, as with Northwood (Mx, Wt) and Norwood (Mx). Heywood (La) means 'high wood', but Heywood (W) and Haywood (Ha, Nt, Sa, St) are 'enclosure wood', as is Lockwood (WRY) too. Broadwood (D, So) is self-explanatory, but Smallwood (Ch) is 'narrow wood', and not 'small wood' as the modern form would sug-gest. The first element often not surprisingly denotes the trees growing there, hence Ashwood (St), Hazelwood (Db) and Hazlewood (WRY), as well as Ewood (WRY) and Linwood (L), named from the yew and lime respectively. Others are from birds or animals – hares in Harewood (He, WRY) and Harwood (La, Nb), eagles in Arnwood (Ha), jackdaws in Cawood (La, WRY), and cranes in Cornwood (D, Wo).

In some cases the wood was named from a natural feature, as in Dunwood (Ha) 'hill', Ewood (La) 'river', Hockerwood (Nt) 'hump of ground', and Hopwood (La, Wo) 'enclosure in waste'; others from the nature of the ground, level in Evenwood (Du), foul in Fulwood (La, Nt), stone, ie. stony in Stowood (O), and wet in Weetwood (Nb). There are also Brandwood (La), Brentwood (Ess), and Burntwood (St) each meaning 'burnt wood'. Stobswood (Nb) seems to be 'wood of the stump', perhaps one which had been cleared, while Sherwood (Nt) 'shire wood' apparently means 'wood belonging to the shire', though it might be 'shire wood' because it was near the shire boundary. Occasionally the wood was named from its owner – Inta in Intwood (Nf), Paca in Packwood (Wa), and a lady called Gōdgifu in Goodwood (Sx).

Forest, a French loan word, on the other hand, is rare in place-names. It occurs, however, in The New Forest (Ha), first recorded in 1086, when it had been newly created as a royal forest. But usually this word has been added to older names as in Epping Forest (Ess), Inglewood Forest (Cu), Peak Forest (Db), Rockingham Forest (Nth), and Selwood Forest (So-W). Most of these represent old royal forests of the Middle Ages and though used as game reserves were not necessarily forests in the modern sense of the word. OE *fyrhð*, modern *frith*, is also used of a wood or woodland and in such names as Duffield Frith and Chapel en le Frith (both Db) it indicated a district subject to medieval forest law. It has been suggested that for most place-names containing this word a better translation would be 'land overgrown with brush-wood, scrub on the edge of forest'. It usually survives as Frith in minor names, but in some areas of the Midlands and South also as Thrift, as in Marston Thrift (Bd). It is, however, rare in major settlement-names but one example is certainly Pirbright (Sr) 'pear-tree scrub'.

There is little doubt that OE *wald* meant 'forest', though much later it denoted open high ground as in Lincolnshire Wolds and Yorkshire Wolds, where independent reference to Wolds does not seem to have been recorded much before the end of the 13th century. The earlier meaning seems to be the usual one in place-names such as The Weald (K-Ha), Weald (O), North Weald and South Weald (Ess), as well as Wield (Ha), Old (Nth) from a dialect form, and Cotswold (Gl) 'Cōd's woodland, forest'. It is found in a few names in East Anglia like the self-explanatory Northwold (Nf), Southwold (Sf), Methwold (Nf) 'middle', and Hockwold (Nf) 'where hocks grow'. Elsewhere there are several *wold*s with a personal name as first element, Cuca in Cuxwold (L), Cuha in Coxwold (NRY), Stígr in Stixwould (L), and Swiðbeorht in Sibertswold (K) and even with a group-name in Easingwold (NRY) 'Ēsa's people'.

As a simplex name Holt, from OE *holt* 'wood', is found as a major name in at least nine counties. However, it is not evenly distributed throughout the country, for while it is found in the West Riding of Yorkshire a few times, it does not figure in the place-nomenclature

further north. It occurs with the name of a tree as first element sufficiently often that it has been suggested that it was to some extent a specialized term for a single-species wood. Acol (K) and Occold (Sf) mean
'oak wood', Alderholt (Do) and Bircholt (K) are self-explanatory,
Aisholt (So) and Esholt (WRY) are 'ash-tree wood', Buckholt (Ha, Sx)
'beech-tree wood', while Wiggenholt (Sx) was named from the wych
elm. Animals and birds are represented in Eversholt (Bd) 'boars', and
Gledholt (WRY) 'kites'. Bergholt (Ess) and Linkenholt (Ha) both mean
'wood on the hill(s)'. Sparsholt (Brk, Ha) is literally 'wood of the
spear', but what that actually signifies is uncertain. The same can be
said of Throckenholt (C) in which the first element is an adjective
derived from OE *þroc*, a word which survives in dialect as 'the share-
beam of a plough'. Perhaps the meaning of this name is 'wood from
which share-beams were got'.

OE *sceaga*, modern *shaw*, means 'small wood' and in place-
names is only common in parts of the north-west and the West Riding
of Yorkshire. Elsewhere it is rare, though widely distributed. Shaw
occurs as a major name in Berkshire, Lancashire, and Wiltshire, but it
often occurs as a minor name in the north-west. Occasionally it was
named from an owner in Audenshaw (La) and Barnshaw (Ch), from
Aldwine and Beornwulf respectively. It is compounded with animal-
names in Ottershaw (Sr) and Ickornshaw (WRY) 'squirrels', and with
the name of a bird in Crawshaw Booth 'crow' and Dunnockshaw, from
the dialect *dunnock* 'hedge-sparrow', both in Lancashire, while in the
same county is Bickershaw 'bee-keepers small wood', as well as
Bradshaw (also Db, WRY) 'broad', Brunshaw 'small wood by the R.
Brun' and the self-explanatory Openshaw. The first element is the name
of a tree in Aldershaw (St), while in Birkenshaw (WRY), Oakenshaw
(WRY), and Ollerenshaw (Db) it is an adjective, derived from a tree-
name, meaning 'growing with birches', 'with oak-trees' and 'with
alders' respectively.

OE *bearu* means 'grove' and Dr Gelling comments "The way in
which *bearu* is used in place-names suggests that it referred to a wood
of limited extent". It is particularly common in the south-west and over
100 examples have been noted in Devon alone, about one-fifth being
named form an early owner, e.g. Ægel in Aylesbeare, Centel in
Kentisbeare, Locc in Loxbeare, as well as Secg in Sedgebarrow (Wo).
This word is not found at all in some counties, though it seems to be
comparatively frequent, especially in minor names, in others like

Cheshire, Gloucestershire, and the West Riding of Yorkshire. *Beuru* is common as a simplex name, surviving as Bare (La), Beer (D, Do), and Barrow, in at least nine counties, from the dative singular form. In compounds there is reference to birds in the self-explanatory Crowborough (St) and Larkbeare (D), as well as jackdaws in Kigbeare and rooks in Rockbeare (both D). Timber was cut at Timsbury (So) and shafts at Shebbear (D).

It is difficult to distinguish between OE *grǣfe* and *grāf*, both of which seem to denote a 'grove', even in the early spellings of place-names. The former is found particularly in the North-west Midlands, where it is the second element of Congreve (St) 'grove in a coomb', Ramsgreave (La) 'grove where wild-garlic grows', and Youlgreave (Db) 'yellow grove'. While *grǣfe* often survives as -greave especially in minor names and field-names, *grāf* has frequently given Grove in modern spellings, but -grave is not unusual when it is the second element of a compound name. It is probably the source of Hargrave (Ch, Nth, Sf) 'hare' or 'hoar', Musgrave (We) 'mouse', Boxgrave (Sx) 'box-tree', Gargrave (WRY) 'triangular piece of land' and Warpsgrove (O) 'bridle-way'. Staplegrove (So) was a grove where posts were obtained; Blagrove (Brk) is 'dark grove' and Leagrave (Bd) 'light grove', and a few are named from an early owner – Cotta in Cotgrave (Nt) and Fygla in Filgrave (Bk). Again, as with other place-names containing words for a 'wood', *grāf* unlike *grǣfe* is the first element of habitative names, especially those compounded with OE *tūn* 'grove estate' in the common Grafton. It is similarly possible that the settlements so-named "derived special advantages from their management of the grove", as Dr Gelling suggests. One should bear in mind, as pointed out above, the difficulty of distinguishing between *grāf* and *grǣfe* in place-names and it is quite possible that one or two of the examples quoted have been assigned to the wrong word.

There are several Scandinavian terms for 'wood' in English place-names, one of which is ON *skógr*. This word is found particularly in the north-west and in Yorkshire, but it is also found as far south as Norfolk. It occurs in compound names like Briscoe (NRY), Hessleskew (ERY), and Thurnscoe (WRY), named from trees, the birch, hazel and thorn respectively. Swinscoe (St) means 'wood for swine', Litherskew (NRY) literally 'wood of the slope', Myerscough (La) 'marsh wood', and Haddiscoe (Nf) 'Hadd's wood, with the first element a Scandinavian personal name.

ON *lundr* 'small wood, grove' also had a meaning 'sacred grove' in Scandinavia, but as pointed out in Chapter Ten we cannot point to a single unequivocal instance of this usage in this country. It has given Lound (L, Nt, Sf), Lund (ERY, La, NRY, WRY) and Lunt (La) and in compounds often today appears as -land, as in Hasland (Db), Plumbland (Cu), and Shrubland (Sf) named form the hazel, the plum-tree and shrubs respectively. Rowland (Db) means 'grove where roe-deer are found', Timberland (L) 'where timber is got', while others are from the name of an early owner Boie in Boyland (Nf), Snell in Snelland (L), and Tóli in Toseland (Hu). Attention was drawn in Chapter Four to two Scandinavian personal name compounds in *lundr*, Aveland (L) and Framland (Lei), which are the names of wapentakes.

Modern English *hurst* or *hirst* is derived from OE *hyrst*, the meaning of which in place-names is usually 'wooded hill'. It has been demonstrated that the occurrence of this word is heavily weighted to Surrey and the Weald of Kent and Sussex, though it is fairly common in other parts of England. It survives in major names as Hirst (Nb, WRY) and as Hurst (Brk, K, So, Wa). In compound names the first element is, not surprisingly, the name of a tree in Ashurst (K, Sx), Buckhurst (Ess, Sx), Ewhirst (Ha, Sr, Sx), Lyndhurst (Ha) and Salehurst (Sx) from the ash, beech, yew, lime, and sallow respectively, while that in Nuthurst (La, Sx, Wa) and Fernhurst (Sx) is self-explanatory. It is the name of an animal in Deerhurst (Gl) and Hartest (Sf) and in Brockhurst (Wa) 'badger', Gayhurst (Bk) 'goat' and Tickenhurst (K) 'kid', and of a bird in Crowhurst (Sr) and Hawkhurst (K), identical with which, perhaps surprisingly, is Haycrust (Sa). Sandhurst (Brk, Gl, K) and Stonyhurst (La) are self-explanatory and Midhurst (Sx) apparently means '(place) among wooded hills'. Colyhurst (La) seems to be 'coaly wooded hill', and though the exact significance is uncertain, the suggestion that this was from charcoal burning is certainly attractive. In several cases the wooded hill was named from an early owner – Bada in Bathurst (Sx), Billing in Billingshurst (Ha), Broca in Brockenhurst (Ha), and Cibba in Chippinghurst (O), while Doddinghurst (Ess) and Warminghurst (Sx) are derived from group-names – 'Dudda's people' and 'Wyrm's people' respectively.

The commonest of all Old English topographical terms in English place-names is *lēah*, modern *lea*. Though 'glade, clearing' is the meaning in very many place-names, the earliest appears to have been 'wood, forest'. Numerous studies of this word have been made over the past thirty years and as a result we can say that "*lēah* is an indicator of woodland which was in existence and recognized as ancient when English speakers arrived in any regions" to quote Dr Gelling. In this connection it is worth noting that The Weald (K-Sx) is recorded in Old English as *Andredesleage* as well as *Andredesweald*. Later the word came to mean 'meadow, pasture' in some place-names. This is also a very common meaning in field-names, for instance in north-east Lincolnshire where the plural *Leas* is frequent in appellative use as well, as the latest volumes of the English Place-Name Society for that county demonstrate.

In a study of place-names in Warwickshire, Dr Margaret Gelling suggested that isolated names containing *lēah* are likely to refer to woods in open country, while clusters of them may well contain the word in a quasi-habitative sense denoting settlements in forest clearings. Three meanings are to be considered in attempting to translate this word when it occurs in place-names – 'wood, forest', 'glade, clearing in a wood' and in later Old English 'meadow, pasture'; the choice between them will depend on local conditions.

The occurrence of *lēah* in English place-names is widespread though unevenly distributed, for example being less common in the North-west and South-east than in some other parts of the country. As a simplex name it is found in the form Lea in at least six counties, as Lee in at least five, but it is commonest as Leigh in at least sixteen. As the second element of a compound place-name, however, the number must be reckoned in hundreds. It was noted, for example, no less than 147 times in Derbyshire, of which some forty-two are the names of parishes.

As we should expect with so common a place-name element the first part is often a personal name and the following list provides a representative selection: Aldhere in Alderley (Ch), Beorn in Barnsley (WRY), Be(o)cca in Beckley (K, O), Blecca in Bletchley (Bk), Cēolmund in Cholmondeley (Ch) and Chumleigh (D), Cufa in Cowley (Bk, O, St), Dudda in Dudley (Wo), Hocca in Hockley (Ess), Cynemær in Kimberley (Nt), Cyneheard in Kinnerley (Sa) and Kinnersley (He, Wo), Cēnwulf in Knowsley (La), Locc in Loxley (St, Wa), Otta in Otley (Sf, WRY), Wemba in Wembley (Mx), Wendel in Wensley (NRY), and Wilmund in Wymondley (Hrt), each being a masculine name. A few feminine names also occur: Ælfgȳð in Alveley (Sa), Aldgȳð in Audley (St), and Cyneburg in Kimberley (Nf). Several are derived from group-names – 'Citta's people' in Chiddingly (Sx), 'Cnotta's people' in Knottingley (WRY), 'Mada's people' in Madingley (C), as well as 'fen dwellers' in Finningley (Nt).

Practically every kind of native tree appears in names in -ley: alder in Alderley (Gl), ash in the common Ashley, aspen in Apsley (Bd), Aspley (Bd, St, Wa), Espley (Nb), birch in Berkeley (Gl), Berkley (So), box in Boxley (K), bramble in Bromley (Mx), elm in Almeley (He), Elmley (K, Wo), hawthorn in Hatherleigh (D), Hatherley (Gl), hazel in Haseley (O, Wa, Wt), lime in Lindley (WRY), maple in Mapperley (Db), oak in Acle (Nf), Eagle (L), Oakleigh (K) and the common Oakley, plum in Plumley (Ch), spruce in Sapley (Hu), thorn in Thorley (Hrt, Wt), Thornley (Du), willow in Willey (Ch, He, Wa), withy in Weethley (Wa), Widley (Ha), Withiel (So), wych-elm in Weekley (Nth), and yew in Uley (Gl).

Other names denote the crops which grew there: flax in Flaxley (Gl, WRY), and Lilley (Hrt), Linley (Sa), Lindley (Lei, WRY), hay in Fawley (Ha, He), Filleigh (D) and Hailey (Hrt, O), oats in Oteley (Sa) and wheat in Whatley (So) and the common Wheatley. Similarly, many are derived from the names of other plants: bent grass in the common Bentley, broom in Bramley (Db, Ha, Sr, WRY), Bromley (Ess, Hrt, K, St) and Broomley (Nb), chag, a dialect word for broom or gorse, in Chailey (Sx), clover in Claverley (Sa), Cloverley (Sa), fern in Fairley (Sa), Fairlight (Sx), Farnley (WRY) and the common Farleigh and Farley, furze in Farsley (WRY) and Freseley (Wa), gale in Gailey and Wyreley (both St), reeds in Reedley (La), Ridley (Ess, K), Rodley (Gl), as well as Hadleigh (Ess, Sf), Hadley (Hrt, Sa), Headley (Ha, Sr, Wo, WRY) and Hedley (Du, Nb), all meaning 'heath glade or clearing'.

OE *lēah* is also found with the name of an animal, both domesticated and wild: beaver in Bewerley (WRY), boar in Barley (La, WRY), Barlow (Db), as well as Everley (NRY), bull in Booley (Sa), calf in Callaly (Nb), Calveley (Ch), deer in Darley (Db), Durley (Ha), goat in Gateley (Nf), hind in Hiendley (WRY), Hindley (Ha), horse in the common Horsley, sheep in Shipley in many counties, stud or herd of horses in Stoodleigh (D), Studley (O, W, Wa, WRY), wether-sheep in Waresley (Hu), and wolf in Woolley (Brk, Db, Hu, WRY). Here, too, may be included Birley (Db) 'clearing with a byre', Loseley (Sr) 'with a shed or pigsty', and Butterleigh (D) and Butterley (Db, He), names in which *lēah* is likely to mean 'pasture, meadow' since the first element is OE *butere*, modern *butter*, presumably denoting rich meadow or pasture producing good butter.

Occasionally it is found with the name of an insect, as in Brisley (Nf) 'gad-fly', Hamsterley (Du) 'corn-weevil', Midgley (WRY) 'midge' and Beeleigh (Ess), Beoley (Wo) 'bees', with which may be compared Honiley (Wa) 'honey wood or clearing'. More frequently, however, it is the name of a bird as in Corley (Wa) 'crane', Crawley (Bk, Ess, Ha) 'crow', Arley (Ch, La, Wa, Wo), Areley Kings (Wo) and Earnley (Sx) 'eagle', Finchley (Gl), Finkley (Ha) 'finch', Hawkley (Ha) 'hawk', Kitley (D) 'kite', and Shrigley (Ch) 'shrike'. Presumably here the meaning of *lēah* is 'wood'.

Other examples of *lēah* are named from natural features, for example Chinley (Db) 'deep valley' Dingley (Nth) 'dingle', the common Morley 'marsh or moor', Shelley (Ess, Sf, WRY) 'shelf', while Marley (D) means 'boundary wood or glade'. The nature of the ground is indicated in Evenley (Nth) 'level', Hardley (Ha, Wt) 'hard', Rowley, in several counties, 'rough'. Slaley (Nb) 'mud', Softley (Du, Nb) 'soft' and Stanley, also a common name, 'stone, i.e. stony'. The *lea* at Smalley (Db, La) was 'narrow', that at Langley, a common place-name, 'long', Bradle (Do) and Bradley, in almost every county, 'spacious', Mickley (Db, Nb) 'big', while Hanley, Handley and Henley, each repeated in various parts of the country, were named from their 'high' situation. Finally two common names, Staveley and Yardley, have as their first element words meaning 'stave' and 'rod' respectively. Presumably these were the names of woods where staves and rods were got.

The common Scandinavian term in English place-names for a 'clearing' is ON *þveit*, which survives in the North as *thwaite* in the senses 'forest clearing' and 'meadow in a low situation'. Whilst 'clearing' is undoubtedly the meaning in older names, that of 'meadow' is perhaps to be reckoned with when it occurs in minor names and in field-names. It is only common in the North-west, especially Cumberland, but it is found as far south as Norfolk and Suffolk where it survives in the name Thwaite. Occasionally as the second element of a compound name it has been replaced by *field* as in Brackenfield (Db), originally identical with Brackenthwaite (Cu) 'bracken', and in Stainfield (L) with Stonethwaite (Cu) 'stony clearing', both Brackenfield and Stainfield being Scandinavian compounds. Similarly, it has been replaced by *wood* in Eastwood (Nt) compared with Easthwaite (Cu) and in Storwood (ERY) 'brushwood clearing'. In Norfolk, as Dr Gelling has pointed out, it survives in minor place-names as -wick and -wight, in Guestwick, from the Scandinavian personal name Guist, and Crostwick, the first element of which means 'cross' as does that in Crostwight. *Thwaite* occurs with a variety of words, chiefly of Scandinavian origin. Terms for animals are found in Calthwaite (Cu) 'calves' and Storthwaite (NRY) 'stirks'; for crops and other plants in Haythwaite (NRY) 'hay', Haverthwaite (La) 'oats', Linethwaite (Cu) 'flax', Branthwaite (Cu) 'broom', and Seathwaite (Cu) 'sedge'; and for trees in Applethwaite (Cu, We), Hawthornthwaite (La), as well as Roundthwaite (We) 'mountain-ash' and Slaithwaite (WRY) 'sloe'. Braithwaite (Cu, NRY, WRY) means 'broad clearing', Micklethwaite (WRY) 'big clearing', while Castlethwaite (We) is near Pendragon Castle, Huthwaite (Nt, NRY) on a spur of land, and Seathwaite (La) near a lake. There is also a small group named from an early owner, as was the case with Guestwick – Eilifr in Allithwaite (La), Finnr in Finsthwaite (La), and the feminine Gunnhildr in Gunthwaite (WRY), all Scandinavian personal names.

A word found only in the Weald of Kent and Sussex and in bordering areas is OE *denn* 'woodland pasture', chiefly for swine, though occasionally place-names refer to other animals. It has been shown that the implication of the use of *denn* in the names of settlements is that they developed "from the activities of people who looked after animals in pastures separated from their home estates". Further, the (swine-) pasture was between eight and twenty miles from the "parent" village, but there is the well-known example of Tenterden (K) 'woodland pasture of the men of Thanet', Tenterden being no less that 45 miles away from Thanet. In time these denns became independent settlements in their own right. A few such names have a personal name as first element – Beaduríc in Bethersden, Bid(d)a in Biddenden, Ciolla in Chillenden, and Hróðwulf in Rolvenden, all in Kent as are the rest of the examples given unless otherwise noted. Cowden and Marden were apparently woodland pastures for cows and mares respectively; Playden (Sx) is literally 'play woodland pasture', whatever the significance of that happens to be, while Iden, also in Sussex, was noted for its yew-trees and Smarden in Kent for its rich pasture, since the first element means 'butter, fat, grease'.

Several terms for 'enclosure' occur in place-names. OE *gehæg* means 'fence, enclosure', but the prefix *ge-* was lost at an early date and leaves no trace in the names derived from the word. It is the source of Hay and Hey which are common in minor place-names. Rowney (Bd, Hrt) means 'rough enclosure', Woodhay (Brk) probably 'wide enclosure; while Oxhey (Hrt) is self-explanatory, and Broxa (NRY) and Idridgehay (Db) are derived from the Old English personal names Brocc and Éadríc respectively. Alternatively, the first element of Broxa may mean 'badger'. In Middle English the word can denote 'part of a forest fenced off for hunting'; this is the sense in Harthay (Hu) where harts were hunted, and in a number of minor names in parts of Derbyshire. It is especially common in some areas of Dorset and Devon and about 250 examples have been noted in the latter, many probably derived from the name of the medieval holder or owner; it is thought that here the term is used of a farm.

OE *haga* means 'hedge, enclosure' and the corresponding Scandinavian word, ON *hagi* 'enclosure, pasture'. As might well be expected these two words cannot be separated when they are found in areas where Danes and Norwegians settled. The Scandinavian word, however, is probably to be assumed where the first element is also Scandinavian. One or other is the source of Haigh (La, WRY), Haugh (L), and Hough on the Hill (L). The enclosure was for a 'herd of horses' in Stodday (La) and for 'cows' in Whaw (WRY). Breary (WRY) means 'briar enclosure', Thorney (Nt) and Thornhaugh (Nth) 'thorn enclosure', and Galphay (WRY) 'enclosure with a gallows', the gallows itself giving rise to three lost names, including the hill on which it stood.

It was pointed out in Chapter Five that it is difficult to distinguish place-names from OE *hām* 'homestead, village' from those derived from OE *hamm* even when early spellings are available. Furthermore, the etymological meaning of the latter is also difficult to determine but seems to be something like 'land in a river-bend'. From a topographical examination of place-names pretty certainly derived from *hamm* it has been deduced that it denoted land hemmed in by water, land in a river-bend, river-meadow, and promontory into lower land. These meanings have been suggested as a result of a great deal of painstaking research by a number of scholars, one of whom proposed an even more elaborate, indeed over elaborated, classification. It is worth noting, however, that modern dialect *ham* survives in the South and South Midlands as 'flat, low-lying pasture, land near a river'. In place-names, it now seems to be accepted that the earliest senses are likely to be 'land in a river-bend', 'promonotory of dry land into marsh or water' and that 'river-meadow', for example, is a later development of meaning. In a survey of this kind all one can say is that the meaning of *hamm* cannot always be determined in individual names and that, in one or other of the senses noted above, it appears commonest in the South and South Midlands of the country. *Hamm* is the source of the common Ham, Hamp (So) and East Ham and West Ham in Essex. In compounds the first element is sometimes an animal name 'deer' in Dyrham (Gl), 'otter' in Otterham (Co), or a bird-name 'crane' in Cranham (Gl) and 'swan' in Elvetham (Ha). Others are named from a crop, plant or tree as with Barkham (Brk) 'birch', Farnham (Sr) and Fernham (Brk) 'fern', Marcham (Brk) 'wild celery', and Witcham (C) 'wych-elm'. In a few cases the *hamm* was named from an early owner, Bōsa in Bosham (Sx), Cōla in Culham (O), Eof in Evesham (Wo), Fecca in Feckenham (Wo), and Passa in Passenham (Nth). In Kingsholme (Gl) it was possessed by the king. It should be noted here that *hamm* is common especially in the names of smaller places in Devon and these must belong to the later Anglo-Saxon period at earliest. It has been suggested that in Devon in particular it had developed a further sense of an enclosure for agricultural purposes, a cultivated plot of ground in marginal land. As Dr Gelling points out the "use of *hamm* in Devon place-names deserves attention from local historians".

Of the common terms for 'land', OE *land* itself occurs frequently in major names, though it was in fact used in various senses in place-names. In an earlier chapter we saw that it referred to a large area of land in Cumberland, Westmorland, and Holland in Lincolnshire, and this must have been the meaning too in Copeland (Cu) 'bought land', the name of a barony. In many other names it denoted a much smaller area and probably an estate. In compounds the *land* is named from an early owner or holder, Bēga in Byland (NRY), Cada in Cadland (Ha), Cydda in Kidland (Nb), Dot in Dotland (Nb) and þórólfr, a Scandinavian personal name, in Thurland (La). Others are from some natural feature as in the self-explanatory Brookland (K); Bowland (La-WRY) seems to have denoted a district characterized by bends. Burland (ERY) was land with a byre, while other places are named from animals found there: stirks in Strickland (We), a herd of horses in Studland (Do), swine in Swilland (Sf), and boar in Yaverland (Wt). Leyland (La) means 'fallow land', Redland (Gl) 'cleared land', and the common Newland and Newlands 'land newly brought into cultivation'. Indeed, Dr Gelling has suggested that 'new arable area' is a sense developed by *land* and of course this is really obvious in Newland(s). It may be noted here that *land* is also very common in medieval field-names in which its meaning is 'strip of land in the common field'.

The commonest place-name element for 'open land, open country', however, is *feld*, modern *field*, used in place-names of 'open country' or 'cleared space in woodland', as we saw at the beginning of the opening chapter. In Old English texts *feld* seems to have been contrasted with marsh, as well as with woodland and hills. It has been suggested that when the word occurs in village-names it probably means 'open land previously used for pasture'. *Feld* itself is well-represented in place-names recorded before 731, so it is a reasonable assumption that it was used in the formation of place-names in the early Anglo-Saxon period. But a name like Scrafield (L) 'open land with a landslip', a Scandinavian-English hybrid, shows that it continued in use till at least the 10th century.

This word is frequently compounded with a personal name: Ælfstān in Alstonfield (St), Cana in Canfield (Ess), Cāfhere in Caversfield (O), Hygerēd in Hurdsfield (Ch), Luffa in Luffield (Bk), and Wihthere in Wethersfield (Ess). Occasionally, it occurs also with a group-name as in Bassingfield (Nt) 'Bassa's people', Finchingfield (Ess) 'Finc's people', and Itchingfield (Sx) 'Ecci's people'.

There is also a group the first element of which is the name of an animal: wild-cat in Catsfield (Nf), deer in Darfield (WRY), kid in Titchfield (Ha), lamb in Enfield (Mx), sheep in Sheffield (Sx), wethers in Withersfield (Sf) and note too Austerfield (WRY) 'open land with a sheepfold'. In others it is a bird: dove in Duffield (Db, ERY), duck in Duckinfield (Ch), eagle in Yarnfield (St, W), and jackdaw in Cavil (ERY). Netherfield (Sx) is 'open land infested by adders' and Dronfield (Db) 'by drones'. It denotes crops in Hayfield (Db) and Whatfield (Sf) 'wheat', or plants, as in Bentfield (Ess) 'bent grass', Bramfield (Sf), Bromfield (Cu, Sa) and the common Broomfield 'broom', Dockenfield (Ha) 'dock', and Mayfield (St) 'madder'. Few compounds of *feld* and a tree-name occur, but the first elements of Bockenfield (Nb) and Lindfield (Sx) are adjectives, formed from the names of trees, meaning 'growing with beech' and 'growing with lime-trees' respectively.

Sometimes the 'open land' has been named from a near-by river: Blythe in Blithfield (St), Pant in Panfield (Ess), and Sheaf in Sheffield (WRY). The reference is to soil in other 'feld' names like Kelfield (ERY, L) 'chalk', or to the type of cultivation as in Wingfield (Db) 'pasture'. The first element in the common Bradfield means 'spacious', Chalfield (W) 'cold', Micklefield (WRY) 'big'; Shenfield (Ess) and Fairfield (Db) each mean 'beautiful' and the common Whitfield and Whitefield 'white', which may refer to chalky land, or is possibly used in the sense dry, hence 'dry open land', the meaning in fact of Therfield (Hrt). Brafield (Nth) and Brayfield (Bk) each have as first element OE *bræ-gen*, modern *brain*, used in some transferred topographical sense such as 'raised', as has recently been suggested. Wakefield (Nth, WRY) might perhaps mean 'Waca's open land', but is much more likely to be 'open land where festivities take place', from OE *wacu*, modern *wake*, as in Burnley Wakes or Oldham Wakes.

The exact sense of OE *mōr*, modern *moor*, is uncertain, though it seems to have been used in early place-names in the sense both of marshy ground and of barren upland. Today, the meaning 'marshland' is chiefly restricted to the Midlands and South, that of high uncultivated land being found especially in the north. In one or other of its early meanings it is the source of the common Moor or Moore, as well as More (Sa), and sometimes one or other has been added to a place-name as in Ilkley Moor (WRY). *Moor*, however, is not particularly common in major names except when combined with OE *tūn* 'village, estate' in the common Moreton and Morton, of which Dr Gelling has noted no less than forty-five instances. As the second element of a compound name the following may be noted: Barmoor (Nb) 'where berries grow', Radmore (St) 'red', Sedgemoor (So) 'where sedge grows', Stainmore (NRY-We) 'stony' and Wildmore (L) 'uncultivated', as well as a few from the names of early owners – Ceacca in Chackmore (Bk) and Cott in Cottesmore (R).

OE *hǣð*, modern *heath*, means 'heather, uncultivated land covered with heather' and the latter is in all probability the sense in the common Hatton 'heath village, estate'. However, in Hatfield (ERY, Ess, He, Hrt, Nt, Wo, WRY) the meaning must be 'open land where heather grows'. The simplex, Heath (Bd, Db, He, Sa, WRY) is no doubt self-explanatory, as are Blackheath (K, Sr) and Horseheath (C), while the first element in Small Heath (Wa) means 'narrow'; in Hampstead Heath (Mx) and Walton Heath (Sr), *heath* has been added to an older name, a fairly common occurrence.

eighteen

Modern place-names

As we saw at the end of the first chapter, the giving of place-names still goes on today. Indeed, a remarkable number of new names have arisen in the 18th, 19th, and 20th centuries as can be seen from the work of Adrian Room. The names discussed here, are restricted to those given in the past 250 years or so. They fall into a number of clearly defined groups, together with one which can only be called miscellaneous.

The largest of these groups consists of place-names derived from family names. Some of these are used alone, as in the case of Ansdell (La), a district named after Richard Ansdell, a 19th century painter, while Carrington (L, Nt) commemorates the banker Robert Smith, created Baron Carrington in 1796. He owned land in Nottingham and in the South Riding of Lindsey, and the Lincolnshire name came into being when the fens were enclosed in 1812. Downham in Lewisham (K) is the name of a district formed after the first World War, taking its name from that of the Chairman of the London County Council. Fleetwood (La), too, arose from the development of the area and in 1836 was given its name from that of Sir Peter Hesketh Fleetwood on whose estate new docks were built. Moira (Lei) also arose as a result of industrial development, in this case coal, and again the name is that of the land-owner, Francis Rawdon-Hastings, Earl of Moira, from Moira in Northern Ireland. Moira as a place-name is apparently first recorded in 1836. Wentworth (Sr), the site of the famous golf course, takes its name from the house, now the Club House, built about 1800, and named from a former owner Mrs Elizabeth Wentworth.

A few new names derived from family names have had *ton* added, no doubt on the analogy of the large number of old names derived from OE *tūn*. Two near Derby are late 19th century formations – Allenton from the name of the builder of the houses there and Crewton named in

1895 from Sir Vauncey Crewe, a large land-owner in the district, Crewton for some time previously being known as Newton. Beckton (Ess) takes its name, apparently in 1869, from the governor of the Gas, Light and Coke Company, a Mr. S.A. Beck, while Coryton (Ess) probably takes its name from the Chairman of Messrs Cory Brothers and Co who opened an oil refinery there in 1922. In one case, Akroydon in Halifax (WRY), a model-village for mill-workers, the modern name has been given the appearance of an ancient name by the suffix -don being added to the name of a local benefactor Edward Akroyd.

There are more names to which Town is added to the family name. Arkwright Town (Db) is named form that of Sir Richard Arkwright, the inventor of the spinning frame, who bought the manor of Sutton near Chesterfield in 1824. Ellistown (Lei) is, like Moira, another coal-mining village founded by a Mr J.J. Ellis, the colliery being opened in 1875-76. Halse Town (Co) is named from a local businessman and M.P., James Halse, and Kemp Town (Sx) from another M.P., Thomas Read Kemp, who is said to have 'laid out' the district c. 1830.

Several other names owe their origins to titles like Canons Town (Co) from Canon John Rogers, who owned land there, and Princetown (D) from the Prince of Wales, later George IV, who owned Dartmoor as part of the Duchy of Cornwall and who gave the land on which the prison was built from 1806-13. Princetown, of course, became the name of the village which grew up around the prison. The Dukes of Leeds have given their name to Leedstown (Co), while York Town (Sr) takes its name from Frederick, Duke of York, who founded the Royal Military College at nearby Sandhurst in 1812.

The Saviles, who owned land in the township of Thornhill (WRY), are commemorated in Savile Town, as are the Somers in Somers Town (Mx), a name first recorded in 1795. The editors of *The Place-Names of Middlesex* comment that this appears to be the earliest example "of the London use of *Town* to denote an urban unit regularly laid out, usually on a part of an estate hitherto not built over". In actual fact, Camden Town (Mx) is also first recorded in the same year, taking its name from Charles Pratt, Earl Camden.

Other family names have formed compound place-names with a variety of words added or prefixed, a common one being Park. Here, we have Bedford Park (Mx) dating from 1877 and named from the Dukes of Bedford; Northwick Park (Mx) from the Northwick family, lords of the manor of Harrow; Raynes Park (Sr) from the Rayne family which held land there in the 19th century before the construction of the railway and the opening of the station in 1871; Regents Park (Mx) fom the Prince Regent, later George IV, the first reference to the name so far noted being in 1817; and Tufnell Park (Mx) preserves the name of William Tufnell, who held the manor of Barnsbury in 1753, though building apparently did not take place till after 1832.

Only occasional examples of other words used as prefixes or affixes have been noted, like Green in Acocks Green (Wo), which seems to commemorate a family Acock which is recorded in the district in the 17th century; hill in Bexleyhill (Sx), referred to as *Boxall Hill* in 1736 and probably to be associated with a Boxall family, which also gave its name to Boxall's Moor in Linchmere parish; and sand in Blundellsands (La) from the Blundell family, a member of which is said to have bought, in the early 19th century, sandhills for building development. Finally in this group, Saltaire (WRY) according to *The Place-Names of the West Riding of Yorkshire* was founded by Sir Titus Salt in 1813, when he established his mills on the R. Aire. The date is incorrect and should be 1853. The name, of course, is a compound of Sir Titus' surname and the R. Aire, an unusual formation for which no parallel has so far been found.

A particularly interesting name is Maryport (Cu), the history of which is well authenticated, and which may well be the only modern place-name with a feminine forename as first part. The earlier name was *Elnefoot* 'the foot of the R. Ellen', which survived till at least the mid 18th century. A harbour was constructed here between 1750 and 1760 by Humphrey Senhouse, who gave his new port the name of his wife Mary.

We have seen in earlier chapters that there are no older place-names derived from French *ville*. However, particularly in the late 18th and 19th centuries it seems to have been fashionable to form new names with the terminal -ville. Pentonville (Mx) and Pittville (Gl) are named from developers, – Henry Penton M.P. for Winchester, who began to build at Pentonville round about 1773 and Joseph Pitt M.P., who in the 1820s began to develop land he owned, including the Pump Room at Cheltenham. Thornville (WRY), first recorded in 1771, appears to have been a pure invention by a Colonel Thornton. Cliftonville (K) apparently took its name from Cliftonville Hotel which was opened in 1868, and Waterlooville (Ha) derived from an inn called The Heroes of Waterloo. Charterville Allotments (O) are named from the Chartists.

The development was begun in 1847 by Feargus O'Connor "who bought here a farm of 300 acres, divided into allotments with cottages, and set eighty-one North country mechanics to live on them". The source of this information concludes laconically "The scheme was unsuccessful", but the name survives. Bournville (Wo) owes its origin to the estate founded in 1879 for workers at George Cadbury's chocolate factory. It seems that it had been intended to call the district Bournbrook after a Hall on the Bourne Brook, but this was changed to its present name "because it had a French sound".

Coalville (Lei) speaks for itself and is another modern name arising from industrial development. It has been first noted in the form Whitwick-Coalville in 1838, Whitwick being the name of the parish in which Coalville was situated. Woodville (Db), however, has a quite different explanation. It is first recorded in 1836 on the first edition of the Ordnance Survey map as *Wooden Box Station*. The history of the name is given in *The Midland Counties Historical Collector*, ii, number 26, 1 Sept. 1856 and is worth quoting in full. "A populous village of potters has sprung up in its neighbourhood (i.e. Butt House) by the name of 'Wooden Box', or more commonly 'The Box' derived, as is well known, from a hut set up there for a person to sit in to receive the toll at the turnpike. The *Historical Collector* may add that this wooden box was originally a port wine butt from Drakelow Hall. In 1845 the name of the place was changed from Wooden-Box to Woodville, and formed into 'The consolidated Chapelry of Woodville' by an order of the Queen in Council, June 17th, 1847 – See *The London Gazette of July 6th*, 1847".

A whole group of names in -ville in the south of the South Riding of Lindsey (L) originated with the drainage of the fens and the enclosure of the land there. Each, however, is based on an older name so that Eastville is earlier East Fen, Midville Mid Fen, and Westville West Fen. Frithville was in medieval times known as *The Frith*, while Langriville takes its name from a place called Langrick 'long stream or straight stretch of river'. Each was formed into a township by act of Parliament in 1812. It may be noted, too, that Carrington, discussed at the beginning of this chapter, was formed as a township at the same time.

The names of a number of places or districts formed during the past 250 years or so are derived from the names of buildings. Branksome, near Poole, (Do) takes its name from Branksome Tower recorded as such in 1863. The house was probably named from the setting of Sir Walter Scott's *Lay of the Last Minstrel* published in 1805.

Castle Howard (NRY) is the name of the mansion, built by Charles Howard, Earl of Carlisle. Castletown (Do) is named from Portland Castle and St Annes on Sea (La) is from the church dedication, the church itself being built in 1872-73 as the first building of the proposed 'new town'. Seaforth, also in Lancashire, was originally the name of a house owned by Sir John Gladstone, whose wife was a Mackenzie. The head of the clan was Baron Seaforth and Mackenzie, hence the modern name. Stocksbridge near Bradfield (WRY) has a much more prosaic origin for it takes its name from a bridge first recorded in 1841. The same is true of Stonebridge Park (Mx) for *The Stone Bridge* is recorded in a survey by John Rocque of 1741-45, but houses were not built there till 1875, the estate being called Stonebridge Park. The explanation of Strawberry Hill (Mx), like Branksome, has literary associations. The details given in *The Place-Names of Middlesex* provide interesting reading. The editors note that a house nicknamed *Chopped Straw Hall* had been built about 1698 and that this was bought by the writer Horace Walpole in 1748 and rebuilt. In looking through some old deeds Walpole found a reference in one of them to a *Strawberry Hill Shot* and "adopted the name for his new house".

As we shall see in a later chapter there are many minor names and field-names which have been transplanted from places in Britain and indeed abroad. A few such names have become those of places or districts, one of the most well-known examples being Belgravia (Ln). The name of the district is taken from Belgrave Square and this in turn is from Belgrave in Cheshire, owned by the Dukes of Westminster. The area was developed in the 1840's and Room notes a further literary association in that William Thackeray uses the name Belgravia in *Vanity Fair*, published in 1848.

Dresden (St) dates from the middle of the last century when houses were built by the Longton Freehold Land Society, many members of which were china manufacturers. Again according to Room, Dresden was chosen as the name of the new estate because of the famous china produced at Dresden in Germany. Dunkirk (Ch, K, Nt, St) is found fairly frequently in field-names as well, where it often has overtones of remoteness. It may be a 'commemorative' name, though the exact connection with the French Dunkerque has never been properly explained. Perhaps it should be just regarded as a nickname of remoteness rather than associating it with some historical fact like the Duke of York's disasterous siege in 1773.

New Holland (L), first noted in 1828, is said in 1842 to be a "new hamlet ... where a large Inn was built on the Humber bank about ten years ago". According to one theory the name was given by a Mr Thomas Lumley, died 1845, who landed smuggled goods there. Another theory, however, is that it is a transferred name from Holland, one of the three Divisions of Lincolnshire, because both are low-lying, though no evidence has so far been found to confirm this suggestion.

Another name frequently found in minor names is Gospel Oak, of which the Middlesex example has actually become the name of a district. The oak here is mentioned in 1761 and 1819, but has since been cut down. The name arose from the Rogation ceremony of Beating the Bounds, which took place in the week preceding Ascension Day. The village officials accompanied by the vicar walked round the boundary of the parish to make sure no boundary mark had been moved. At each mark the party halted and a passage of Scripture was read or a prayer said. Hence Gospel Oak was an oak tree at which a halt was made and a passage from the Gospels read. This particular Gospel Oak was on the boundary between the parishes of Hampstead and St Pancras.

A number of modern places have developed around a public house. The best known examples are probably Nelson (La), Cliftonville (K), and Waterlooville (Ha), already discussed. Bay Horse (La), Black Dog (D), Cherry Tree (La), and Craven Arms (Sa) each takes its name from that of an inn, as does Triangle in Sowerby (WRY). Triangle was the name of a triangular piece of land on which stood The Triangle Inn. An industrial village developed there in the second half of last century, hence the modern name Triangle. Another West Riding name was originally known by the name of the inn Queen's Head, so recorded in 1821. It was subsequently changed to Queensbury by common consent at a public meeting held 8 May 1863. Swiss Cottage (Mx), too, was was the name of a Chalet-Style inn, the Swiss Tavern, built in 1803-4, changed to its present-day name, and rebuilt almost thirty years ago. Perhaps the most unusual of this type of name is also the oldest so-far noted – New Invention in Walsall (St). The explanation of the name is really not known, but Room records its existence as early as 1663 and comments that "the inn name seems the likeliest derivation".

Some modern place-names appear to have been invented for the purpose. Brierfield (La), for example, is a township which arose in the last century in the cotton manufacturing district of Burnley and Nelson. Situated between the two, it is near to Briercliffe and it has been suggested that the choice of name has been influenced by the form of the latter, though no evidence survives to confirm this. On the other hand, the history of Camberley (Sr) is fairly well understood. It was earlier known as Cambridge Town after the Duke of Cambridge, who built the Staff College there in 1862. The change to Camberley is believed to have been for postal convenience to avoid the clash with the city of Cambridge.

Room notes that the name Peacehaven (Sx) was chosen in a competition held just after the first World War, apparently as a symbol of peace. The place had military associations and had been known as Anzac-on-Sea, because Anzac troops had been stationed there. The choice of the name and the former presence of Australian and New Zealand soldiers may well have been connected.

Sunningdale (Brk) was formed as an ecclesiastical parish in 1841 and as a civil parish in 1894. It included Sunninghill and may well have been named from *Sunning Hill Dale* recorded on a map of Windsor Park, dated 1800.

It will have been noted that names such as Bournville, Maryport, and Saltaire have arisen as a result of industrial development in the 18th and 19th centuries. Indeed, these form an important group of 'modern' names and three or four additional examples are worth quoting. Various reasons have been put forward to explain Etruria (St). What is certain is that it was the name given to the district around Josiah Wedgewood's pottery, in 1769. Wedgewood, himself, had built a house there called Etruria Hall and the name was probably given in an allusion to Etrurian pottery. The construction by Abraham Darby of the first coldcast iron bridge in the world quite naturally gave rise to Ironbridge (Sa) as we saw in an earlier chapter, while Port Sunlight (Ch), originally the name of an industrial estate, is from Sunlight Soap made at a factory there. Stourport (Wo) developed around "the basin that linked the Stour with the canal first planned here in 1756 by James Brindley". The canal was known as The Staffordshire and Worcestershire Canal and connected The Trent and Mersey Canal with the Severn at Stourport. Room notes that the latter appears to be the only "new town" to be situated on a canal.

Just as some modern place-names have arisen as a result of industrial development, so others are the result of the rise in the popularity of seaside resorts in the late 18th and particularly in the 19th century. Fairhaven (La) appears in one sense a typical modern name with its overtones of agreeableness, especially for a part of the seaside resort of Lytham. New Brighton (Ch) is also typical, but in this case of transferred names. It apparently dates from developments in the 1830s and quite clearly was named after Brighton (Sx), already firmly established as a resort. It seems to be first recorded on the Tithe Award Map of 1841. In Bournemouth (Do), three districts Northbourne, Southbourne, and Westbourne, which developed in the late 19th century, incorporate the name of the stream which gave its name to Bournemouth itself. Clearly they were so-named in contrast to each other. Southport (La), however, has not been properly explained. According to Room, a William Sutton built an hotel here, later called Duke's Folly. At a dinner to celebrate its opening the resort was named South Port by a Dr Barton, for what reason is quite unknown.

On Ptolomy's map of c. 150, *Morikambē* seems to denote the Lune estuary but the name has no continuous history. The present-day Morecambe (La) is clearly an antiquarian reintroduction of the Greek form of what is a Celtic name. The identification seems to have been made by the Lancashire historian Whitaker in 1771 and this led to the adoption of Morecambe Bay as a name. It was then used for the town which grew up as a result of the holiday industry in the 19th century. So, the old Celtic name was reintroduced and the name "caught on".

Westward Ho! (D) is unique as the only place-name in England with an exclamation mark as part of the name. It takes its name from the title of Charles Kingsley's novel of 1855, many scenes of which are actually set in the area. A company was formed to develop a resort here and an Hotel, the Westward Ho! Hotel was opened in 1865 and by the 1870s it had become an established seaside resort. Westward Ho! is probably also unique in being the only English place-name to be directly taken from the title of a novel.

At least two names originated from the settlement in this country of Moravians. One is Fairfield in Droylesden (La) and this would appear to be of the complementary type for a model village developed in 1783 by refugees. The Moravians also bought an estate at a place called *Fall Neck* in Pudsey (WRY), where they also established a model village. Their original home was at Fulneck in Silesia, so that it is easy to see how the earlier name was adjusted to the present-day Fulneck.

Finally, place-names are still being given today. The Ministry of Defence sold to developers the residential part of the Royal Air Force airfield at Binbrook (L). The houses were sold to private individuals and it was decided in 1991 that they should be consulted about the name of the 'new village'. From a number of suggestions the name they chose was Brookenby. It is clear that this is only one example of a new name for similar developments, for Cherry Park is the name which has been given to the residential area of the former airfield at North Coates also in Lincolnshire.

nineteen

Street-names

Most of the names discussed in this chapter are of medieval origin. Later street-names are often derived from the name of a local landowner or tenant and, though invaluable for the local historian, they are comparatively easy to interpret. Salthouse Lane (Lincoln) is a good example of this. It is first recorded in 1842 and in the Census Return for 1851 a Charles S. Salt was living at No. 3 and Frederick Salt at No. 30. The name clearly has nothing to do with a *salthouse* and has been named from the Salt family.

Many medieval street-names have been lost because of the constant rebuilding in larger towns. Enough of them, however, survive to make it possible for us to obtain an idea of their general character. They give useful information on the early history and development of the particular town, especially on the various trades found there as well as their location. If we added to the surviving names all those now lost, a comprehensive picture of a medieval town could be obtained.

It is impossible at present to give examples of street-names from all the medieval towns in England, for detailed surveys of many are not yet available, but in what follows as wide a selection as possible has been illustrated. Numerous other examples will be found in the volumes of the English Place-Name Society and in Eilert Ekwall's *Street-Names of the City of London*, as well as in local studies already published for towns in counties not yet completed by the Society.

Most street-names end in *street* or *lane*. The distinction between the two seems to have been that *street* denoted a wider and more important way than *lane*, but this is not one which is, or perhaps even could be, consistently maintained. Of the two, *street* is by far the commoner, but in the North and North Midlands is often replaced by *gate*, from ON *gata* 'street'. This is not always easily distinguished from OE *geat*, modern *gate*, 'opening', the usual term for the entrance to a walled town, though as a rule the context will make it clear which is intended. For example, Bailgate (Lincoln) is today the name of a street, but originally it denoted one of the gates to the Bail, the wall of the outer court of the castle.

Three other terms, *row, alley,* and *hill,* are found less frequently. *Row* is used of a number of houses standing in a line, or of a street, particularly a narrow one, formed by two such lines of houses and often with a first part denoting the trade carried on there. Many such names have been lost; for example, in Norwich no less than thirteen have been noted in early sources but which no longer survive. *Alley* seems to refer to a passage into a house, or to a narrow lane, and *hill* is usually self-explanatory.

Most street-names are descriptive of size, situation, or importance. High St 'chief or principal street' is particularly common, and the comparable Highgate is found in the North, as in Kendal. King St, however, as the name of an important street, is usually modern, but an early example survives in Chippenham (W), while the first element in Coney St (York) is from ON *kunungr* 'king'. In York too, as well as Pontefract, there is the Scandinavian compound Micklegate 'great street', identical with which is Mitchelgate in Kirkby Lonsdale. An apparently unique name for a street meaning 'main street' is Boroughgate in Appleby, while Hare Lane, earlier Hare St, in Gloucester must have been an important thoroughfare since it is derived from OE *herestrǣt* 'army road, highway'.

North, South, East, and West St are self-explanatory, as are the corresponding Northgate, Southgate, Eastgate, and Westgate in the North and North Midlands. However, Eastgate and Westgate (Lincoln) and Northgate and Westgate (Gloucester), now the names of streets, were originally gates. Nether and Upper St, i.e. 'lower' and 'higher', are found in many towns, as well as Middle St, paralleled by Middlegate (Newark, Penrith). Similarly comparable to Broad St is Broadgate. A rare name is Small St in Bristol, in which *Small* is used in an earlier sense 'narrow'. Old St is uncommon in medieval street-names, as is New St. There are many examples of the latter in more modern names, for the most part formed with the extension of a town from its old centre.

A street paved with stones is sometimes called Stoney St, while Stonegate occurs in York. Comparable are High, Low, and Middle Pavement (Nottingham) and The Pavement (York), as well as Chiswell St (Finsbury) 'flint or pebble street'. Other references to the surface are not common, though occasional examples of Clay St are found as at Colchester. Honey Lane, on the other hand, is found in many small towns and villages, perhaps for a muddy or sticky way, but occasionally it may simply mean that honey was produced there. There are also Wet Lane, Stinking Lane, and Featherbed Lane, the last perhaps referring to a soft or muddy road. Other interesting names include Full St (Derby) 'dirty street', Lurk Lane (Beverley) 'dirty lane', and the occasional Summer Lane denoting a lane usuable only in summer. In London there is Addle St, probably one 'full of cow-dung', as well as two Pudding Lanes. These may simply have been lanes where puddings were sold or perhaps sticky like a pudding, or even, as Ekwall suggested, lanes down which *puddings* 'butchers' offal' were taken for disposal in the Thames.

The common term for cul-de-sac is Blind Lane, but Bag Lane and Pudding-bag Lane are also found, and, in Abingdon, Turnagain Lane, a name also found in London, which is earlier *Wendagain* 'turn back'. A secluded way is often called Love Lane and another name for a similar lane was Grope Lane, often with an early form *Gropecuntlane*. Apart from Grape Lane (York), the name has dropped out of use because of its suggestive connotations. As an 18th century local antiquarian put it, the York example "tends not a little to obscenity". A comparable name for a street of ill-repute may be Mutton Lane, if mutton was used of a loose woman, a prostitute, and Mab Gate in Leeds if *mab* here means 'loose woman'. It is hardly surprising that other similar ones, recorded in medieval sources, have subsequently been lost.

Streets and lanes named from their length or shape are fairly common; Long Lane and Long St are obvious examples, but they are rarely recorded at an early date, unlike Long St in Sherborne in Dorset which has been first noted in 1397. More interesting is Endless St (Salisbury), so named since it leads out beyond the limits of the city. Crooked Lane and Winding Lane are self-explanatory, but Crink Lane (Southwell) is less obvious and is derived from *crink* 'twist, bend', and there are in fact several sharp turns in the lane itself. In Lincoln a piece of land inside the Roman wall was known as The Bight 'land in the bend'. This became the name of a street, East Bight, which runs east-west, then bends to the south at an angle of 90 degrees. Its continuation to the west as early as the 13th century became known as West Bight.

Other common names indicate the place to which they led. Most explain themselves as with Bridge St and the corresponding Briggate

(Knaresborough, Leeds), Bridgegate (Rotherham) and Bridge Gate (Derby) both earlier *Briggate*, Castle St, as well as Castlegate (York) and Castlegate (Newark, Nottingham), Marsh Lane and Marsh St (Newbury), Mill Lane and Mill St, as well as Millgate (Macclesfield). In Hitchin, Portmill Lane led to the 'town mill' and in Finsbury, Turnmill St is named from a mill with a wheel. Streets or lanes which led to a well or spring are common enough, as in Well St, but Wallgate in Macclesfield is misleading, since it too means 'street leading to the well', *wall* representing the West Midlands dialectal form of *well*. In Beverley the Scandinavian compound Keldgate appears to be unique as a street-name, for it also means 'well street'. The self-explanatory Holywell St occurs several times, and in Totnes there is a Leechwell St, apparently from a spring 'where leeches are found'. Three wells in Colchester have given their names to streets: Childwell Alley led to a 'children's spring', Stanwell St to a 'stony well', and East and West Stockwell St to a 'spring marked by a tree-trunk'. Conduit St in Westminster and elsewhere was named from a water-channel and Fishpool St in St. Albans from the abbey fish ponds. Other streets take their names from the stream or river towards which they led like Ock St (Abingdon) the R. Ock, Ousegate (Selby, York) the R. Ouse, Skellgate (Ripon) the R. Skell, and Thames St (Wallingford) the R. Thames. Here, too may be included Ferry St (Lambeth) leading to a ferry across the Thames, from which Horseferry Road (Westminster) is also named, and Heath St (Barking) which led to a *hythe* or landing-place on the river.

In a number of towns including Gloucester, Lincoln, Nottingham, and Sherborne, there are streets called Newland(s), each leading to land newly brought into cultivation on the outskirts of the town. Such names are clearly of considerable importance for the local historian for some are recorded early like that in Lincoln, first noted in the late 12th century and that in Gloucester in the early 13th. They clearly throw light on the development of the town itself.

Numerous streets are named from the village or town to which they led and most are obvious enough. Some of the 'miscellaneous' destinations are unusual, some of special interest. Laith Gate (Doncaster) presumably led to a 'barn' and is a Scandinavian compound, Sheath St (Northwich) to a 'salt-pit', and Yield Hall Lane (Reading) to the Guildhall. Gallows St has occasionally survived to today, along with Gallowgate (Newcastle upon Tyne), Richmond (NRY), and Gallowtree Gate (Leicester), but Gallows St (Warwick) has replaced an earlier

Warrytreestreet 'street leading to the felon's tree, i.e. gallows'. Pillory St in London and Nantwich is self-explantory. Litchdon St (Barnstaple) was the way to the medieval 'cemetery' and with this can be compared Lich St (Worcester) literally 'corpse street', leading to the cemetery belonging to Worcester Cathedral, and also Dead Lane, once common in many towns but now frequently lost. On the other hand Bury St and Bury Lane, found in the South, usually represents OE *burh* in one of its post-conquest senses of 'manor, manor-house'.

Church St or Church Lane is found in many towns in England, and the Scandinavian compound Kirkgate occurs for example in Leeds, Ripon, and Wakefield. Many old streets are named from the dedication of the church to which they lead, often in the forms St. Giles St (Northampton) or simply as Magdalen St (Colchester, Exeter). Names of this type are usually self-explanatory, but Bow St (Durham) is from the church of St. Mary le Bow, Gillygate (York) and Gilly Gate (Pontefract) from a church dedicated to St. Giles, and Sidwell St (Exeter) from one dedicated to the virgin St. Sidwell. In London Foster Lane and Sise Lane are also from church-dedications to St. Vedast and St. Sithe respecively, while a unique name, St. Aldate St survives in Gloucester from a church dedicated to St. Aldate. Here too belongs Ladygate (Beverley) 'street leading to the church of Our Lady'.

Spital St, which is not uncommon, along with Hospital St (Nantwich) take their names from a medieval hospital. Abbey St and Abbeygate (Leicester) are, of course, named from an abbey, while College St in Northampton takes its name from the college of the clergy of All Saints there. Cross St is another common name and there are also occasional examples of compounds such as High Cross St in London and High Cross in Truro, as well as reference to a coloured cross in Red Cross St (Leicester, Ln) and White Cross St (Ln), though this last might well refer to a stone cross. Rood St and Rood Lane, from OE *rōd* 'cross', are rare, though the latter survives in Coventry and London. In Newport (Wt) there is a Holyrood St 'holy cross street'.

Street names from clerics include Archdeacon St (Gloucester), Bishop St (Coventry), Canon Row (Westminster), Preston St (Exeter) and Priestgate (Peterborough), both 'street of the priests', Monk St and the equivalent Monkgate (York), and Mincing Lane (Ln) 'lane of the nuns'. More common are Friar(s) St and Friar(s) Lane as well as Friargate (Derby, Penrith) and Friary St (Guildford), from one or other of the mendicant orders. More specifically there is Whitefriargate

(Hull) from the Carmelites, Blackfriargate (Hull) from the Dominicans and Greyfriars (Cirencester, Gloucester), Greyfriar Gate (Nottingham) and Grey Friars Lane (Coventry) from the Franciscans. Crouch St (Colchester) and Crutched Friars (Ln) take their names from the order of Crutched Friars or Friars of the Holy Cross, and The Minories in London is named from the abbey of the Minoresses, nuns of the second order of St. Francis known also as the Poor Clares.

The Bedern (York) means 'prayer house' and Little Sanctuary (Westminster) was a precinct of the abbey in which refugees could seek protection. In London, the neighbouring Amen Lane, Ave Maria Lane and Creed Lane are all later names, perhaps from the Rogation Ceremony of Beating the Bounds, or in imitation of Paternoster Row, though this is recorded from the early 14th century as *Paternosterstrete*, which Ekwall believed means 'street of the makers of rosaries'.

People of the same nationality lived together in medieval towns, a fact reflected by such names as Lombard St (Ln), Danesgate (Lincoln), though this seems to have originally meant 'Danish street', Flemingate (Beverley), Frenchgate (Richmond, NRY) and French Gate (Doncaster), French Row (St. Albans) as well as Petty France (Westminster) 'little France', and Scot Gate (Doncaster). Jews were usually segregated and so have given rise to such names as Jewbury (York) 'jews' quarter', Jury St (Warwick), Jewry St (Ln, Winchester), and Old Jewry (Ln).

A further group is named from animals or birds which were kept or found there. Occasional examples have been noted of Cock Lane (Ln), Culver St (Salisbury) 'doves' and Hengate (Beverley), of Cowgate (Norwich), Dog Lane (Nantwich) and Huggin Lane (Ln) 'hogs'. Boar Lane, however, is more likely to refer to an inn-sign. Stodman St (Newark) is earlier *Stodmare Street*, where the stud-mare was kept. Although Cat St (Oxford) is referred to in a medieval document as 'the street of the mouse-catcher', Cat was later taken to be a shortened form of *Catherine*, which was at one time the official name of the street. The place where bear-baiting took place has given Bear Lane in Bristol, with which can be compared Bearward St in Northampton, where the keeper of the bears lived. Bull-baiting is reflected in Bull Ring in Beverley, Birmingham, and Grimsby. In areas where Scandinavian influence is prominent Hungate is not uncommon as in Lincoln, Market Weighton and York, as well as Hounds Gate in Nottingham 'street where dogs are kept or found'.

Some of these names may perhaps refer rather to streets where such animals or birds were sold. This is perhaps the more likely explanation of Cowgate (Leicester, Norwich, Peterborough), Rother St (Stratford on Avon) 'cattle' and Sheep St, also in Stratford on Avon. Other commodities were (prepared or produced and) sold in Bread St (Bristol, Ln), with which may be compared Bakehouse St (Leicester), Corn St (Bristol), Fish Row (Salisbury), Fish Street Hill (Ln), Milk St (Exeter), Oaten Hill (Canterbury), Oat Lane (Ln), Oatmeal Row (Salisbury), Pepper Alley (Southwark), Pepper Lane (Coventry), Pepper St (Middlewich, Nottingham), Rye St (Bishop's Stortford), Salt Lane (Salisbury), Wheat St (Nuneaton), and Wine St (Bristol). Lime St in London and Wood St in Kingston on Thames as well as London are probably obvious enough, but Woodgate in Leicester appears to have been the way along which wood was transported into the town. Rather less obvious names of this type are Cowl St (Evesham) 'coal', Crock St (Barnstaple) 'pots', Hart St (Ln) probably 'hearthstones', and Whimple St (Plymouth) 'wimples'.

Gold St in Northampton is certainly where gold articles were made, for medieval sources indicate that goldsmiths had shops on the east side of the street. Silver St in London is comparable to Gold St and indeed is a fairly common 'lost' name in towns, like Lincoln. Though there are two lost Silver Lanes and a Silver St in the latter, the modern Silver St only dates from the late 18th century and this is paralleled elsewhere. Indeed, it has been suggested that others similarly only recorded late may well be transferred names from the well-known London street. So many street-names illustrate the kind of work going on there that it is surprising to find Do Little Lane in London, a lane which apparently served simply as a passage from one street to another.

Most towns have their Market Place, but in many cases Place has replaced an earlier *stead*, a word of similar meaning. Occasionally there is Market Hill (Cambridge, Watford) but more often Market St. Sometimes a particular commodity was sold there, as at Corn Market, a not uncommon name, Fishmarket (Hastings), Haymarket (Westminster), and Bigg Market (Newcastle upon Tyne) where barley was sold. Butter St (Alcester) was earlier *Buttermarket Street* and Butter Cross (Oakham, Winchester) a cross where butter was sold. There is also Beastmarket Hill in Nottingham and Horse Market in Northampton, and the annual sale of horses in various towns is still commemorated in Horse Fair (Banbury, Ripon), The Horsefair (Malmesbury), and Horsefair St (Leicester). Perhaps the most unusual name of this type is St. John Maddermarket, the name of a street in Norwich. St John refers to the church dedicated to St. John the Baptist, while Maddermarket was where madder was sold, presumably for the red dye got from the plant. In the recent survey of the place-names of Norwich no less than twenty lost names of markets have been recorded in the city, including an Apothecary, Leek, Pudding, Southbread, Tallow, Wastel 'bread made of the finest white flour', and Whitebread Market, the last two having identical meanings.

Towns were sometimes given the right to hold markets on particular days of the week, often one on Saturday and another on some other weekday. There are frequent references to these in medieval sources, where *Saturday Market* and *Weekday Market* are common names. These rarely survive, but there is still a Saturday Market and Wednesday Market in Beverley, a Weekday Cross in Nottingham, which was originally called *Weekday Market*.

OE *cēap* 'market' is the source of Cheap or Westcheap (now Cheapside) and Eastcheap in London, as well as Cheap St in Newbury and Sherborne, while Wincheap St in Canterbury, first recorded in the early 13th century, appears to mean 'waggon market'. A derivative of, *cēap* OE *cēping* has given rise to The Chipping in Wotton (Gl), Mealcheapen St (Worcester) 'meal market', and Cross Cheaping (Coventry), named from a cross near which the market was held. Another, and later derivative of the same word ME *chepere* 'market man', is the source of Chipper Lane, earlier St, 'street of the marketmen'.

One of the most famous names associated with the sale of food is The Shambles in York, formerly *Fleshshambles* 'flesh benches', so-named from the stalls set up for the sale of meat in the open air. An identical name with similar early forms is found also in Chesterfield and Ripon, and these can be compared with Fishamble St in Dublin. Many other medieval towns had their Shambles, though The Shambles in Worcester used to be called Baxter St and then later Baker St. The place where meat was sold was also called The Butchery (Ely) and there is a Butchery Green in Hertford and a Butchery Lane in Canterbury. Comparable names are Poultry in London and Nottingham and Poultry Cross in Salisbury where poultry was sold.

Often names indicating streets where various food or other articles were sold have as first element an occupational term. Many of those current in medieval times have been lost but others still remain and the nature of the goods (produced and) sold there is often obvious enough. There is Baxter's Row (Carlisle) and Baxter Gate (Doncaster) 'bakers';

Butcher Row (Coventry, Exeter, Ludlow, Salisbury, Shrewsbury), Butcher's Row (Bristol) as well as Fletcher Gate (Nottingham) 'flesh-hewer, i.e. butchers', the original spelling being later confused with *fletcher* 'arrow-maker'; Fisher St (Carlisle, Paignton), Fisher Row (Chesterfield), Fishergate (Norwich, Nottingham, York), Fisher Gate (Doncaster) and Fisher's Lane (Cambridge) 'fish-sellers'; Saltergate (Chesterfield, Lincoln) 'salt-merchants', though in some cases this denotes a road used by salt-merchants; Spicer St (St. Albans) and Spiceal St (Birmingham) 'spicers, i.e. grocers'; as well as Cook St (Coventry) and Cooks Row (Wimborne Minster) 'cooks', and Petty Cury (Cambridge), this last literally meaning 'little kitchen'.

Several are named from cloth-workers: wool-dealers lived in Woolmonger St (Northampton), dressers of wool in Wolsdon St (Plymouth), wool-combers in Cumbergate (Peterborough), makers and sellers of stockings in Hosier Lane (Ln), dealers in silks and velvets in Mercers Row (Northampton) and Mercery Lane (Canterbury). A similar name to the last is Drapery (Northampton) where cloth and linen workers or dealers lived. Cloth-finishers are commemorated in Tucker St (Bristol), cloth fullers in Walkergate (Beverley) and Walker Lane (Derby), dyers in Lister Gate (Nottingham), while bleaching was done in Blake St in York. Felt-makers carried on their trade in Felter Lane, also in York, rope-makers in Roper Gate in Pontefract, shoe-makers in Soutergate in Barton upon Humber, tanners in Tanner St in Barking and Winchester, as well as Barker Gate in Nottingham, saddlers in Sadler Gate in Derby and Sadler St in Durham, and makers of pilches, i.e. outer garments made of skin, in Pilcher Gate in Nottingham. Here we may note Rack St, from *rack* 'frame for stretching cloth' and Tenter Yard, from *tenter* a word with a similar meaning, for both are found in some towns.

Metal-workers, too, are well-represented in street-names: smith, a general term for a worker in metals, is the source of Smith St (Exeter, Warwick), goldsmith of Goldsmith St (Exeter) and Goldsmith's Lane (Wallingford), bridle-smith of Bridlesmith Gate (Nottingham), and wheel-makers of Wheeler Gate also in Nottingham. Billiter St (Ln) was the home of bell-founders and Skeldergate (York) of shield-makers. Ironmonger Lane (Ln) and Ironmonger Row (Coventry) are self-explanatory and Iron Gate in Derby also refers to workers in iron. Other trades recorded in surviving street-names include carters or carriers who are represented in Carter Gate (Nottingham, Scarborough), as well as Catherine St (Salisbury), where this modern form is due to popular etymology, coal-dealers in Colliergate (York), potters in both Crocker St (Newport, Wt) and Pottergate (Lincoln, Norwich), and water-bearers or carriers in Waterbeer St (Exeter), a medieval name and not as one might assume, a modern depreciative name. Birchin Lane (Ln) 'lane of the barbers' seems to be the only surviving example so far noted of a street named from this trade. As is to be expected, few street-names are from agricultural workers, but exceptions are Blossom St in York and Blossomgate in Ripon 'street of the ploughmen', and perhaps Stramongate in Kendal 'the street of the dealers in straw'. Stramongate appears to be unique as a name, the first element being a medieval occupational name recorded only in this street-name but not in any other early sources.

Another unique name is Bellar Gate in Nottingham 'street of the bellman or town crier', but a few others refer to sports or entertainments. Gluman Gate (Chesterfield) means 'street of the minstrels', Gigant St in Salisbury 'of the fiddlers' and we have already seen an example of this type of street-name in Bearward St in Northampton, also found elsewhere in medieval documents but subsequently lost. The meaning of Blowhorn St (Marlborough) is uncertain, but it is possible that a trumpeter lived or performed here. Bowling Alley is still fairly common, though usually recorded only in later sources and there is Bowlalley Lane in Hull similarly a late name. Threadneedle St (Ln) perhaps takes its name from a children's game and Pall Mall in Westminster is almost certainly from the game of *paille maille* or *pelmet*, introduced into England during the reign of Charles I.

It will have been noted that several of the street-names discussed above are unique and this is certainly true of two interesting names. Dollar St in Cirencester means 'street of the hall where charitable gifts were doled out' and Doomgate in Appleby denoted a street where trials were held, the first element being OE *dōm* 'judgement'.

Chancery Lane in London was formerly *Chancellor's Lane* and earlier still was *Convers Lane* from the Domus conversorum, the home for converted Jews. Fetter Lane also in London preserves ME *faitor* 'imposter, cheat', which was used particularly of beggars who sham illness or deformity. The exact significance of a third London street-name, Maiden Lane, found also in other towns, is uncertain, but it could well have had the sense of 'prostitutes' lane'.

Many streets recorded in later sources are taken from the signs of inns or taverns. Perhaps the most famous of these is Elephant and

Castle, an old coaching inn, now the name also of the crossroads. Other names of lanes or streets derived from the sign of the Angel, Bear, Bush, Dun Cow, Greyhound, Harp, Hart, Ship, Star, Sun, Swan, Whitehorse, and Woolpack can be found in many towns and the list could indeed be extended almost indefinitely.

Another group of street-names is that named from buildings like Old Bailey in London, The Baile in York, and North and South Bailey in Durham, each of which is derived from Old French *baille* 'outer defensive work of a castle, prison'. Barbican in London refers to the outer fortification of a town, and Warser in Warser Gate in Nottingham means 'building by the wall', i.e. the Anglo-Saxon wall of the city. The Brittox (Devizes) was originally a place fortified with stockades, and Garret Hostel Lane (Cambridge) a watch-tower or look-out place in a hostel on the site of what is now Trinity College.

It is an interesting and perhaps surprising fact that a number of street-names derived from the name of a person or of a family have survived to the present day. Baldwin St (Bristol) first recorded in the mid 13th century commemorates the name of a *Baldewin Albus* who was granted land in Bristol c. 1160; Bleke St in Shaftesbury is named from the *Blick*s, first mentioned there in 1314; the first element of Colegate in Norwich, mentioned as a street-name as early as c. 1220, is either the Old English personal name *Cola* or Scandinavian *Koli*, probably the latter, which would give a Scandinavian compound since the second element is *gata*. It may well not be sheer coinicidence that the family name *Cole*, which is derived from either of these personal names, is well-evidenced in Norwich, certainly from 1278. Three street-names in towns in Cheshire belong here: Jordangate in Macclesfield takes its name from a *Jordan* of Macclesfield who died in 1356, the street-name being first noted in 1339; Lewin St in Middlewich found in a document dated c. 1300 is derived from the Old English personal name *Lēofwine*, Middle English *Lewin*, but in this case no one of this name has been recorded locally; and the *Minshull*s, burgesses of Knutsford, lived there certainly from the second half of the 14th century, and Minshull Lane itself dates from at least 1430.

A few miscellaneous names are worthy of note. Carfax in Oxford means 'place where four roads or streets meet' and is comparable with Five Ways in Birmingham; Eden St in Kingston on Thames is 'heathen street', though the reason for such a name is unkown; Galliard St in Sandwich takes its name from *Galliots Bridge*, the first element of which is apparently ME *galliot* 'small galley or boat'; Land of Green Ginger is thought to have been named from one of the old gardens in Hull in which pot-herbs of that name were grown; Stepcots Hill in Exeter is a narrow street with a series of steps and no doubt originally flanked by cottages; and Whip-ma Whop-ma Gate in York may take its name from a whipping post and pillory at the end of the street.

twenty

Field-names

Field-names have been defined as the names of all pieces of land forming part of the agrarian economy of a town or village. Each piece of land has its own name, but even those which are probably comparatively old are rarely recorded before the 16th century. Many, in fact, date from the period of the enclosure of the common land and the redistribution of the open fields in the 18th and 19th century. Nonetheless, most country parishes contain some names surviving from at least the 13th or 14th century, though the size and shape of the particular field may now be very different. A major source of information for later field-names is to be found in the many Tithe Apportionment documents of the first half of the 19th century and it is not unusual to find a hundred or more names recorded there for each parish, while in Killingholme in north Lincolnshire over 250 separate field-names were actually collected from pre-1500 documents. Only a selection of field-names can be provided here, but the reader wishing to seek further information should consult John Field's excellent *English Field-Names: a Dictionary* and *A History of English Field-Names.*

Often enough the names of the old open fields still remain as, for example, *North*, *South*, *East,* and *West Field*, though what was once North Field may now be divided in Far and Near North Field, Lower and Upper North Field, or even Big and Little North Field. Here *field* is used in some such sense as 'unenclosed land used for agriculture'. The open fields were divided into smaller areas and the term for such divisions is often *Furlong*, though this could mean 'piece of land the length of a furrow'. *Acre* originally meant only a plot of land irrespective of its size, but early became used as a measurement of area. Ten Acres and Fifteen Acres are common enough today, but perhaps a surprising number bear little relation to the actual size of the present field. Indeed, though

Hundred Acres in a very few cases is the size of the field, it usually denotes a very small area of land. In a similar way Thousand Acres is used ironically for very small fields.

Dole(s) or *Doale(s)* refers to a share or shares of the common field and the equivalent Scandinavian word giving *Dale(s)* is very common in parts of the East Midlands. The singular form *Dale*, of course, cannot always be distinguished from *Dale* 'valley', but usually the topography will show which word is intended. Another fairly common term is *Flat*, sometimes denoting a piece of flat ground, but perhaps more often the sense is 'larger division of land in the common field'.

A number of modern field-names commemorate the strips of land in the common fields like *Brade*, *Braid*, and *Broad*. These are derived from OE *brǣdu* 'breadth', which in Middle English denoted a broad strip of land, especially one in the village field. It is sometimes found in the compound *Gorebroad* or *Goarbroad* meaning 'broad strip in a triangular corner of the common field' as well as *Shovelbroad* 'strip of land as broad as a shovel', a name surviving in a variety of spellings including *Shoebroad*. The first element of *Gorebroad*, *Gore*, is sometimes used alone or as the second element of a compound in the sense 'triangular piece of land, land in the angle where two furlongs meet'. *Balk* and *Baulk* often survive and referred to a strip of land left unploughed to mark the boundary between adjacent strips or used as an access path. Mr John Field points out that tethered animals often grazed the balks. *Butt*, sometimes preceded by a numeral, originally denoted a strip abutting on a boundary, a short strip or a ridge at right angles to another, but occasionally however the reference is to an archery butt.

Head is more common earlier than it is in modern field-names, but it is frequently found in the compound *Headland(s)* denoting the strip of land left for turning the plough. *Land* itself, however, is very common and is a "basic unit of ploughing in common arable fields". It denoted a strip of arable land in the common field, a selion, and is often found preceded by a numeral. References to as many as *Twenty Lands* have been noted in many counties. *Ridge(s)* and *Rigg(s)*, from the equivalent Scandinavian word, are normally used in field-names of cultivated strips of land, again often with a numeral as in *Five Ridges* or *Six Riggs*. A fairly frequent term for a strip of land is *Shot*, *Shoot*, *Shutt*, or *Shute*, all variant modern spellings of the same word. John Field explains this word as 'a block of arable land, consisting of a number of selions or lands, all running in the same direction, and having at either end a headland on which the ploughteam could turn'. He further points out that it is synonymous with furlong or flat. A compound derived from the ultimate source of *Shot* is *Cockshoot* and *Cockshut*, a natural glade where woodcocks shoot or dart, examples of which are recorded from the 13th century.

Various terms for land for cultivation are common. *Breach* or *Breech*, even *Bridge*, *Brick* or *Breck*, refer to land (newly) broken up for cultivation. Consequently, in the North and East Midlands *Breck* is easily confused with Scandinavian *brekka* 'slope', which gives similar forms, but again topography will usually decide between the two. Confusion can also take place with *Brake* 'thicket, waste-land covered with brushwood'. *Inhams* and *Innams* are from an English word meaning 'land taken in or enclosed', while the Scandinavian term for such land is *Intake* or *Intack*. Surprisingly this is uncommon in medieval sources, though it continued in living use into the 19th century to give such names as *Railway Intake,* and no less than fifteen *Intakes* are recorded in the 1850 Tithe Award for Thornton Curtis in north Lincolnshire.

Mead and *Meadow* are very common and *Meadow* appears as a field-name in almost every parish. On the other hand *Pasture*, apart from an occasional example is rarely found before the 16th century. In Scandinavianized districts of the country, however, *Ing* 'meadow, pasture' is the usual word, often surviving in the plural *Ings*, and like *Meadow* is very common in early documents. *Grounds* on the other hand is very rare in such records, but does occur in Enclosure and Tithe Awards referring to a large piece of grassland, especially one lying at a distance from the farm or village, as John Field points out. A strip or measure of grassland is also sometimes called *Swathe*, common also in the plural and preceded by a numeral.

OE *lēah* 'forest, wood, glade, clearing', which as we saw in Chapter Seventeen is very common in the names of major places, is equally common in field-names meaning 'meadow, pasture'. It survives in a variety of forms such as *Lea, Lees,* and *Leys*. These forms are difficult to separate from *Leas(e)* and *Leaz(e)* from OE *lǣs* 'pasture, meadowland'. However, recent research has shown that *lea* and the plural *leas* are so common as appellatives in 16th and 17th century Glebe Terriers that most of the names in *Lea(s)*, etc. are to be derived ultimately from OE *lēah* in its developed sense 'meadow, pasture'. It may be noted here that the dative singular of *lǣs*, *lǣswe*, frequently survives to the present day as *Leasowe* and even *Leaser, Leasure* , and *Leizure*.

Wang and *Wong* could be derived from either OE *wang* or ON *vangr*, but since the names are common only in the Danelaw counties the Scandinavian word is almost certainly the source. The meaning is 'garden, in-field, piece of land near a house', to which Field adds 'enclosed land among open strips'. 'Vegetable garden' is the usual sense of the field-name *Lawton* or *Laughton*, though when such names are old they may denote herb-gardens.

Several place-name elements used in field-names in the original sense 'clearing' include OE *rod* 'clearing in woodland', which survives as *Rood* or *Road* and in the North in the distinctive dialect form *Royd*. *Ridding*, even *Riding*, *Reading,* and *Reeding* are all modern forms of OE *ryding* 'clearing in woodland' and also 'land taken into cultivation from waste' and are common field-names. However, *Stubbing* and *Stocking* each denoting a place where trees have been stubbed, hence 'clearing', are less common, though both are recorded at least from the 13th century. Incidentally, examples of *Stocking Leg* have been noted, where the reference is to the shape of the field. The only loan-word from French denoting 'clearing in woodland' is *Assart*, sometimes shortened to *Sart* or *Sarts*, though neither are particularly common.

Words referring to plots of ground or enclosures are, as is to be expected, very frequently found. *Close*, also a French loan-word, in the sense 'enclosure', appears in numbers in most Tithe Awards, though it is comparatively rare in medieval sources. *Croft*, on the other hand, is certainly as common in the 13th and 14th centuries as today, if not more so. It denotes a small piece of land, often attached to a house and "almost invariably enclosed". Field points out that variant forms of *Croft*, such as *Croat*, *Crout*, *Crowd*, were first noted in the English Place-Name Society's surveys for Surrey and Hertfordshire and that subsequent surveys have reinforced these "and indeed additional variants". The plans accompanying Tithe Awards frequently show that a *Croft* was indeed often a small enclosure of arable or pasture *near a dwelling*. *Inland* is a similar term for land near a house or building and also for land cultivated for the owner's use. Similarly *Eddish* 'enclosure' occurs in some parishes, though in dialects it has an additional meaning 'stubble, aftermath', and so, on occasion, may have the same sense in field-names as *Fog* 'aftermath, long grass left unmowed during winter'. *Math*, itself, 'mowing, cutting of grass' is found occasionally and it is used either of grass for mowing or of the place where it was cut. It has been noted in such a name as *Seven Days Math*, as well as *Day Math*, *Day's Mo(w)th* and *Demath*.

Lot 'share, allotment of land', the self-explanatory *Piece*, and *Parcel* 'piece of land' occur in many Enclosure or Tithe Awards, as does *Plot*. Similar terms for a small piece of land are *Plat*, *Pleck*, and *Pingle*. This last denotes a small enclosure and is almost as common in some areas today as it was in the 13th or 14th century. *Pingle* is a nasalized form of ME *pightel*, which survives as *Pightle* or even *Pickle*. The geographical distribution of these two words has never been studied in detail and is an area well worth close attention. *Yard* certainly sometimes has its usual modern sense of a small uncultivated piece of land attached to a building and often surrounded by a wall or the like, but more often in field-names it has its earlier meaning 'enclosure'. This is also the meaning of *Garth*, a word of Scandinavian origin, which is common in the North and East Midlands both in medieval and modern names.

The commonest term for an 'enclosure for animals' is *Fold*, but *Pen* is sometimes found, as well as a derivative *Penning*, while *Hitch* is used specifically of an enclosure of hurdles for sheep. In many parishes, however, the name *Pinfold* occurs for the pound in which stray animals were put. Many parishes too had their rabbit-warren and the name for this, derived from ME *coninger*, survives in a variety of forms – *Conegar, Conegree, Conery, Coneygar, Coneygree, Coninger, Conyer, Conygre*. Indeed, Mr Field has noted several dozen variant forms of this name. Rabbit-warrens were established particularly in sandy parts of villages and some survive to the present. The similar name *Coneyearth* is occasionally found, but in Scandinavianized parts of the country the normal term for a rabbit-warren is *Coneygarth*, the second element of which is *Garth* noted above.

Some of the words for topographical terms which are not very common in place-names occur more often in field-names, like *Bottom* and *Botham* 'valley bottom' and *Bye* 'corner of land in a river-bend'. Similarly, there are *Dimble* or *Dumble* 'hollow' and *Dimple* or *Dumple* 'deep hole'. These are sometimes confused in modern forms, but the topography will usually make it clear which is the correct etymology.

Most of the field-names discussed so far are common, though some appear to have a particular regional distribution. This is, in fact, an area deserving of much greater study and is one in which local people could well play an important part. Other field-names can be said to be met with regularly, but much less frequently. So, we can expect to come across occasional examples of *Stitch* 'a bit, a piece, an allotment of land', *Screed* 'narrow strip of land', *Slang* 'narrow piece of land', *Sling* and *Slinket* 'long narrow piece of land', *Spong* 'narrow piece of land', *String* 'narrow strip (often in woodland)' and *Tail* 'long narrow strip of land'. Used as a noun *Long* denotes a long piece of land, while a derivative of this, surviving as *Langet* and *Lanket*, is found in some areas with a similar meaning. *Hirn, Hiron,* and *Iron* are variant spellings of OE *hyrne* 'nook or corner of land, spit of land in a river bend'. *Island* may denote a field surrounded by a wood or by other fields, or even one with trees in the middle, and *Roundabout(s)* has similar meanings.

Names denoting wet or marshy ground include *Featherbed, Forty* 'projecting land or island in marshy ground', though the latter as a first element is of course usually the numeral, *Gall* 'barren wet land', along with *Bog, Gog,* and *Quab. Slob* and *Lag* are recorded from southern counties of a marshy field, as are *Flash* and *Flosh* in the north, while *Honey, Pudding,* and *Treacle* are used generally for sticky or muddy land. *Frog* is apparently sometimes used in a similar way.

A pool is sometimes called *Plash* or *Plaish*, while *Stank* is the term for a stagnant pond and *Stew* for a pond for keeping fish till ready to eat. Other types of land do not seem to have such a variety of names. Rocky ground is sometimes called *Cloudy* and the noun *Cloud(s)* is also found for 'rock(s)'. *Cat's Brain* refers to mottled soil, often rough clay mixed with stones or clay overlaid with marl, and *Marl* itself as well as *Marled*, is a common descriptive term. *Checker* or *Chequer* also occurs for ground that has a variegated appearance, where as John Field notes "alternative patches of light and darker soil give the bare earth the appearance of a chess board".

Names such as *Distants, Hem, Sheath, Skirts* and *Mare, Mear, Meer* or *Mere* all denote land on or near a boundary, but the last group of these may represent OE *mere* 'pool'. *Ball*, too, sometimes has the meaning 'boundary', since in some areas it was used of a mound piled up as a boundary mark.

Several terms for gates or openings are fairly common in field-names, particularly *Lidgate*, surviving also as *Lidget* and *Ledget*, 'swing gate', and a name of similar meaning is *Clapgate. Cripplegate* usually refers to a low opening in a wall or fence which allows sheep to pass through. *Hatch* is used of a hatch-gate or wicket and *Hatchet* and *Hacket* are weakened forms of *Hatch-gate*.

Several miscellaneous names, each occurring regularly but not frequently, are worth noting. *Day(s) Work* was a field that could be ploughed in one day and similar examples with numerals as high as *Twelve* have been noted; *Farthing* usually means 'fourth part' and *Half*, as a noun, is sometimes used in the sense 'half-share' or 'half acre'; *Kitchen* usually refers to land cultivated for domestic purposes; *Hopping* means 'hop-garden'; a name like *Lammas Close* or *Lammas Croft* illustrates the custom by which certain land became common pasturage between August 1st and the following spring; *Pest* and *Pesthouse* are named from hospitals for those suffering from the plague; and *Bedlam* is a derogatory name for a field, from the Royal Bethlem Hospital, London, for the insane. *Saintfoin*, even *St. Foin*, are forms of *Sainfoin*, a valuable fodder plant as its name from French *Sain Fein* 'healthy hay' implies. Being leguminous it is also used to improve the soil. *Several(s)* refers to land held in separate or private ownership, particularly that enclosed, as opposed to common land. In Scandinavianized areas *Storth* is found as a field-name for a plantation or land with brushwood, while another Scandinavian word has given *Carr* 'marsh', especially one overgrown with brushwood, and *carr* itself still survives as a noun in some local dialects.

The terms so far considered most frequently occur as the second element of a compound. In a survey of this kind little attention can paid to the first elements of such compounds, since they literally run into tens, indeed hundreds of thousands. However, it should be pointed out that many such are the names of individuals or families, even in names recorded from the 13th and 14th century. In later records, like Tithe Awards, family-names are found very frequently. In many cases, even in early ones, the person or family can be identified as living in the parish. This is a source of considerable importance for all interested in genealogy and it gives ample scope for important work based on local documents. Those dated from the 18th and 19th century are easy to read, while the hands of earlier scribes *can* be transcribed with patience, practice, and some teaching.

Many field-names repeated in various parts of the country are nicknames of a fanciful type. However, it was thought readers might find it more interesting to see examples from a single county. The volumes, especially the most recent volumes, of the English Place-Name Society often provide lists of various types of fanciful field-names, but only one monograph has so far appeared dealing solely with one county.

This is H G D. Foxall's excellent *Shropshire Field-Names*, published by the Shropshire Archaeological Society. All the following examples are in Shropshire and so provide some indication of the variety of such names within a single shire.

Sometimes fanciful names are complimentary referring to productive land such as *Blest Acre, Cream Pots, Filpots, Have a Good Heart, Honest Meadow, Paywell Field, Providence, Rich Land, Sweet Field,* as well as *Syllabub Close,* Syllabub being "a rich mixture of cream and wine", referring to the quality of the land. Much more common, however, are derogatory names like *Awkward Croft, Bare Arse, Barebones, Beggarall* or *Buggerall, Clam Croft, Dangerous Furlong, Famish Croft, Goodfornothing Acre, Hard Bargain, Hunger Hill, Isle of Want, Judas Field, Labour in Vain, Little Worth, Long Purgatory Meadow, Nasty Field, Peck and Hope, Place of Pain, Sorrowful, Starveall, Thirsty Field,* and *Unlucky Leasow.* Some similar field-names refer to places in cold, exposed places like those containing *Cold,* of which *Cold Comfort* and *Cold Harbour* have been noted in Shropshire, as well as the comparable *Windy Batch* and *Windy Harbour.*

A further group of nicknames describes the shape of the field, as for example the common *Shoulder of Mutton* and *Boot Leg,* as well as *The Angle, Bear's Arse, Cocked Hat, Coffin, Crooked, Elbow Piece, Ell Piece, Hammer Head, Harp, Knee Croft, Leg and Foot, Leg of Mutton, Peacock's Tail, Punchbowl Field, Round O, Rump of Beef, Shapeless, T Meadow, Umbrella Piece,* and *Why Croft,* which is shaped like the letter Y. Small Fields are sometimes named ironically as with *Handkerchief* and *Petticoat Park,* and though names in *Penny,* like *Halfpenny Croft* and *Penny Croft* may similarly denote little fields, usually they refer to the rent, as must have been the case with *Half Guinea Pleck, Penny Rent,* and *Ninepenny Task.*

A considerable number, named from distant counties and places, are usually called nicknames of remoteness, for the fields with such names are for the most part a good distance from the farm to which they belong or are situated close to a parish boundary. In Shropshire there are *America, Barbados, Belle Isle, Boston, Corsica, Flanders, Gibralter, Hudson's Bay, Jericho, New England, Newfoundland, New York, Pensylvania, Stockholm Field, West Indies,* while *Botany Bay* may have been just such a name or that of a piece of land "so difficult to work that it was regarded as in the nature of penal servitude". This type is not confined to those names adopted from abroad, but includes some from distant parts of England and the British Isles, like *Batterea Road*, *Carnarvon*, *Cumberland*, *Dorset*, *Ireland*, *London*, *Londonderry*, *Rutland Bank*, *Salisbury*, *Westminster,* and from nearer to Shropshire, *Nantwich Leasow* and a series comprising *Birmingham*, *Brinncham*, *Brunicham,* and *Brimicham*. *Scotland* can be a nickname of remoteness, but certainly on occasion is a name for land subject to *scot*, a tax. Besides these, as nicknames for remote fields, we can add *End of the World*, *World's End,* and *No Man's Land*.

Here, too, belongs a group named from battles such as *Bunkers Hill* 1755, *Portobello* 1739, and perhaps *Dunkirk* 1793, though these do not appear to be so well-represented in Shropshire as they are in some other counties.

Some names indicate that the rent from the field was used for a charitable purpose as in the case of *Poors Meadow* and *Poors Piece*, for the parish poor, and *Charity Butts*, for some local charity. But most such names have a religious association, sometimes a saint's name usually from the dedication of the local church, hence *St. John's Ground* or *St. Peter's Patch*. In many cases the rent was assigned to some specific purpose, as is indicated in *Bell Croft* and *Bell Meadow*, *Chantry Furlong* and *Chantry Leasow*, *Roof Leasow*, *Steeple Furlong,* and *Bobbington Steeple Piece*. *Rope Meadow* probably belongs here with reference to land given for the upkeep of the bell ropes and *Pew Field* may well be a comparable name. That allocated to individual clerics is indicated by *Parson's Meadow*, as well as *Glebe Croft*, the land assigned to a parson as part of his benefice. But most interesting of all those with religious associations are names derived from the Rogation Ceremony of 'beating the parish bounds'. On many parish boundaries names commemorating this are to be found, and in Shropshire Foxall noted *Bannerings*, *Epistle Field*, *The Proverbs* and *The Psalms*, as well as eight examples of *Gospel*, including *Gospel Ash* and *Gospel Oak*, an ash-tree and an oak-tree at which a passage from the Gospels was read during the parish perambulation. Interestingly, no example of *Amen* was found in Shropshire, although *Amen Corner* is a common name elsewhere.

Many field-names of the fanciful type defy interpretation, though someone, somewhere, may well be able to propose a satisfactory and convincing explanation. Foxall refers to a selection of such names as "a mere drop in the ocean" and these include *Anagron*, *The Aptical*, *Bamberline*, *Bombolin*, *Clequirley*, *The Corder Warders*, *Donacles*, *The*

Funstages, *The Grudy*, *The Last Skin*, *The Occoptts*, *Pindle Rindle Field*, *Scrill Scroll*, *Stredbow*, *The Striddle*, and *Thread Barber*.

Fanciful names, however, are by no means only of recent origin and similar ones can be found in the early records of many counties. The following may be taken as typical of those so far recorded by editors of the English Place-Name Society. Of the complimentary type are *Parodys* 1320 (WRY) and *Godesworlde* 1407 (Sx), while *Karlingten* 1267 (WRY) 'old woman's troubles', *Foresakenelond* 13th (Ess) 'forsaken land', *le Sullen* 1369 (Sr) literally 'the sullen', *Wabigan* 13th (ERY) 'woe-begone', and *le Schold in Wityng* 1275 (Nt) 'the scold in reproach', all names for fields difficult to work, are derogatory. A number of others commemorate a now long-forgotten tragedy, as in *Dedesmonnesdike* 1270 (Gl) 'dead man's dike', *Dedemanyslane* 1370 (Ess) 'deadman's lane', and *Dedquenesike* 13th (Nth) 'dead woman's stream', while *Thertheoxlaydede* 13th century 'where the ox lay dead' is described by the editors of the Buckinghamshire survey as "a picture in miniature of a medieval farming tragedy".

Only rarely does the place-name researcher find a name which gives particular pleasure. Just such a name, however, is *Disnayland* found in an unpublished land-charter, dated 1386, for Usselby in north Lincolnshire. The document was actually witnessed by a Thomas *Dyseney de Kingerby* (Kingerby is an adjacent village). The field was, therefore, named from a branch of the *Disney* family, which also gave its name to Norton Disney (L) and from whom the founder of the famous Disney Cartoon Films was descended. Clearly the modern Disneyland has no copyright to that name since it was already that of a piece of land in Lincolnshire way back in the 14th century.

Bibliography

A full bibliography to 1990 is to be found in:

J. Spittal and J. Field, *A Reader's Guide to the Place-Names of the United Kingdom*, Stamford 1990

Dictionaries and Works of Reference

E. Ekwall, *The Concise Oxford Dictionary of English Place-Names*, Oxford 1960

J. Field, *English Field-Names: A Dictionary*, reprinted Gloucester 1989
A History of English Field-Names, London 1993

M. Gelling, W.F.H. Nicolaisen and M. Richards, *The Names of Towns and Cities in Britain*, revised reprint, London 1986

O.J. Padel, *Cornish Place-Name Elements*, EPNS 56-57, EPNS 1985

A. Room, *A Concise Dictionary of Modern Place-Names in Great Britain and Ireland*, Oxford 1983
The Street Names of England, Stamford 1992

A.H. Smith, *English Place-Name Elements*, EPNS 25-26, Cambridge 1956

County Surveys and Monographs

A.M. Armstrong, A. Mawer, F.M. Stenton and Bruce Dickins, *The Place-Names of Cumberland*, EPNS 20-22, Cambridge 1950-52

K. Cameron, *The Place-Names of Derbyshire*, EPNS 27-29, Cambridge 1954
The Place-Names of Lincolnshire, EPNS 58, 64-66, 71,73, EPNS 1985, 1991, 1992, 1996, 1997 (several volumes to follow)
A Dictionary of Lincolnshire Place-Names, EPNS 1988

R. Coates, *The Place-Names of Hampshire*, London 1989

B. Coplestone-Crow, *Herefordshire Place-Names*, British Archaeological Reports, British Series 214, Oxford 1989

Barrie Cox, *The Place-Names of Rutland*, EPNS 67-69, EPNS 1994

The Place-Names of Leicestershire, EPNS 75, 1998

J. McN. Dodgson, *The Place-Names of Cheshire*, EPNS 44-47, Cambridge 1970-72, EPNS 48, 54, 74, EPNS 1981, 1997

W.H. Duignan, *Notes on Staffordshire Place-Names*, London 1902

E. Ekwall, *The Place-Names of Lancashire*, Manchester 1922

A Fägersten, *The Place-Names of Dorset*, Uppsala 1933

J. Field, *Place-Names of Greater London*, London 1980

M. Gelling, *The Place-Names of Oxfordshire*, EPNS 23-24, Cambridge 1953-54

    The Place-Names of Berkshire, EPNS 59, Cambridge 1973, EPNS 60-61, EPNS 1974-76

with H.D.G. Foxall, *The Place-Names of Shropshire*, EPNS 62-63, 70, EPNS 1990, 1995 (several volumes to follow)

J. Glover, *The Place-Names of Kent*, London 1976

J.E.B Glover, A Mawer and F.M. Stenton, *The Place-Names of Devon* EPNS 8-9, Cambridge 1931-32

    The Place-Names of Hertfordshire, EPNS 15, Cambridge 1938

    The Place-Names of Northamptonshire, EPNS 10, Cambridge 1933

    The Place-Names of Nottinghamshire, EPNS 17, Cambridge 1940

    The Place-Names of Wiltshire, EPNS 16, Cambridge 1939

    with A. Bonner, *The Place-Names of Surrey*, EPNS 11, Cambridge 1934

    with F.T.S. Houghton, *The Place-Names of Warwickshire*, EPNS 13, Cambridge 1936

    with S.J. Madge, *The Place-Names of Middlesex (apart from the City of London)*, EPNS 18, Cambridge 1942

H. Kökeritz, *The Place-Names of the Isle of Wight*, Uppsala 1940

A. Mawer, *The Place-Names of Northumberland and Durham*, Cambridge 1920

    and F.M. Stenton, *The Place-Names of Bedfordshire and Huntingdonshire*, EPNS 3, Cambridge 1926

    The Place-Names of Buckinghamshire, EPNS 2, Cambridge 1925

    with J.E.B. Gover, *The Place-Names of Sussex*, EPNS 6-7, Cambridge 1929-30 and F.T.S. Houghton, *The Place-Names of Worcestershire*, EPNS 4, Cambridge 1927

A.D. Mills, *The Place-Names of Dorset*, EPNS 52, 53, 59-60, EPNS 1977-89 (two volumes to follow)
Dorset Place-Names: their Origins and Meanings, reprinted Winchester 1991

J.P. Oakden, *The Place-Names of Staffordshire*, EPNS 55, EPNS 1984 (several volumes to follow)

O.J. Padel, *A Popular Dictionary of Cornish Place-Names*, Penzance 1988

P.H. Reaney, *The Place-Names of Cambridgeshire and the Isle of Ely*, EPNS 19, Cambridge 1943
The Place-Names of Essex, EPNS 12, Cambridge 1935

K.I. Sandred and B. Lindström, *The Place-Names of Norfolk*, EPNS 61, 72, EPNS 1989,1996 (several volumes to follow)

W.W. Skeat, *The Place-Names of Suffolk*, Cambridge 1913

A.H. Smith, *The Place-Names of Gloucestershire*, EPNS 38-40, Cambridge 1964-65
The Place-Names of the East Riding of Yorkshire and York, EPNS 14, Cambridge 1937
The Place-Names of the North Riding of Yorkshire, EPNS 5, Cambridge 1928
The Place-Names of the West Riding of Yorkshire, EPNS 30-37, Cambridge 1961-63
The Place-Names of Westmorland, EPNS 42-43, Cambridge 1967

J.K. Wallenberg, *Kentish Place-Names*, Uppsala 1931
The Place-Names of Kent, Uppsala 1934

Studies on the Significance of English Place-Names

K. Cameron, ed. *Place-Name Evidence for the Anglo-Saxon Invasion and Scandinavian Settlements*, EPNS 1977, a Collection of Eight studies
"The Significance of English Place-Names" in *Proceedings of the British Academy* 62, Oxford 1976
"Viking Settlement in the East Midlands. The Place-Name Evidence" in *Giesener Flurnamen-Kolloqium*, Heidelberg 1985

G.J. Copley, *English Place-Names and their Origins*, Newton Abbot 1968

Archaeology and Place-Names in the Fifth and Sixth Centuries, British Archaeological Reports, British Series 147, Oxford 1986

E. Ekwall, *English River-Names*, Oxford 1928
English Place-Names in -ing, Second Edition, Lund 1962
Selected Papers, Lund 1963
Old English wīc in Place-Names, Uppsala 1964

G. Fellows-Jensen, *Scandinavian Settlement Names in Yorkshire*, Copenhagen 1972
Scandinavian Settlement Names in the East Midlands, Copenhagen 1978
Scandinavian Settlement Names in the North-West, Copenhagen 1985

H.D.G. Foxall, *Shropshire Field-Names*, Shrewsbury 1980

M. Gelling, *Place-Names in the Landscape*, London 1984
Signposts to the Past, Second Edition, Chichester 1988
and Ann Cole, *The Landscape of Place-Names*, Stamford 2000

D. Hooke, *The Anglo-Saxon Landscape: the Kingdom of the Hwicce*, Manchester 1985

K.H. Jackson, *Language and History in Early Britain*, Edinburgh 1953

C. Johansson, *Old English Place-Names and Field-Names in lēah*, Stockholm 1975

A. Mawer and F.M. Stenton, ed. *Introduction to the Survey of English Place-Names*, EPNS 1, Cambridge 1924

A.D. Mills, *A Dictionary of English Place-Names*, Oxford 1991

P.H. Reaney, *The Origins of English Place-Names*, London 1960

A.L.F. Rivet and C. Smith, *The Place-Names of Roman Britain*, London 1979

K.I. Sandred, *English Place-Names in -stead*, Uppsala 1963

N. Wrander, *English Place-Names in the Dative Plural*, Lund 1983

Numerous articles on various aspects of English Place-Names in *Nomina*, the Journal of the Society of Name Studies and in *The Journal of the English Place-Name Society*, now in its 26th number. All the volumes of the EPNS, both those published by the Cambridge University Press and those later volumes published by the Society itself can be obtained from

The Secretary
The English Place-Name Society,
The University
Nottingham, NG7 2RD

Index

Place-Names